WILLIAM MORRIS

Decor & Design

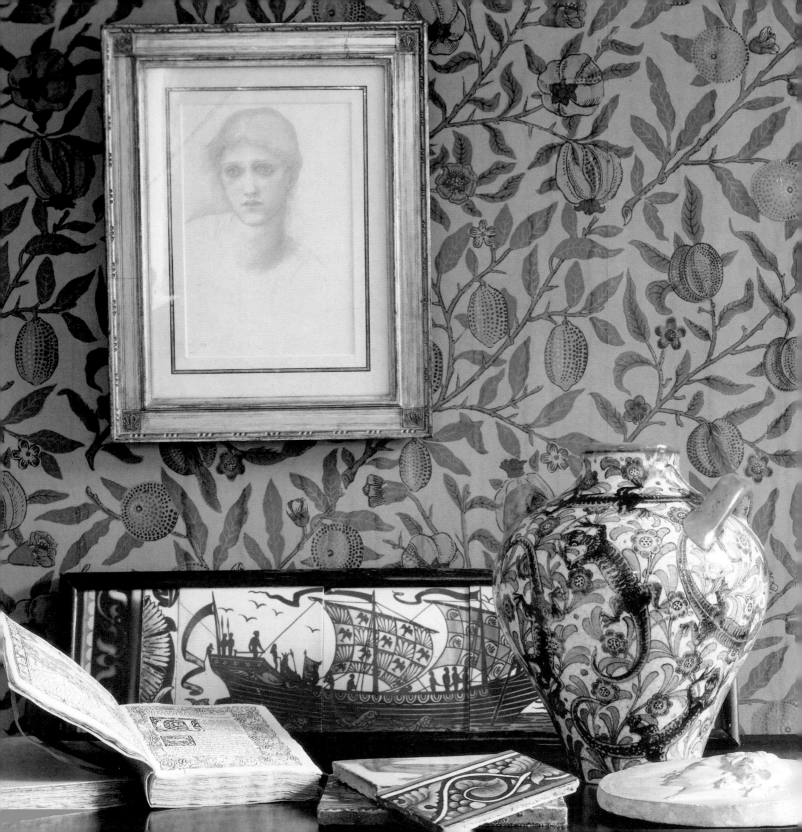

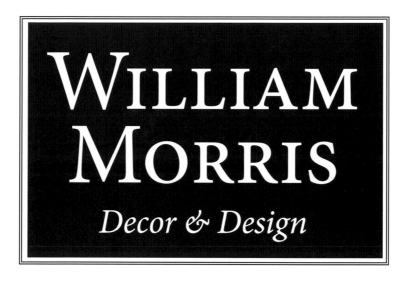

WILLIAM MORRIS
Decor & Design

Elizabeth Wilhide

PAVILION

To M.L.

Published in the United Kingdom in 2016 by
Pavilion
1 Gower Street
London
WC1E 6HD

ISBN 978-1-910904-86-2

A CIP catalogue record for this book is available
from the British Library

10 9 8 7 6 5 4 3 2 1

Reproduction by Mission, Hong Kong
Printed by Toppan Leefung Printing Ltd, China

This book can be ordered direct from the publisher at www.pavilionbooks.com

CONTENTS

INTRODUCTION: WILLIAM MORRIS: HIS LIFE & WORK 6

1 WILLIAM MORRIS AND NINETEENTH-CENTURY INTERIORS 35

2 DECORATING WITH PATTERN 60

3 WALLS AND FINISHES 84

4 CURTAINS AND WINDOW TREATMENTS 118

5 FURNITURE AND FURNISHINGS 142

GLOSSARY OF PATTERNS 167

COMMERCIAL SUPPLIERS 187

SELECT BIBLIOGRAPHY 189

ACKNOWLEDGEMENTS 190

INDEX 191

INTRODUCTION

'My work is the embodiment
of dreams in one form or another. . . .'

Letter to Cormell Price, Oxford, July 1856

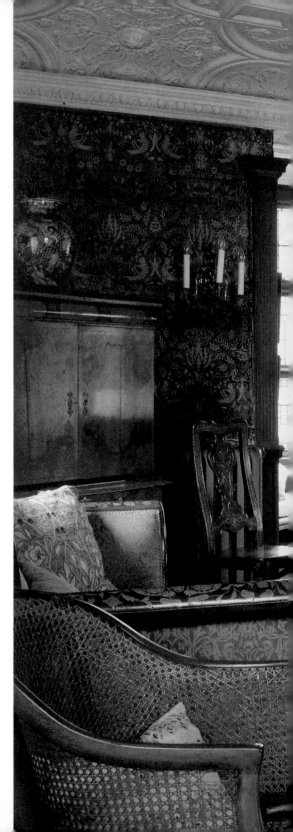

RIGHT The Drawing Room, Wightwick
Manor, West Midlands, with fireplace tiles
by de Morgan, and painted glass illustrating
William Morris's epic poem, *The Earthly
Paradise*. The mock-Elizabethan house
(built 1887-93) was designed by Edward
Ould for Theodore Mander, a partner in a
prosperous paint business.

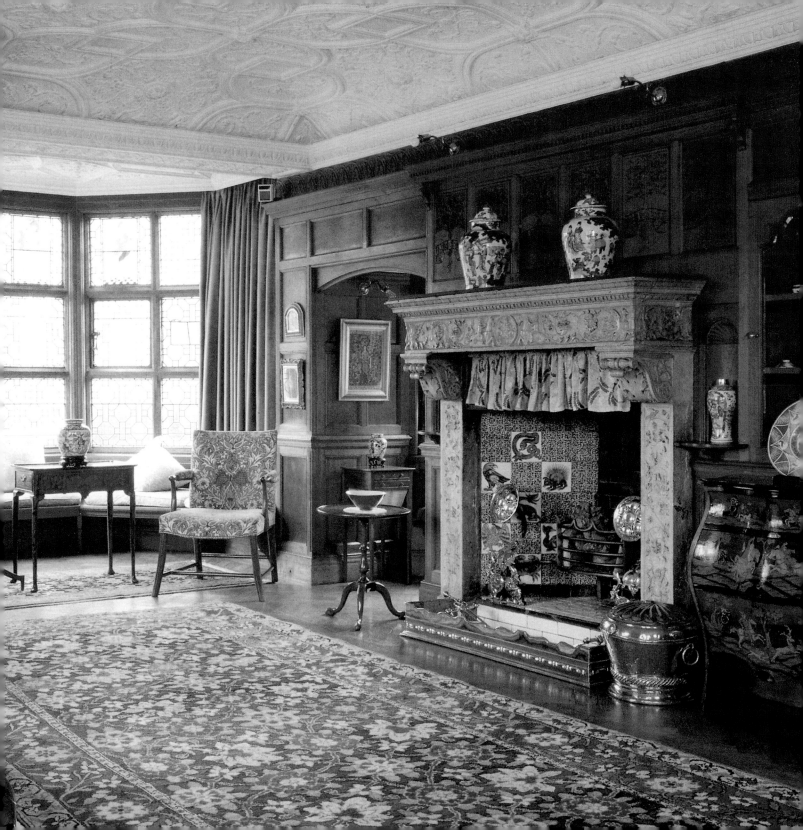

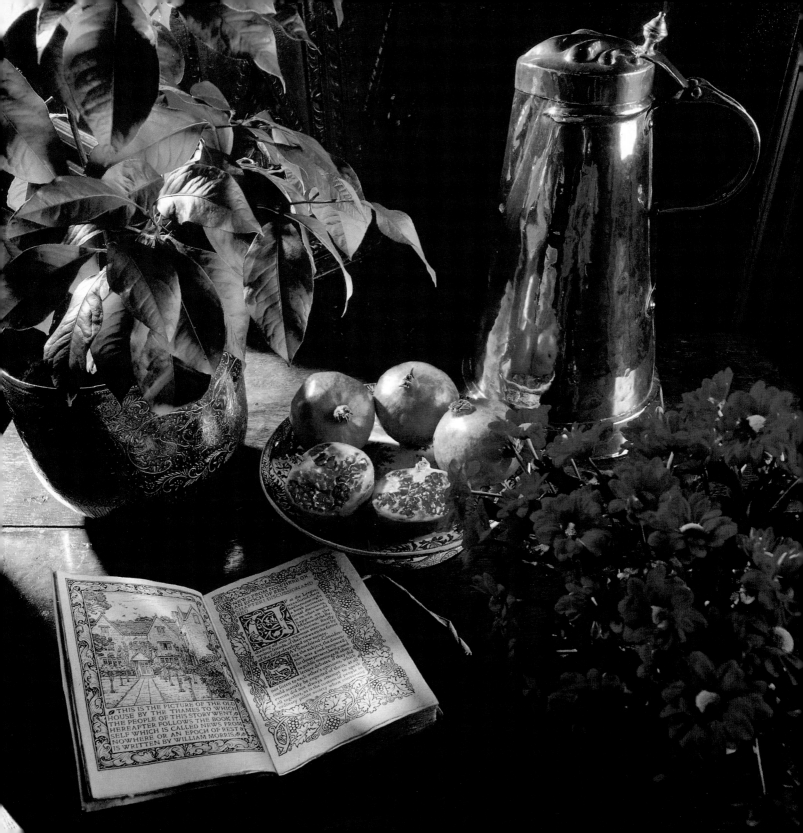

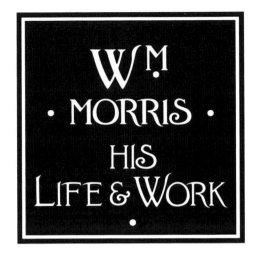

WM · MORRIS · HIS LIFE & WORK

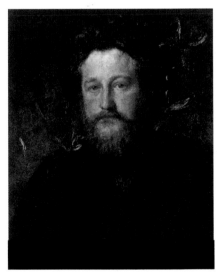

ABOVE William Morris painted in 1870 by G F Watts, the leading portraitist of the latter part of the nineteenth century. This portrait was believed by many at the time to be one of Watts' finest works..

OPPOSITE In the Great Parlour at Wightwick, with *News from Nowhere* showing the woodcut of Kelmscott Manor.

WILLIAM MORRIS DESIGNED WALLPAPER AND TEXTILE PATTERNS WHICH HAVE remained in production for over a century. His work in the field of the applied arts inspired an entire generation of designers and architects; his concern with decorative honesty and truth to materials had a direct bearing on the principles of what was to be the Modern Movement. He transformed the whole status of decorative art, challenging the mass-produced mediocrity of the nineteenth century and re-establishing the value of handcrafted work.

During his lifetime, Morris was renowned not as a designer but as a writer of visionary, romantic verse, much of which retold classical myths and medieval tales. He was one of the first to translate the Icelandic sagas; his own poetry was so well regarded that he was offered (though did not accept) the Poet Laureateship on the death of Tennyson.

Politically, Morris was a key figure in early socialist groups, a tireless and impassioned campaigner and speaker. His commitment to improving working conditions was evident in his early cooperative endeavours and in the organization of his own firm. His vision of a future Britain, where art, peace, decency and harmony with nature have triumphed, is described in *News from Nowhere*, a classic of Utopian literature.

William Morris was also a painter, weaver, typographer, illuminator, and a designer of stained glass, tiles, furniture, tapestries and carpets. And his lifelong interest in architecture had at least two important consequences: the building of the influential Red House, which was specially designed by Morris's friend Philip Webb, and the founding of the Society for the Protection of Ancient Buildings, which continues its work to the present day.

Few people have had the energy, imagination, intellect or will to accomplish so much in one short lifetime. This book, as its title suggests, is concerned with William

Morris the designer, with his impact on the decorative arts and with the relevance of his approach to design and decoration today. But it is impossible to appreciate the meaning of Morris's design work without the broader context of his other passions and activities. In any event, these other interests do not reside in distinct, watertight categories: they are all of a piece. Morris the poet is also Morris the lover of nature and history; Morris the designer is also the Morris who wanted art for all.

One hundred years ago William Morris was best known as a poet whose medieval romances had captured public imagination. He was already a public figure when, at the mature age of 49, he allied himself with the socialist cause, disconcerting friends and supporters. With typical energy, he threw himself into political work and his death, thirteen years later, was greatly mourned in radical circles.

Today, William Morris the poet is largely forgotten. William Morris the political thinker has been reappraised by succeeding generations of critics, at one time disparaged as reactionary and historicist, more recently reinstated as an important theorist of the early socialist movement. But what has never been in dispute and never forgotten is his work as a designer, chiefly as a designer of pattern. The name William Morris is synonymous with a particular type of design, a flowing, intense evocation of the natural world, described with great clarity and skill. In these patterns can be found all of Morris's passionate observation of nature and all of his deep dedication to history and man's place in it. Morris insisted on integrating life with art, and art with life, and he rejected the destructive and spiritless specialization of industrialization, with its remorseless separation of work, leisure and creativity. This holistic attitude meant that he simply could not conceive a design without considering how it would be made, the techniques and materials which would be used, the eventual purpose to which it would be put and the conditions under which it would be produced.

A Morris design celebrates the natural world. All of Morris's work, with its emphasis on harmony with our natural environment, is particularly timely today. But his patterns also display the value of artisanship and the intimate connection between form, function and beauty. It is the unique combination which holds a particular attraction and relevance for us now.

EARLY LIFE

William Morris was born on 24 March 1834, at Elm House in Walthamstow, to the northeast of London. Although by the 1880s Walthamstow could be described by Morris as 'terribly cocknified and choked up by the jerry-builder', during his childhood it was 'a pleasant place enough', no more than a country village.

Morris was the eldest of five sons, the third of nine children altogether. His father was a successful broker and the family prospered, moving from Elm House to a grander Georgian house, Woodford Hall, in 1840. Woodford Hall stood on the edge of Epping Forest. Its extensive grounds and the neighbouring wildness of the Forest were a stimulating environment for a small, imaginative boy, who not only had his own pony but also his own set of toy armour.

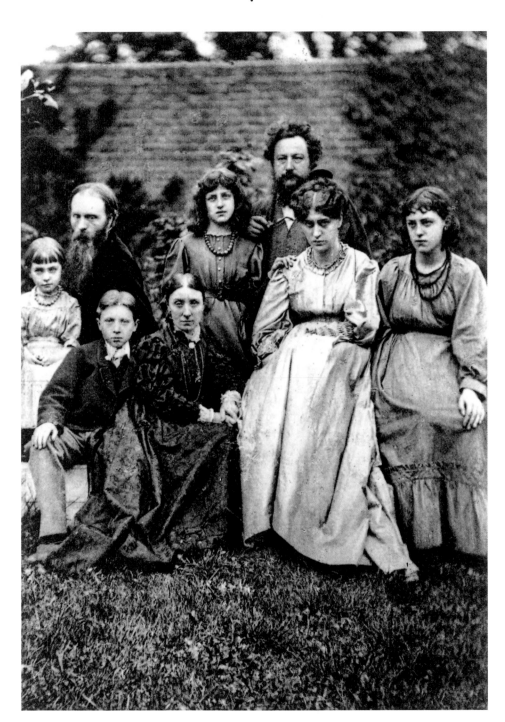

LEFT A double family portrait – the Morrises and the Burne-Jones – photographed in the garden of The Grange, the Burne-Jones' family home in Fulham, west London. The two families often took holidays together; Morris was a regular visitor to The Grange for Sunday morning breakfasts. Clockwise, from the far right: Jenny Morris, Janey Morris, Georgiana Burne-Jones, Philip Burne-Jones, Margaret Burne-Jones, Edward Burne-Jones, May Morris and William Morris.

Morris spent an idyllic childhood, riding in the Forest with his brothers and sisters and inventing games of chivalry and adventure. An early and voracious reader, his head was full of the novels of Sir Walter Scott. The old Essex churches also made a lasting impression, as did a visit to Queen Elizabeth's Lodge in Epping Forest, where he was struck by the romantic sight of a room hung with 'faded greenery'.

In 1847, the idyll came to an abrupt end with the death of Morris's father. A few months later, Morris was sent away to school, to Marlborough College, then recently established. He was miserable at school, a place he later described as 'very rough' and, even more bitterly, as a 'boy-farm', admitting that he had 'a hardish time of it, as chaps who have brains and feelings generally do at school'. One consolation, however, was the setting of the school, in beautiful countryside near the ancient stone circle at Avebury. Morris explored the vicinity thoroughly, absorbing the local history and making detailed observations of the architecture, artefacts, and the natural landscape. His unhappiness threw him on to his own resources and he became a 'great devourer of books', feeding a prodigious memory and capacity for retaining detail. It was at Marlborough, too, that he became an Anglo-Catholic.

These early experiences had a critical influence on the development of Morris's sensibilities both as a poet and designer. A pervading nostalgia for a romantic past can be traced to those blissful hours of play in the Forest, the tangible sense of history to his direct observations of ancient churches and prehistoric monuments, and the avid reading of medieval works in the library at Marlborough. A delight in nature is already being expressed: in a letter to his sister Emma, the closest of his siblings, he wrote, 'So for your edification, I will tell you what a delectable affair a watermeadow is to go through. . . .'

OXFORD

Just how dreadful a place Marlborough must have been can be gathered from the fact that in 1851 a mutiny occurred among the boys in protest against the poor running of the school. Instead of returning there, Morris remained at home and was tutored privately for Oxford admission.

In 1853, Morris went up to Exeter College to read theology, intending to enter the clergy. Within a few days, he had met Edward Burne-Jones (1833–98) and a friendship began which was to last a lifetime.

Over thirty years later, Morris described Oxford as 'a vision of grey-roofed houses and a long-winding street, and a sound of many bells'. Still essentially medieval, Oxford impressed Morris with its beauty, although he was less captivated by academic life. Together with Burne-Jones, and a close-knit set of friends that included Charles Faulkner, Morris devoured poetry, especially Chaucer, Malory, Keats, Tennyson and Shelley, read novels, studied Carlyle and Ruskin and pored over illuminated manuscripts in the Bodleian. All of this reading and the discussions it provoked nourished a growing conviction that society would be better organized along the lines of the religious communities of the Middle Ages.

The work of Ruskin was particularly influential. *The Stones of Venice* (1853) 'seemed to point out a new road on which the world should travel'. From Ruskin Morris learned that 'art is the expression of man's pleasure in his labour', and that with the Renaissance and its divisive distinction between designer and craftsman, the free, creative and fulfilling work of the medieval artisan was destroyed. Through Ruskin's lectures, Morris and Burne-Jones also learned about the Pre-Raphaelite Brotherhood. Millais' *The Return of the Dove to the Ark* was exhibited in an Oxford shop in 1854. This, and other works by Holman Hunt, Ford Madox Brown and Dante Gabriel Rossetti, seemed breathtaking and original. The heightened sense of beauty and the intense medievalism of these paintings began to convince Morris and Burne-Jones that their futures lay in the direction of art, not theology.

In 1855 Morris and Burne-Jones travelled in northern France, visiting (revisiting in Morris's case) the great medieval cathedrals of Chartres, Rouen and Evreux. Although it was architecture which made the holiday such a turning point in his life, it is typical of Morris that in letters home he is almost as lyrical in his descriptions of the surrounding landscape. One night, 'the most memorable night of my life' as Burne-Jones recalled, while walking on the quay at Le Havre, Morris and Burne-Jones finally resolved to give up any notions of becoming clergymen to 'begin a life of art'. Morris had decided to become an architect, Burne-Jones a painter.

Morris left Oxford in 1856 with a pass degree in theology, but much more besides. He had made lasting friendships with people who would later become his working colleagues; his mind was enriched with his intense study of the medieval period, with the history and architecture of Oxford itself and the beauty of its setting: years later, the flowers of Oxford's watermeadows, the snakeshead fritillary and wild tulip, would reappear in his designs. He had searched for a vocation and believed that he had discovered one in architecture. And, almost in passing, he had begun to write poetry, with a facility that made him doubt its value, although those who heard or read it were not so dismissive.

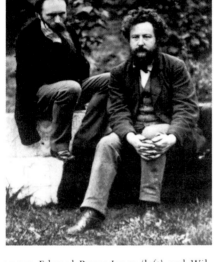

ABOVE Edward Burne-Jones (left) and William Morris (right) in the 1860s. Lifelong friends and artistic collaborators, their relationship was severely strained, but not broken, by Morris's commitment to socialism in the 1880s. Their last great joint endeavour was the Kelmscott Press.

When Morris left the university in 1856 he stayed in Oxford, apprenticed to G. E. Street, later principally known as the architect of the Law Courts in the Strand, then architect of the Diocese of Oxford. During this time, Morris was also involved in the publication of the *Oxford and Cambridge Magazine*, to which he gave financial support as well as numerous editorial contributions. He was in comfortable financial circumstances, having inherited an annuity of £900 on coming of age two years earlier.

Street was a leading figure of the Gothic Revival. Although Morris stayed in his office only nine months, he must have been influenced by Street's view of the architect as a complete artist, involved not only in building, but also in the design of glass and fabric: Street was particularly interested in historic textiles and ecclesiastical embroidery. Morris was put to work copying a drawing of the doorway of St Augustine's, Canterbury, an exercise so tedious that it led him to reconsider architecture as a future.

APPRENTICESHIP AND MARRIAGE

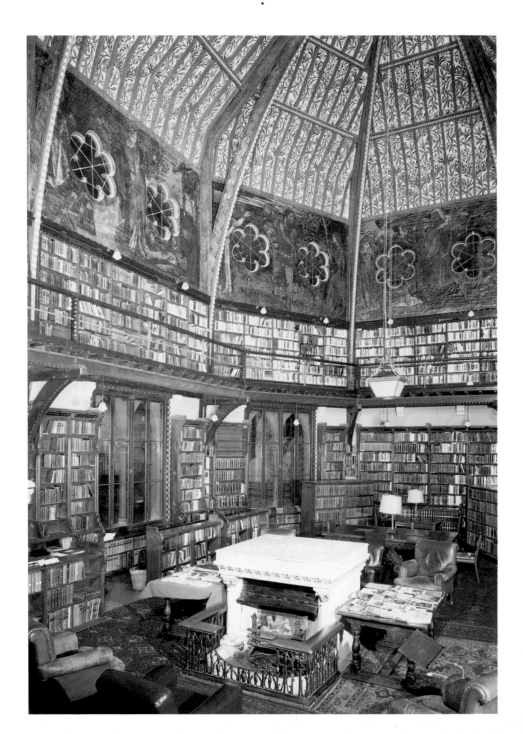

RIGHT The Oxford Union library (originally the Debating Hall) showing the murals and decorated ceiling begun in 1857 by Rossetti and his team of artists. Much acclaimed when they were first completed for their use of pure colour, the murals swiftly deteriorated because Rossetti was ignorant of the proper methods of preparing the surface, and are now badly discoloured. The ceiling patterning is by Morris.

It was in Street's office that Morris met another person who was to be of prime importance in the development of his life and work. This was Philip Webb (1831–1915), who later would design Red House for Morris, as well as Standen for the Beale family, which Morris would decorate, and other influential late nineteenth-century houses.

When Street moved offices to London, Morris went too, and joined Burne-Jones in his lodgings in Bloomsbury. After a short while, they moved again, to Red Lion Square, to a studio that had formerly been occupied by Dante Gabriel Rossetti (1828–82). Burne-Jones already knew and admired Rossetti; now Morris also fell under his spell. Inspired and charmed by this charismatic figure, Morris determined to abandon architecture and take up painting.

In the meantime, unable to find furniture that he liked for the studio, Morris designed chairs, a table and an enormous settle. His new friend Webb designed a wardrobe. The furniture was made up by a local carpenter and decorated by Rossetti and Burne-Jones with scenes taken from Morris's own poems, from Chaucer and from Dante's *Beatrice*. This communal effort, both in terms of design and execution, prefigured the work of the 'Firm'.

In 1857, Morris and Burne-Jones joined Rossetti in another collective enterprise in Oxford where, with other artists, he was engaged in the decoration of the new Oxford Union debating hall. The ten bays between the windows in the gallery were to be painted with scenes from Malory's *Morte d'Arthur*, almost a sacred text in that circle. The work was organized in an amateur way, spirits were high and there was much practical joking. Morris designed a suit of armour and had it made by a local blacksmith as a reference for his own mural.

Burne-Jones later recounted with amusement what happened when the helmet first arrived from the forge. Morris tried it on and was unable to lift the visor. Looking down from his vantage point in the gallery, Burne-Jones saw Morris 'embedded in iron, dancing with rage and roaring inside'. Morris was much more satisfied with the mail coat when it was finished and wore it at dinner.

The Oxford Union murals, brilliantly coloured and boldly drawn, were a technical disaster. Soon after the work was completed, it began to deteriorate because the surface had not been properly prepared. Morris went on to paint the ceiling with a twining pattern of leaves and stems. In 1875 he was asked back to the Union to redecorate.

Artists working on the murals modelled for each other, but female models were harder to come by. One evening at the theatre Rossetti was struck by the extraordinary beauty of a young woman. He asked her to model and she agreed, posing for him as Guenevere and for Morris as Iseult. Morris fell deeply in love.

Jane Burden, an ostler's daughter, was the personification of the Pre-Raphaelite ideal. In the slang of the day, she was a 'stunner'. Her slender figure, thick wavy black hair and pale melancholy expression made a lasting impression on everyone who saw her. Even then her particular type of beauty was so strongly associated with the Pre-Raphaelite vision that it was difficult to tell which came first, a fact noted by the novelist Henry James when he met her in 1869: 'It's hard to say whether she's a grand synthesis of all the Pre-Raphaelite pictures ever made – or they a "keen analysis" of her – whether she's an original or a copy. In either case she's a wonder.'

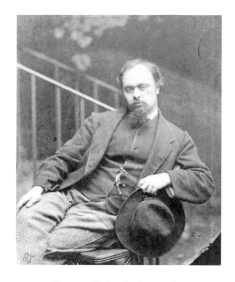

ABOVE Dante Gabriel Rossetti, photographed by Charles Dodgson (Lewis Carroll) in 1863, the year after the death of his wife Lizzie Siddal, a Pre-Raphaelite model and aspiring artist. Rossetti was stricken by guilt and grief at her death, which was thought to be suicide.

Jane was the subject of Morris's only painting in oils, *La Belle Iseult*. By 1858 he proposed marriage and she accepted. In April 1859 they were married at Oxford.

To some of Morris's friends they made an unlikely pair. Morris, who had been given the nickname 'Topsy' at Oxford because of his unruly mop of black hair, was untidy, violently energetic and prone to sudden rages of frustration. His friend Webb later told May, Morris's daughter: 'When a difficult point arose your Father would beat his head with his fists, till I thought it would stun him.'

By contrast, Jane ('Janey' throughout her life to family and friends) was quiet and languid. Like many Victorian ladies, she enjoyed poor health. It is likely that at the time of her marriage she was already in love with Rossetti; Rossetti, although engaged to Lizzie Siddal, may already have returned her affections. The anguish their relationship caused was to blight Morris's family life.

In 1859, however, these difficulties were in the future. Morris had just published *The Defence of Guenevere and Other Poems*, dedicated to Rossetti, and considered by many critics today to be his best work of poetry. The same year, he commissioned Webb to design a house, a venture which marked the true beginning of Morris's career and a turning point in the decorative arts in Britain.

RED HOUSE

In 1860 William and Jane Morris began their married life together in Red House. Soon it became the weekend retreat for the newly married Rossetti and Lizzie Siddal and Edward and Georgiana Burne-Jones, and for Webb, Charles Faulkner and his sisters. Morris's two daughters, Jenny and May, were born there in 1861 and 1862.

Webb's first commission, Red House, Bexleyheath, Kent (then about ten miles from London) marks an important stage in the development of English domestic building. 'More a poem than a house, but admirable to live in too', according to Rossetti, it was functional yet romantic, and 'very medieval in spirit', just as Morris had intended. According to John Mackail, Morris's biographer, the house was so skilfully sited by Webb that, although it stood in an orchard, hardly any trees had to be cut down and 'apples fell in at the windows as they stood open on hot autumn nights'. The planning, layout and decoration of Red House are described in more detail in the following chapter but here it is important to note that Morris believed attractive surroundings were a vital stimulus for producing good work. Red House was not only the 'embodiment of dreams' but a setting which would itself inspire and stimulate ideas.

Like the studio at Red Lion Square, Red House was decorated and almost entirely furnished through the communal efforts of Morris and his friends. Morris believed passionately that what was commercially available was debased and ugly: almost the only articles which he could bring himself to buy for the house were Persian carpets and Delft china. Webb designed much of the furniture for Red House, from the massive oak dining table to copper candlesticks. The settle from Red Lion Square was installed in the drawing room, whose walls were decorated with murals painted by Burne-Jones. Morris designed wallhangings which were embroidered by his wife and Lizzie Siddal. In the

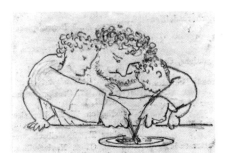

ABOVE A pen and ink sketch of Morris and his two little daughters, drawn by Burne-Jones about 1865. Burne-Jones made similar drawings of Morris – affectionate caricatures – all through their friendship.

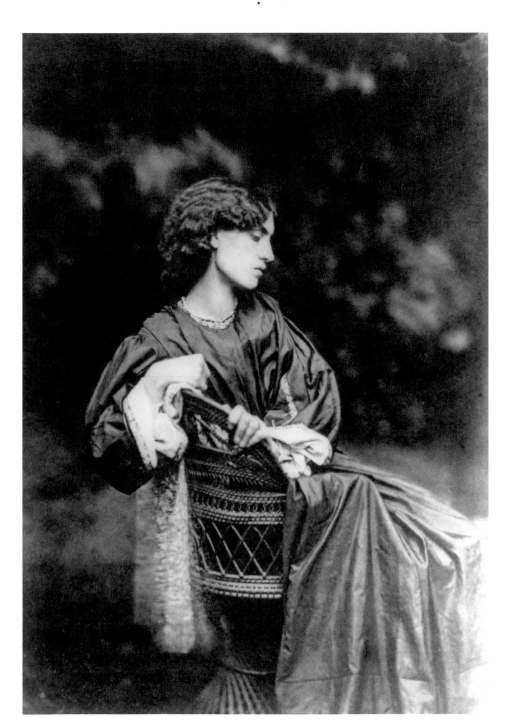

LEFT Jane Morris, posed by Rossetti but photographed by a professional photographer, in the garden of Rossetti's London home in Cheyne Walk, summer 1865, shortly before the Morrises left Red House and moved to Queen Square. At this time, Jane also posed for drawings, possibly intended as studies for an oil portrait. Over the next few years, the mutual attraction between Rossetti and Jane deepened.

bedroom, the hangings featured a daisy motif, inspired by an illuminated manuscript Morris had seen in the British Museum. With Burne-Jones, Morris also designed stained glass, a decorative departure for domestic buildings.

ॐ

THE FIRM

The decoration and furnishing of Red House soon led Morris and his friends to the idea that they should set up as an artists' cooperative, producing all kinds of decorative work by hand on a commercial basis. Morris, Marshall, Faulkner and Co. – 'Fine Art Workmen' – was established in 1861 with seven founder members who included, as well as the named partners, Rossetti, Burne-Jones, the Pre-Raphaelite painter Ford Madox Brown and Webb. Premises were taken at Red Lion Square, with an office, showroom, workshops and a small kiln for glass-making and firing tiles.

Under-capitalized but with high ideals, the 'Firm' launched itself with a prospectus proclaiming the importance of the work of artists in design and decoration and setting

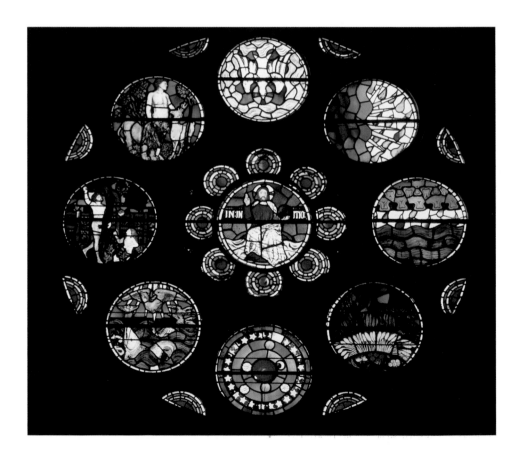

RIGHT One of the Firm's first commissions was to design stained glass for All Saints, Selsley, Gloucestershire in 1862. The architect of the new church, G F Bodley, commissioned the Firm to do the work after admiring the stained glass they showed at the International Exhibition. Six of the nine roundels in this window are by Morris, including Christ in Majesty.

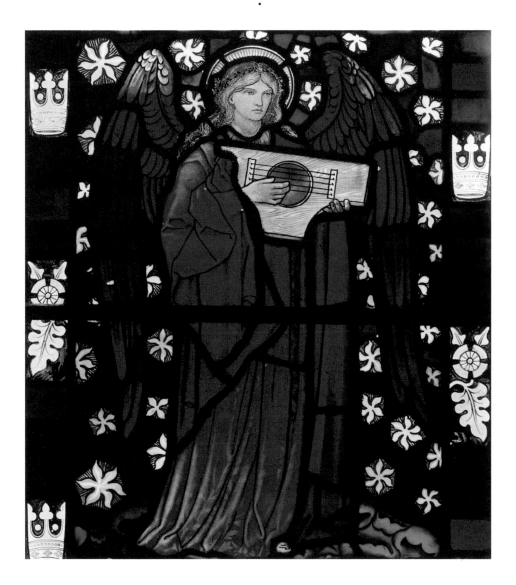

LEFT An angel with a dulcimer, 1882, from St Peter and St Paul, Cattistock, Dorset. The Firm's distinctive stained glass work was a return to the spirit of the great medieval tradition, using bold outlines and a mosaic of pure colour for a rich, glowing effect. Morris's instinctive colour sense was invaluable in this respect; although Burne-Jones, Webb and Rossetti drew many of the figures and animals in the Firm's designs, Morris was responsible for turning those drawings into stained glass, choosing the colours and setting the leaded lines.

out areas of specialization, including mural painting, carving, stained glass, metal work and furniture making. Initially the greatest demand was ecclesiastical, and they found a steady market for stained glass, tiles and church hangings to complement the medieval character of the new Gothic revival churches. In 1862 the Firm won two gold medals for their exhibits at the International Exhibition, South Kensington Museum (later the Victoria and Albert Museum). The stained glass in particular was so successful that it was initially thought to be original medieval work and there were calls for it to be disqualified.

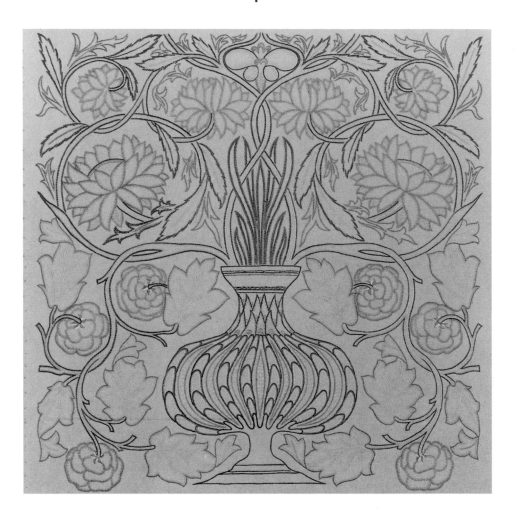

RIGHT *The Flowerpot*, designed by Morris and worked by May in about 1880, in silk and gold on a linen ground. The panel was available in kit form from Morris and Co, to be made up at home into a cushion cover or firescreen. Embroidery was an important part of the output of the Firm from the very beginning.

In stained glass, as in the other areas of decoration with which he became concerned, Morris was quick to grasp and master the potential of the medium, instinctively knowing what the material could do best. Morris supplied glass for over four hundred buildings during his lifetime but the best examples date from this early period, when he designed more than one hundred windows himself as well as providing backgrounds for Burne-Jones's figures and Webb's animals. The Firm returned to the medieval notion of using coloured glass in a mosaic to tell a story, rather than merely painting on to glass. Its use of pure colour, strong outline and detail was much admired.

The Firm had another popular line in handpainted tiles for panels and fireplaces. Faulkner's sisters Kate and Lucy did much of this work. Morris began a collaboration with the artist William de Morgan (1839–1917) who was to become a ceramicist noted for his natural forms and Islamic motifs.

Embroidery was also a large part of the early output. Jane, her sister Bessie and Georgiana Burne-Jones tackled much of the work, under Morris's direction. Morris had taught Jane medieval techniques which he discovered by laboriously unpicking old examples. It was Jane who discovered the length of indigo serge in a London shop which together they transformed into the *Daisy* hanging for the bedroom at Red House. According to Jane, when she took the fabric home, Morris 'was delighted with it and set to work at once designing flowers. These we worked in bright colour in a rough simple way.' Most of the Firm's first commissions for embroidery were ecclesiastical.

Webb was the Firm's principal furniture designer. Many of the early pieces were huge, one-off commissions, medieval in character and richly painted. These, naturally, were expensive.

Towards the middle of the 1860s matters in both Morris's business and private lives came to a head. The casual disorganization of accounts and work had taken their toll. At the same time, Morris's private income had dropped due to a decline in the value of his shares. When Faulkner, who had been running the business side of the Firm, returned to Oxford in 1865, an old Etonian called Warington Taylor who had fallen on hard times himself took over as manager. Despite suffering from consumption, which meant that he had to move to Hastings for his health, Taylor managed to stabilize the Firm, forcing Morris and Rossetti to adopt more rational, businesslike methods and castigating Morris, in particular, for any private over-expenditure. In a painfully honest letter to Rossetti, Taylor gave this vivid account of Morris's muddled working methods: 'Morris will start half a dozen jobs; he has only designs for perhaps half of them, and therefore in a week or two they have to be given up. They are put away, bits get lost, have to be done over again: Hence great loss of time and money.'

There was physical illness as well as poor financial health. In 1864 Morris suffered a severe bout of rheumatic fever which weakened him considerably. The Burne-Jones family fell ill with scarlet fever. Tragically, an infant son died and Georgiana came close to death herself. For financial reasons, Ned Burne-Jones was unwilling to move to the country, and by now Morris was physically unable to commute to London. When new premises for the Firm were taken in Bloomsbury, Red House had to be abandoned. Morris and his family went to live at Queen Square, literally above the shop. The move from Red House was an emotional wrench. Many of the larger pieces of furniture and, of course, all the mural decorations, had to be left behind. Morris was so distraught that he could never bear to return.

It was also about this time that family life became a source of intense private grief. Jane's attraction to Rossetti had developed into love. She began spending more time with him, posing for the first of many drawings, photographs and paintings in which he recorded her strange, brooding beauty. The attachment between Janey and Rossetti soon became too obvious to hide; it was a double betrayal for Morris, who lost a friend and mentor as well as a wife.

QUEEN SQUARE

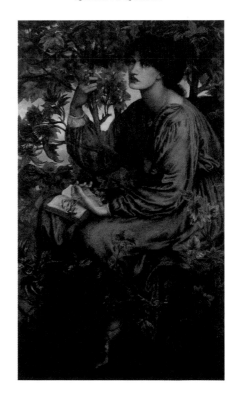

ABOVE *Day Dream* by Rossetti. The face and form are recognizably Jane Morris. This is a late work, dating from the mid 1870s.

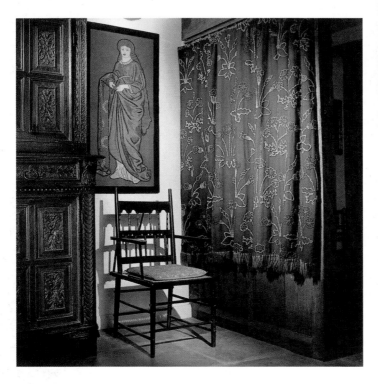

ABOVE The *Daisy* hanging, designed by Morris in 1860 and worked by Jane on a length of indigo serge which she discovered in a London shop. The hanging was originally made for the bedroom at Red House and featured one of Morris's favourite motifs. It won a medal at the International Exhibition in 1862.

RIGHT In 1866 the Firm were asked to decorate a room at the South Kensington Museum: it was the intention of the museum's founder, Henry Cole, to create a museum which was itself a work of art. The Green Dining Room (now the William Morris Room, Victoria and Albert Museum) was a cooperative effort. Webb designed the ceiling and frieze. Burne-Jones and Charles Fairfax-Murray painted the figure panels and fruits on gold backgrounds, which symbolize months of the year.

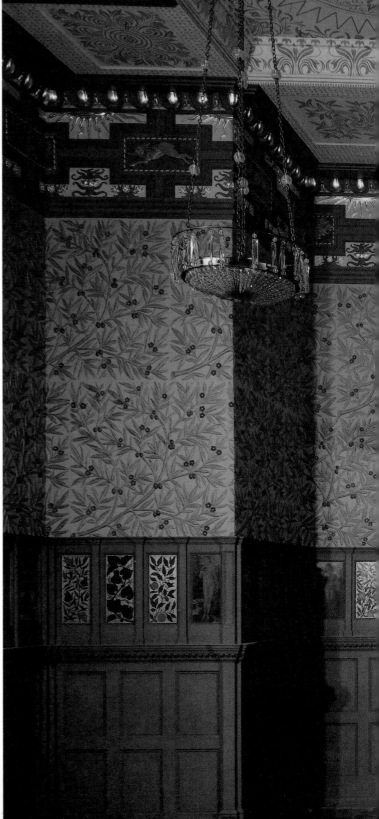

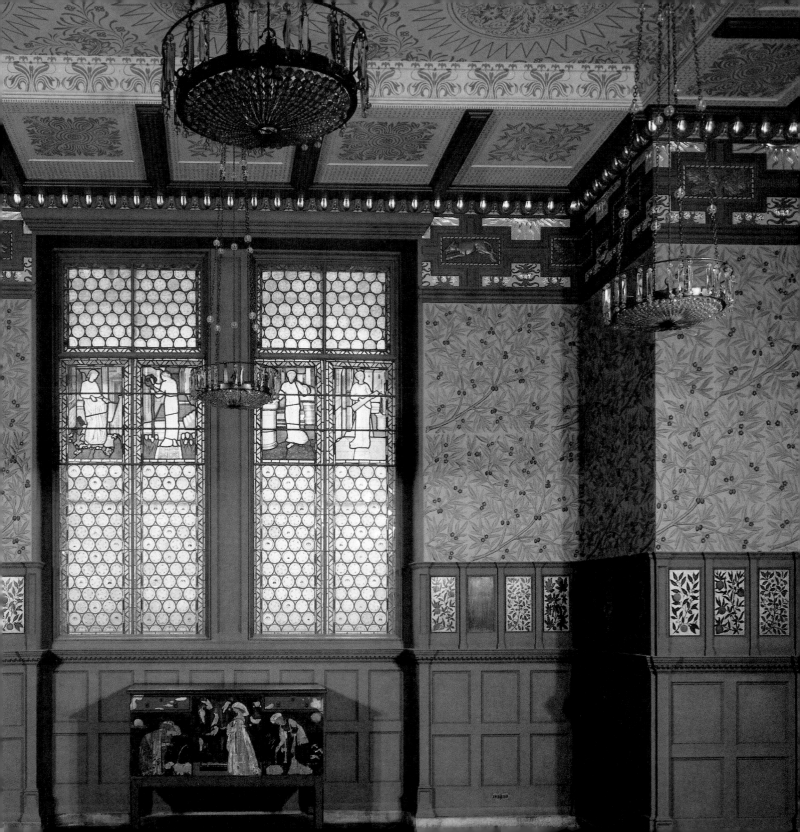

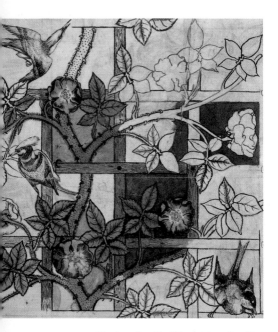

ABOVE Design for *Trellis*, 1862, the first wallpaper pattern William Morris attempted; the birds are by Webb. The design is said to have been inspired by the rose trellis that extended along one side of the garden at Red House.

OPPOSITE *Blue Silk Dress (Mrs William Morris in a Blue Silk Dress)*, 1868. William Morris commissioned Rossetti to paint this portrait of his wife, which captures Janey at 28, in the fullness of her beauty. It is a picture ripe with sensuality and suppressed longing; the period during which it was painted marks the beginning of the affair between Rossetti and Janey. The picture was intended to hang in the drawing room at Queen Square, but Morris was dissatisfied with it and returned it to Rossetti to be reworked.

In the second half of the decade the Firm consolidated its reputation with two important official commissions. The first was to refurbish the Green Dining Room at the South Kensington Museum (now the William Morris Room at the Victoria and Albert). The second was to redecorate the Armoury and Tapestry Room at St James's Palace, beginning an involvement which continued until the early 1880s. There were numerous private commissions as well, with Morris increasingly occupied in decorating houses designed by Webb.

Two of the Firm's most popular and influential furniture designs date from this time. Unlike the monumental, richly decorated earlier examples, both were based on plain traditional country pieces. The 'Morris' chair was designed by Webb in 1866 after a prototype which was originally discovered in Sussex by Taylor. The range of 'Sussex' rush-seated chairs also first came out in 1866. Cheap and simple, they were enormously popular and remained in production for 80 years.

Between 1864 and 1866 Morris produced his first three designs for wallpaper. None were well received at the time, although *Daisy* was later to be the Firm's bestseller for fifty years. All three papers were expensive to produce, requiring twelve blocks each to print. *Trellis* was supposedly inspired by the rose trellis in the garden at Red House. *Daisy* featured a favourite motif which also appeared on embroidered hangings, tiles and small stained glass panels. *Fruit* or *Pomegranate*, as it was also known, was the most sophisticated of the three designs.

Throughout the 1860s, Morris was engaged in writing an epic cycle of narrative poems, which was published in three volumes, the first in 1868, the second two in 1870. *The Earthly Paradise*, with its direct and accessible language and narrative style, set the seal on Morris's reputation as a poet. In structure the work is similar to Chaucer's *Canterbury Tales*. Set in the fourteenth century, it tells how travellers escaping the plague journey in search of 'earthly paradise' but arrive instead at a 'western land'. Over the course of a year the 'wanderers' tell stories to their hosts, who return the favour. There are twenty-four stories in all, retellings of myths, romances and sagas, as well as an introductory poem for each month. The latter part of *The Earthly Paradise* was written as Morris's family life was disintegrating and after he had left Red House. As the affair between Janey and Rossetti slowly and inexorably developed, Morris felt bitterly isolated and helplessly unable to alter the situation. Not only was his preoccupation with poetry indicative of a more inward-looking and solitary disposition, this portion of *The Earthly Paradise* can be read all too easily as a bleak, despairing autobiography.

From the introduction to *September*:

> *Look long, O longing eyes, and look in vain!*
> *Strain idly, aching heart, and yet be wise,*
> *And hope no more for things to come again*
> *That thou beheldest once with careless eyes!*
> *Like a new-wakened man thou art, who tries*
> *To dream again the dream that made him glad*
> *When in his arms his loving love he had.*

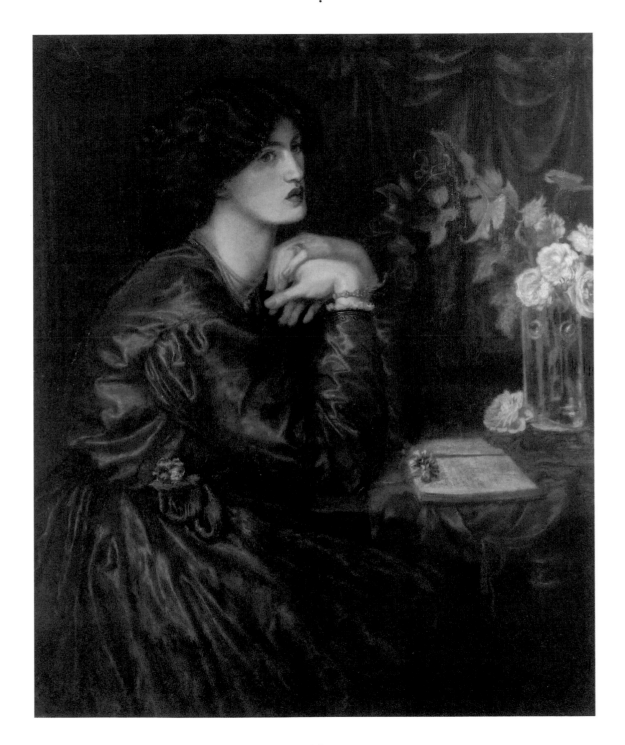

KELMSCOTT

In 1871 Morris bought the lease of 'an old stone Elizabethan house' in the Cotswolds. Kelmscott Manor near Lechlade in Gloucestershire was not actually Elizabethan but dated from a later period. Nevertheless it was a perfect country retreat, with nearby watermeadows bordering the upper reaches of the Thames and a garden which was to inspire many of Morris's most memorable patterns. The house, with its grey stone gables, is described in Morris's utopian work, *News from Nowhere*.

The original tenancy was taken jointly with Rossetti, a tacit acknowledgement of his continuing involvement with Jane. There seems to have been the intention that Kelmscott would provide a place for Rossetti and Jane to be alone.

Rossetti, never very stable, grew increasingly unbalanced. Guilt over the death of his wife in 1862 (presumed to be suicide) had precipitated the process of decline that the stress of his affair with Jane accelerated. Drink and drug dependency eventually led to a suicide attempt in 1872. Two years later Jane finally put a stop to the relationship.

In the intervening time, Morris found Rossetti's presence unbearable. Twice during the early 1870s he embarked on long journeys to Iceland, leaving Rossetti and Jane behind at Kelmscott. Iceland provided just the revitalizing element Morris needed. He had become interested in Icelandic sagas during his work on *The Earthly Paradise* and in typical fashion followed this up by learning the language and translating sagas himself. The raw beauty of the country, the courage of the people in facing the hardship of their

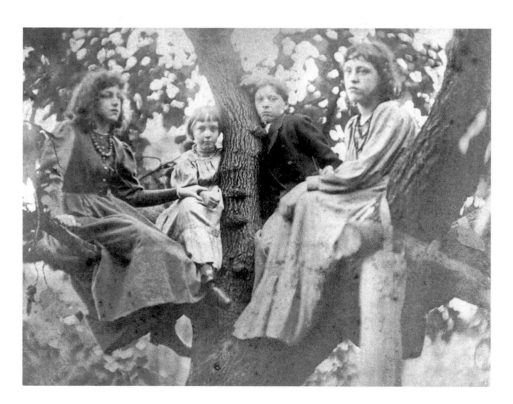

RIGHT The Morris and Burne-Jones children photographed in the garden of The Grange, summer 1874. (From left to right: May Morris, Margaret Burne-Jones, Philip Burne-Jones, Jenny Morris.) The onset of Jenny's epilepsy, two years later, ended her hopes of an academic career.

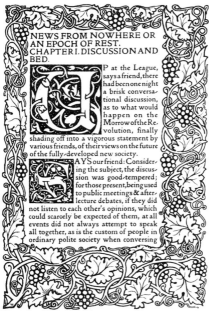

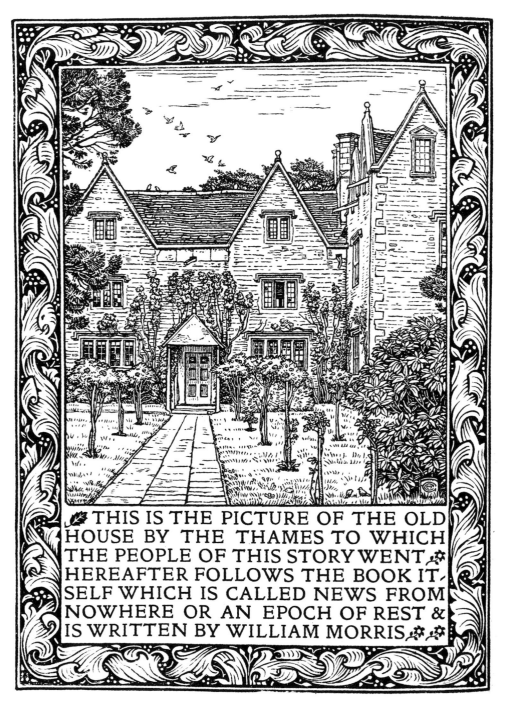

THIS IS THE PICTURE OF THE OLD HOUSE BY THE THAMES TO WHICH THE PEOPLE OF THIS STORY WENT HEREAFTER FOLLOWS THE BOOK IT SELF WHICH IS CALLED NEWS FROM NOWHERE OR AN EPOCH OF REST & IS WRITTEN BY WILLIAM MORRIS

LEFT Kelmscott Manor, near Lechlade, Gloucestershire, Morris's beloved country home. This drawing of the east front, by C M Gere, was used as the frontispiece for *News from Nowhere* (above), Morris's utopian work. A house very like Kelmscott Manor is described in book. After Morris's death, Janey maintained the tenancy and was finally able to buy the property before her death. May also lived there for many years.

living conditions and the sheer rigours of what was at that time very difficult travelling impressed and inspired him. 'A piece of turf under your feet, and the sky overhead, that's all; whatever solace your life is to have here must come out of yourself or these old stories,' he noted in his journal, referring to the power and relevance of the sagas. Iceland also saw the beginnings of his awakening political conscience. 'I learnt one lesson there, thoroughly I hope,' he later wrote, 'that the most grinding poverty is a trifling evil compared with the inequality of classes.' Although the people of Iceland were poor, they were not oppressed or degraded.

By 1874 the joint tenancy with Rossetti was at an end, Rossetti's affair with Jane was over and Morris could begin to find solace in Kelmscott himself. It remained his country home until his death: 'As others love the race of men through their lovers or their children, so I love the earth through that small space of it.'

But there was one more personal sorrow to come. In 1876 Morris's beloved elder daughter Jenny was diagnosed as an epileptic. The condition, which could not be regulated in those days, was probably inherited from Morris's side of the family; some of Morris's stupendous rages may also have been epileptic in nature.

MORRIS AND CO.

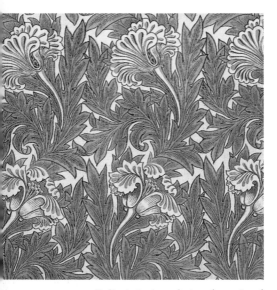

ABOVE *Tulip* (1875), a design for printed cotton, or chintz, from Morris's most naturalistic period.

For several years the Firm had been run mainly by Morris without much participation from the other partners. Reorganization was in order. The old partnership was dissolved fairly amicably and Morris and Co. was formed in 1875.

By now the market for their work was largely domestic, as opposed to ecclesiastical. At the beginning of the 1870s Morris had begun to design wallpaper again; the period between 1872 and 1876 was his most fruitful, when designs such as *Willow, Jasmine* and *Larkspur* were produced.

The year 1875 also represented a turning point in Morris's involvement with textile design. Early experience in this field had been disappointing and unsatisfactory. The new aniline dyes produced harsh colours which were also technically unsound: they faded and bled. At this point Morris began to collaborate with Thomas Wardle, the brother of his new business manager George, who had a dyeworks in Leek, Staffordshire, experimenting with the techniques of vegetable dyeing. Morris found the work absorbing, particularly the challenge of indigo dyeing. He studied old herbals and medieval treatises, creating colours by such arcane means as boiling twigs and crushing the carcases of insects.

Over half of the forty chintz designs Morris produced during his lifetime date from the period 1876–83. The beautiful hand-printed cottons for which he is best-known include the flowing, naturalistic *Tulip* (1875), *Honeysuckle* (1876) and *Snakeshead* (1876–77). During the second half of the 1870s Morris also became interested in weaving, taking inspiration from both medieval and Eastern sources. This, in turn, led him on to tapestry weaving and carpet design, driven by an ambition to recapture the height of perfection displayed in Persian carpet-making. At this stage, naturalism in his designs gave way to a more abstract and Eastern style.

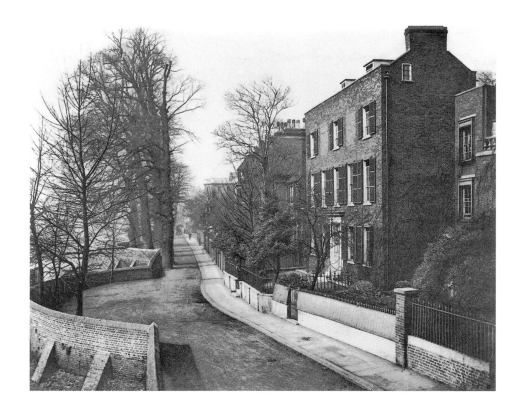

LEFT Kelmscott House on the banks of The Thames at Hammersmith, west London. After several London moves, Kelmscott House was the place Morris and his family finally settled in 1878. Spacious, with river views from its first floor drawing room, it also had an orchard and kitchen garden, and a coachhouse, where meetings of the Socialist League were held in the 1880s.

Morris's expanding interests together with his need to earn a living from the company made it necessary to move premises. Earlier, the company had taken showrooms at the corner of Oxford Street and North Audley Street, which enabled the retail side of the business to be moved away from Queen Square. Morris's London home, too, was no longer over the shop. In 1872 the family had moved to Turnham Green, near the Burne-Jones's in Fulham. In 1878 they moved again, for the last time in London to Hammersmith, to a Georgian house on the river which Morris decided to rename as Kelmscott House.

Morris finally found the workshop space he needed in Surrey. Merton Abbey was situated on the banks of the River Wandle. Originally established by the Huguenots as a silk-weaving factory, it was at that time being used as a print works. Morris retained the old buildings with their red tiled roofs and weather-boarding and converted them into workshops for printing, glassmaking, weaving and dyeing. Carpet looms were built and pits for indigo dye vats were dug. The river water was found to be ideal for madder-dyeing.

All in all, Merton Abbey, with its buttercup meadows, willow and poplar trees growing beside the riverbank and millpond, with its garden full of cottage flowers and the rushing stream turning the water wheel, was a setting fit to inspire Morris's finest work.

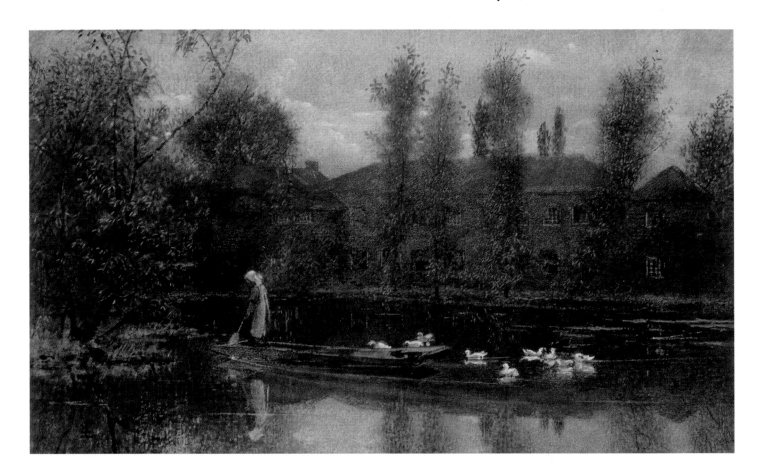

ABOVE *The Pond at Merton Abbey*, gouache and watercolour by L L Pocock. The idyllic setting of the works, on the banks of the River Wandle in Surrey inspired many of Morris's designs.

Mackail, Morris's biographer, describes lengths of cotton 'bleaching on grass thickly set with buttercups' and 'trout leap[ing] outside the windows of the long cheerful room where the carpet looms are built'. George Wardle, Morris's business manager, described it more succinctly as 'altogether delightful'. It certainly was a fulfilment of Morris's particular vision to create a working environment where dyes could be made from the twigs of trees growing nearby and processed using local river water, where cloth could be bleached in the sun and dried after dyeing on the meadows and where there was an abundance of natural beauty to fuel the imagination.

The years following the move to Merton Abbey were prolific, even by Morris's standards. Nineteen new designs for chintzes were produced between 1881 and 1883, including *Strawberry Thief*, one of his best-known. Most of these were floral designs but the scale of the patterns varied from small repeats to large, more diagonally stressed designs. And, although Morris and Co. was never highly profitable due to Morris's exacting standards, this was a successful time for the business, with its growing reputation for quality, and a fashionable artistically-minded clientele.

At Merton Abbey, Morris employed a number of former Spitalfields weavers to help produce the handwoven textiles, chiefly in wool. The size of the new premises meant that he could design and produce larger carpets and tapestries. Carpet-making was very labour-intensive and very expensive. The Howard family commissioned Morris to design a carpet for the library at their home, Naworth Castle. It took a year to complete.

Morris had long been interested in tapestry, which he called 'the noblest of all the arts of weaving'. Characteristically, he taught himself the difficult technique of high-warp weaving from a pre-Revolution French manual, building a loom in his bedroom at Kelmscott House and rising at five in the morning to get in a few hours' practice before the day began. As with the stained glass the Firm produced earlier, tapestries were communal design efforts. Burne-Jones, who remained Morris's principal designer, drew the figures, Webb the animals and Morris and J. H. Dearle tackled the backgrounds. Dearle, who began as an assistant in the glass studio in 1873, went on to run the works at Merton Abbey during the last years of Morris's life.

Embroidery remained an important part of the Firm's output. As well as specially commissioned wallhangings, the Oxford Street showroom sold embroidery kits to be made up at home and a popular range of embroidered accessories, including ladies' bags, covers for photograph frames and books, gloves and even bell pulls. May, Morris's

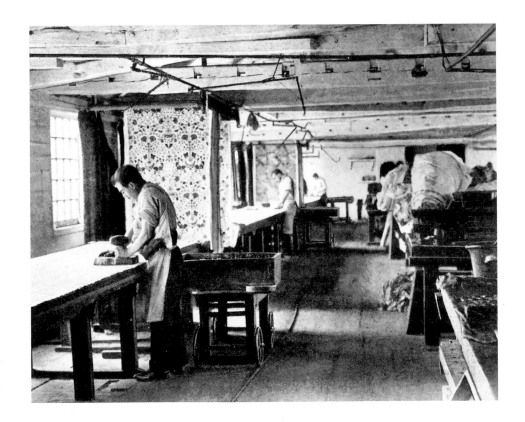

LEFT Hand block-printing of chintzes at Merton Abbey. The print shop was on the first floor; it echoed to the thud of wooden blocks hit by mallets. In contrast to the usual harsh conditions of Victorian factories, the Merton Abbey workshops were light and airy, the setting healthy and pleasant.

younger daughter, was a talented embroiderer and designer herself. From 1885 she was in charge of this part of the firm's business and later in life campaigned, lectured and wrote widely on the subject of embroidery.

PUBLIC LIFE

Morris became a socialist in 1883 at the age of 49 when he joined the Democratic Federation led by Hyndman. It was a move which consternated many of his friends, particularly Ned Burne-Jones, and earned him a hostile press. Since the publication of *The Earthly Paradise*, Morris had been a public figure, much admired and respected for his poetry. His public advocacy of the socialist cause was a significant propaganda coup and an act of some personal courage.

Iceland had aroused his social conscience but his first real political activity came about in 1876 during the controversy over the Eastern Question, where he supported the Liberal leader Gladstone against the imperialist foreign policy of Disraeli. Once Gladstone came to power, however, Morris became severely disillusioned with the Liberals. About the same time as he became involved with the Eastern Question campaign Morris threw himself into another public debate. This concerned the common nineteenth-century practice of 'restoring' ancient monuments and churches by dismantling additions made over the years in an attempt to arrive at the 'original' building. Morris saw this as nothing less than architectural vandalism, a wanton destruction of the 'living history' of these buildings in favour of some arbitrary notion of authenticity. In 1877 he founded the Society for the Protection of Ancient Buildings – 'Anti-Scrape' as he called it – to act as a pressure group opposing the practice. 'Anti-Scrape' mounted opposition to the restoration works proposed for St Mark's, Venice in 1879. More than 100 years later the society is still active and follows Morris's original manifesto.

After founding SPAB, Morris began a series of lectures on art and architecture to popularize the ideas of the society and help raise money. The early lectures were a success and he was soon in great demand as a speaker. Throughout the 1880s, all the strands of his life came together in his speeches, as he related art to society, discussed in detail the nature of design and pattern-making, and campaigned against the tawdry products of industrialization in favour of handcrafted work. In his words, it was 'Socialism seen through the eyes of an artist'.

A year after he joined the Democratic Federation, the organization split into factions. Morris resigned and, together with Eleanor Marx, helped to establish the Socialist League. His tireless political work was supplemented by generous financial support, and May Morris was always by his side. Weekly meetings of the local Hammersmith branch also took place in the coachhouse of Kelmscott House.

Morris believed that a just society would come only through revolution and considered himself to be a communist. He was fully aware of the irony that only the wealthy could afford his best work; even his chintzes and wallpapers were relatively expensive. He was once overheard to complain bitterly that he spent his life 'ministering to the swinish luxury of the rich'.

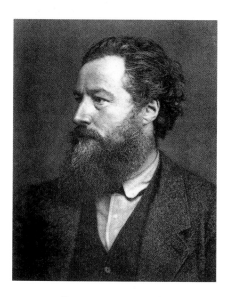

ABOVE William Morris in 1876. A stocky untidy man, he characteristically dressed in rather shabby suits of blue serge or work smocks; his hands were habitually stained from the dye-vat.

The gruelling round of public speaking and appearances eventually left little time for the Firm. But Morris continued to write poems and political tracts. In 1890 he published *News from Nowhere*, his great Utopian novel. The narrator of the story falls asleep one night in nineteenth-century Hammersmith to awaken the next morning far in the future. Following a revolution in 1952, the industrialized landscape has been replaced with a rural paradise, where work is pleasure and there is no money. There are small communities living close to the land, creating beautiful handcrafted work very like that produced by Morris and Co.

Morris suffered a breakdown in health in 1891 when a severe attack of gout weakened his kidneys. His illness came a year after the breakup of the Socialist League, and disillusionment as well as the strain of campaigning may have contributed to its onset. Jenny was also seriously ill at the same time, which caused great anguish.

Although he remained an active socialist, Morris was forced to conserve his energies. But during the last years of his life, he became preoccupied with an entirely new interest – the art and craft of printing. In 1891, he founded the Kelmscott Press, based in Hammersmith, and set to work with Burne-Jones designing type and illustrations, cutting wood blocks, and ordering paper and ink, going back to fifteenth-century sources to learn the techniques. This collaboration with Burne-Jones restored their friendship, which had been strained by the years of political activity. Over fifty books were printed by the press, including Ruskin's 'On the Nature of the Gothic' from *The Stones of Venice*, *The Earthly Paradise* and a edition of Chaucer which was four years in the making. Although the press never made a profit and closed down in 1898, its influence on the quality of commercial printing was considerable and it helped to stimulate a revival of the private press.

Early in 1896 it became obvious to his friends and family that Morris's health was failing. Diabetes was diagnosed and in April he visited Kelmscott Manor for the last time. The final weeks were spent at Kelmscott House, where Georgiana and Ned Burne-Jones were frequent visitors. There had always been a deep affection between Georgiana and Morris. Like Morris, Georgiana had her emotional troubles and had been a particular support when Morris's marriage nearly broke down.

William Morris died on 3 October, at the age of 62. According to Jane, among his last words were: 'I want to get mumbo-jumbo out of the world.' Three days after his death, his coffin was taken by train to Lechlade, loaded on to an open hay cart 'festooned with vines, with alder and with bullrushes' and driven along country lanes to Kelmscott. His grave is marked by a simple stone in the Cotswold tradition designed by Philip Webb.

Jane Morris maintained the lease of Kelmscott Manor and was finally able to buy the property in 1913, just a year before her death. Jenny, increasingly invalid, survived until 1935. May edited Morris's *Collected Works* after his death, and became a leading figure in embroidery and textile design. After Jane's death, she lived at Kelmscott Manor and died three years after Jenny, in 1938.

LAST YEARS

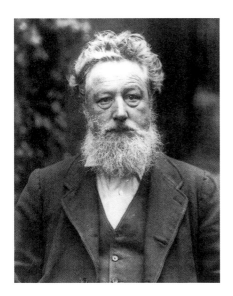

ABOVE William Morris in 1889, seven years before his death. Of his final illness, one of his doctors commented 'no doubt the disease was being William Morris and working 18 hours a day'. Morris is buried in Kelmscott churchyard.

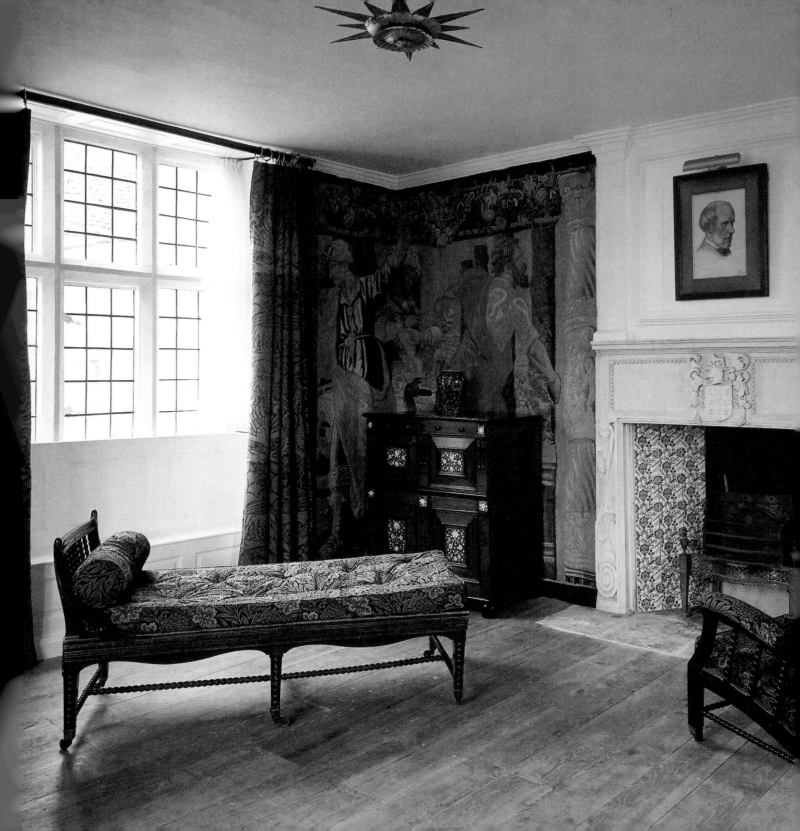

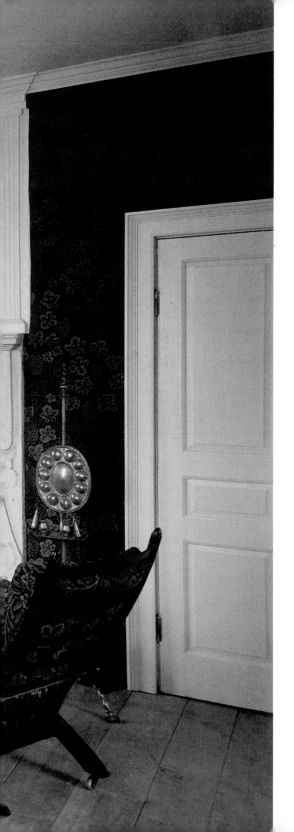

CHAPTER ONE

Forget the spreading of the hideous
town;
Think rather of the pack-horse on the
down,
And dream of London, small, and white,
and clean,
The clear Thames bordered by its garden
green . . .

The Earthly Paradise

LEFT The Tapestry Room at Kelmscott Manor. Morris loved the faded colour of the old hangings, which depicted the story of Samson.

35

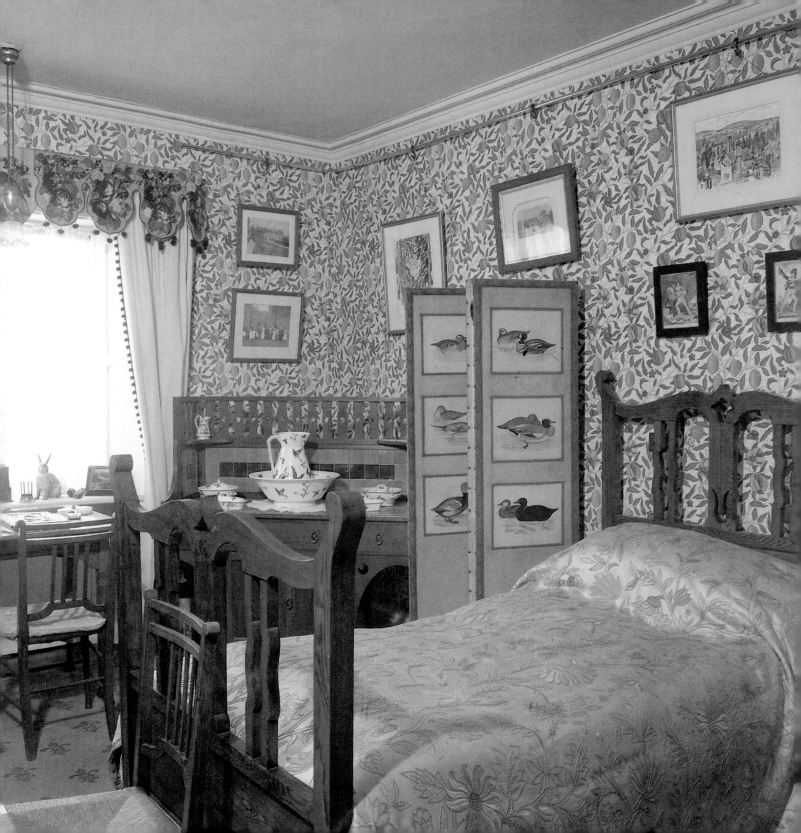

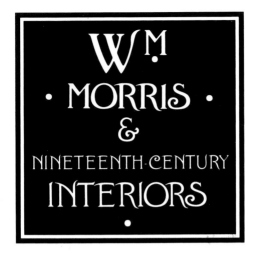

Wᴹ·MORRIS·&·NINETEENTH·CENTURY·INTERIORS

'THE PRESENT AGE IS DISTINGUISHED FROM ALL OTHERS IN HAVING NO STYLE which can properly be called its own,' declared an English guide to interior decoration published in 1840. By the time of the Great Exhibition in the middle of the century, this stylistic confusion was even more apparent. A fascination with the past at its most extreme was displayed in antiquarianism. This often co-existed with a taste for the exotic. Neo-Rococo, neo-Renaissance, Gothic Revival, Oriental, Moorish, Grecian, Baroque – the list of past styles borrowed for the design and furnishing of houses was seemingly endless. Above all, the Victorian age was one of eclecticism.

Industrialization and a rising middle class had created an expanding market for household goods. Status-hungry and fashion-conscious, this newly prosperous section of the population were eager consumers of the products of furniture makers, drapers and builders, with all their borrowed grandeur, imprecise terminology and derivative detailing. As new manufacturing techniques and new-materials were introduced throughout the century, traditional craft skills were jettisoned and, within a few generations, all but forgotten. 'Shoddy is King,' observed William Morris.

Although essentially confident and forward-looking, the Victorian middle class could also be insecure in matters of taste, which had formerly been the province of the wealthy landed gentry. Coupled with a tendency to acquisitiveness, this led to an over-abundance of objects on display in the home and a density of furnishing and drapery which could be breathtaking. The stifling, claustrophobic clutter of High Victoriana reached its zenith in the 1880s but the tendency is apparent much earlier. Compared to the spare elegance of many Georgian interiors, the Victorian room was very well furnished indeed. Superficially, the designs of William Morris could be seen as one more Victorian revival, a fascination with medieval style, a fantasy played out to its limits. But, although there is undoubtedly an element of romantic idealism – even, perhaps,

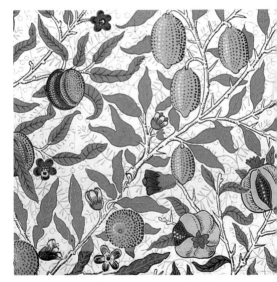

ABOVE *Fruit* or *Pomegranate*, 1864, the most sophisticated of Morris's early wall-paper designs.

OPPOSITE A bedroom at Cragside, North-umberland, with walls papered in *Pome-granate*. The golden fabrics and printed patterns echo the warm wood tones.

escapism — there is also a much more serious issue underneath it all. Morris was concerned to bring art back into people's lives. He did not merely want art for an élite, but for everyone. 'I do not want art for a few, any more than education for a few or freedom for a few . . .' he said memorably in a lecture in 1877. He was drawn to the medieval period as a source of inspiration because, like Ruskin, he believed that it represented the last period of honest design. He viewed the Renaissance, with its creation of specialists such as architects removed from the direct process of craft-making, as beginning a process of deterioration which led inexorably to the shoddy reproduction Rococo table or neo-Baroque sideboard. By contrast, the medieval period stood for honesty, truth to materials, the exercise of skill and artisanship. One might compare this with the value that is often placed today on the indigenous crafts of the Third World or pre-industrial cultures, with 'ethnic' patterns and handcrafts having a similar apparent honesty and directness. To Morris, the medieval woodcarver or stonemason must have seemed as instinctively expressive and unselfconscious in his work as the African basket-weaver or Indian dhurrie-maker does to us today.

There is another important difference between Morris and other designers who were drawn to historical sources. This is the fact that he was violently opposed to reproduction. As his friend and lifelong colleague Edward Burne-Jones put it, 'All his life, he hated the copying of ancient work as unfair to the old and stupid for the present, only good for inspiration and hope.' Morris's genius was his ability to create something entirely new out of his enthusiasm for the past.

A final, obvious distinction is that Morris's particular vision entailed that everything should be made by hand, displaying the stamp of individuality absent from mass-produced goods. His notion of 'craft' and the attendant revival of lost skills has remained a powerful force in modern design.

THE VICTORIAN INTERIOR 1860–1890

To understand the impact of William Morris and the Arts and Crafts movement it is necessary to place their radical ideas in the context of what was typical of the time. This is not a straightforward task, since the Victorian period was by no means consistent and homogenous and, like any other period, resists generalization. Nevertheless some common characteristics can be described and some trends discerned without too much distortion.

The period from the middle of the century to its close saw an explosion in house-building, rapidly expanding existing towns and cities and leading to the establishment of new centres. The process was accelerated by the spread of the railway. In Britain, where the pressure on space had always been intense, a great deal of new domestic building took the form of terrace or 'row' houses, extending up through several storeys to give the Victorian family enough room to accommodate themselves and their servants.

The architectural detailing of many of these houses was stylistically very varied. Gothic met Italian Renaissance met Classical Greek; mass-produced decorative

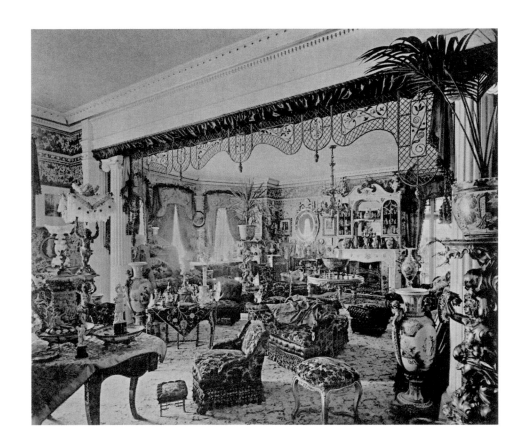

LEFT The Drawing Room, Wickham Hall, Kent in 1897. This late Victorian interior, with its lavish window drapery, ornaments of all descriptions and occasional tables laden with curios is the ultimate in conspicuous consumption.

flourishes embellished doorways and surmounted windows adding prestige. Angled bay windows replaced the Georgian bowfront as a common feature of elevations in many middle-class homes.

Indoors, similar effects were created with mouldings, archways, brackets and decorative plasterwork. Many of these architectural elements were not created *in situ* but applied ready-made. In main rooms, ceilings often had an elaborate central rose, a relief decoration in plaster from which the light fitting would be suspended. The cornicing (crown moulding) might also be very elaborate, classical in spirit although less refined than Georgian examples.

Of central importance was the fireplace, often light-coloured marble in a classical design – 'after Adam'. Black marble was a common choice for dining-room fireplaces. Other materials included painted wood or plaster surrounds and cast-iron with inset ceramic tiles.

Wallpaper was first mass-produced in Britain in 1841. It soon took over from fabric and wood panelling to become virtually the sole wall treatment in the ordinary domestic interior. Wallpaper, however, continued to simulate the effect of fabric coverings, which could be afforded only by the very rich. Stripes and floral sprigs were common. Crimson flocked paper with a relief surface was a popular choice for dining rooms. As the century progressed, patterns became denser and colours more brilliant with the introduction of chemical or aniline dyes: purple, yellow, sage green, maroon, Prussian blue and mahogany comprised the typical High Victorian palette. The effect of a dado was often created by using two contrasting papers, one from skirting board to chair rail, the other, 'filling' paper up to the picture rail. The lower paper, particularly in those hallways where there was no dado panelling, was often a heavy relief paper to resist wear. Lincrusta and Anaglypta came into production at the end of the 1870s in designs simulating wood, plasterwork or leather. Lighter designs were often displayed in drawing rooms and bedrooms, both deemed 'feminine' in spirit. Dining rooms and libraries, by contrast, were essentially 'masculine' and more sombre in mood.

Woodwork, which included deep skirting boards, panelled doors, architraves, staircases and picture rails, was painted a dark 'wood' colour or 'grained' to restore the impression of wood.

Floors were often carpeted, sometimes wall-to-wall, but more often leaving a margin of dark stained wood around the perimeter. Floral patterns predominated. Oilcloths were a cheap alternative to carpet, later superseded by linoleum. Hallways, kitchens and bathroom floors (where these existed) were often tiled in geometric patterns.

The characteristic gloom of the High Victorian interior, which deepened as the century progressed, was largely a function of an excessive use of fabric. Very little went undraped in the typical drawing room of the 1880s.

The window alone might be covered in anything up to four layers. First there was often a deep flat pelmet or lambrequin (an ornamental drapery or board fixed above the window to conceal the curtain rail), elaborately shaped and trimmed and extending about a third of the way down the window. Alternatively, the pelmet might consist of swagged drapery, artfully arranged over an ornate pole. Beneath the pelmet were heavy dark outer curtains in damask, figured satin, heavy silk or merino, caught back low down. Under the outer curtains came 'sub-curtains' in lace or muslin. Finally, next to the lower panes of glass might be 'glass curtains' or a decorative roller blind. During the summer, the outer curtains might be replaced with others in lighter fabric or left off altogether.

The intention appears to have been to exclude as much light as possible. Gloom was certainly fashionable and in a sense it was also an indication of status. A man would have to be fairly successful for his wife to languish all day in semi-darkened rooms, burning expensive candles if she wanted to read or attempt a little embroidery but otherwise doing very little except receive callers. Daylight, of course, was a precious resource for those who needed it to illuminate their work, but a comfortable middle class family employed others to do their household chores. Gloom expressed the prevailing Victorian mood of melancholia, associated with gentility, artistic sensitivity and spirituality.

Aside from the window, there were half a dozen other places for drapery. Understandably, doorways were one of them. Portières or door curtains fulfilled the important function of excluding draughts in these imperfectly heated houses; stylistically they could be highly elaborate. As in the case of window treatments, the effect was often unintentionally hilarious. A photograph of one draped dining room doorway in a fashionable Liverpool home of 1891 shows a pair of swords hanging from either side of a spear from which is ingeniously suspended a fringed pelmet. Three lengths of heavy gold rope awkwardly half-hoist a dark velvet curtain encrusted with deep scrolled embroidery, altogether more amateur theatricals than interior decoration.

Less understandable than portières, perhaps, were curtains for alcoves, mirrors and fireplaces. Picture frames, plant pots and pianos were also covered in cloth; there were tablecloths, antimacassars, runners, embroidered firescreens and framed samplers. Festoons of drapery might be tied between chair legs. Furniture was often upholstered in dark serviceable plush; chintz loose covers were for summer use or more intimate places such as bedrooms. Trimming in the form of deep fringing, gimp and tassels added to the overall effect. Upholstery was plump and overstuffed with horsehair; a deep buttoning was fashionable for a time, accentuating the curvaceous lines of the furniture.

As the interior gloom deepened, clutter also increased. Again, this over-abundance was perhaps an expression of prosperity – a form of conspicuous consumption – so much was collected and proudly displayed. Memorabilia, souvenirs, and exotica from colonial outposts mingled with framed photographs, *objets* and potted ferns and palms. Towards the end of the period a craze for Japanese decorative arts took hold, and fans, Japanese prints and screens were added to the *mélange*.

The nineteenth century saw an increasing separation of activities in the home, with different rooms being assigned to different uses in a manner that would have been unthought of a century previously. In a similar fashion, there were more types of furniture than ever before. Particularly Victorian was the 'whatnot', essentially a little display stand or cabinet for all the curios and mementoes. Furniture styles were as varied as architectural ones. Early on there was a fashion for 'naturalistic' pieces, which were curved, comfortable and often decorated with carved flowers and leaves. These tended to be well-stuffed, sometimes deep-buttoned pieces; examples included circular sofas, pouffes, and the *crapaud* (French for 'toad'), a squat deep-buttoned easy chair. Suites of drawing-room furniture might be reminiscent of eighteenth-century French designs; the Renaissance was a more common style for the dining room; while 'Adam' was the term generally given to the lighter painted bedroom pieces. Spindly Japanese 'art' furniture was very popular, as was bamboo for occasional tables and plantstands.

Most of what was available to the middle classes after 1870 was mass-produced or reproduction. At the top end of the market some very skilful copies of fine furniture were produced, but in general the standards of craftmanship and design were low. About this time antiques began to be avidly collected by the rich. For all the rampant eclecticism of the age, the plethora of stylistic sources and the emphasis on the display of personal taste, there was something remarkably similar and indelibly Victorian about many of these interiors. By the 1880s comfortable middle-class drawing rooms in Melbourne, Manchester or Philadelphia displayed striking similarities. The spread of the British Empire, together with improved communications, had helped to promote this conformity of taste. Throughout the second half of the nineteenth century countless books and magazines offered advice on interior decoration and furnishing. The home, if not a castle, could always have the trappings of one.

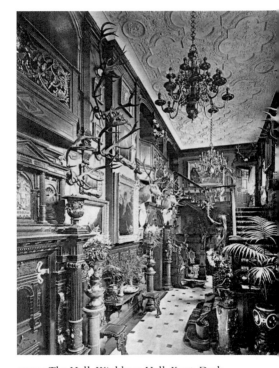

ABOVE The Hall, Wickham Hall, Kent. Dark wooden panelling, hunting trophies and the sheer density of ornament and elaboration is suggestive of ancestral wealth and grandeur.

THE WILLIAM MORRIS INTERIOR

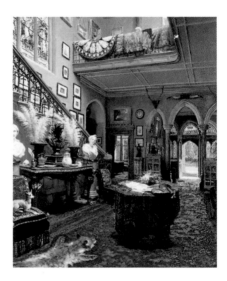

ABOVE *A Country House Hall* by Jonathan Pratt. The fussiness and clutter of this typical Victorian interior contrasts sharply with Red House.

'Masses of sordidness, filth and squalor, embroidered with pompous and vulgar hideousness,' was Morris's vivid and outspoken condemnation of the products of the Industrial Revolution. Many of the worst decorative excesses of the Victorian interior came well after Morris had formulated his design philosophy. But he was obviously more than acquainted with the stylistic confusions which reigned mid-century and deeply affected by the theorists of the Gothic revival who maintained that Gothic was the only true path in design. For Morris, however influenced he was by Ruskin and medievalism, Gothic was just a starting point and his own ideas quickly matured into a consistent and distinctive approach.

Throughout Morris's life, individual buildings and architecture in general played a central role in his vision. He never thought what people used or lived with in their daily life or how they decorated their homes was unimportant, and his writings, lectures and especially the decoration and furnishing of his own houses leave us in little doubt as to what he valued and sought in design. His central philosophy can perhaps be best summarized by his famous 'golden rule': *'Have nothing in your houses which you do not know to be useful or believe to be beautiful.'* This guiding principle occurs at the end of a passage where he describes what he considers to be the necessary decoration and furnishing of a living room, an inventory which might have been written today:

First a book-case with a great many books in it: next a table that will keep steady when you write or work at it: then several chairs that you can move, and a bench that you can sit or lie upon; next a cupboard with drawers; next, unless either the book-case or the cupboard be very beautiful with painting or carving, you will want pictures or engravings, such as you can afford, only not stopgaps, but real works of art on the wall; or else the wall itself must be ornamented with some beautiful and restful pattern: we shall want a vase or two to put flowers in, which latter you must have sometimes, especially if you live in a town. Then there will be the fireplace of course, which in our climate is bound to be the chief object in the room.

This is all we shall want, especially if the floor be good; if it be not, as, by the way, in a modern house it is pretty certain not to be, I admit that a small carpet which can be bundled out of the room in two minutes will be useful, and we must also take care that it is beautiful, or it will annoy us terribly . . .

. . . This simplicity you may make as costly as you please or can, on the other hand: you may hang your walls with tapestry instead of whitewash or paper; or you may cover them with mosaic, or have them frescoed by a great painter: all this is not luxury, if it be done for beauty's sake, and not for show: it does not break our golden rule: 'Have nothing in your houses which you do not know to be useful or believe to be beautiful.' (The Beauty of Life, 1880).

This eloquent plea for quality and simplicity was an indirect attack both on consumerism and on the sham, shoddy goods being peddled to the mass market. Morris believed in quality because well-made goods lasted longer and were a better use of resources and labour. But he also was opposed to accumulation for the sake of it: 'I have

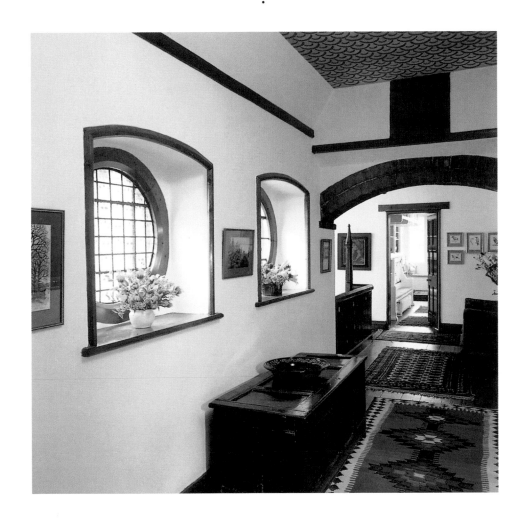

LEFT The Upper Landing at Red House.
Visitors at the time Morris lived there, in
the early 1860s, found it shockingly simple.

never been in any rich man's home which would not have looked the better for having a
bonfire made outside it of nine-tenths of all it held.'

Morris's own interiors, to our eyes comfortable and well-furnished, must have
seemed positively minimal to Victorians. There is evidence for this in accounts of the
time. A visitor to Red House in 1863 found it 'grand and severely simple,' while George
Bernard Shaw recalled the shock of seeing, at Kelmscott House, a dining table without a
tablecloth: 'a thing common enough now among people who see that a table should be
itself an ornament and not a clothes horse, but then an innovation so staggering that it
cost years of domestic conflict to introduce it.'

There is also an indication that Morris foresaw a time when it would be possible to
move away from strict separation of functions within a house to a more generous,
communal way of life. To Yeats he commented: 'The house that would please me would

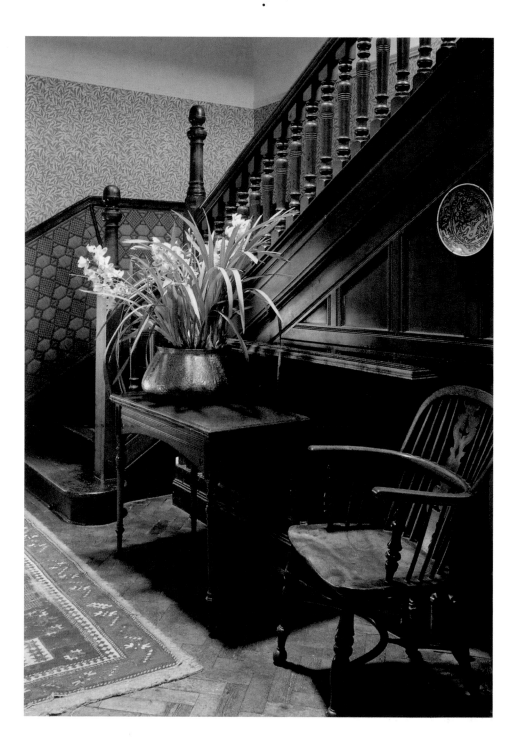

RIGHT The staircase at Wightwick Manor. Here the decoration, including *Willow Bough* paper above the dado, complements rather than obscures the strong architectural character.

be some great room where one talked to one's friends in one corner, and ate in another, and slept in another and worked in another.'

Although Morris is best known today for his rich and highly decorative patterns, one of the ways in which his work has influenced modern design is in the emphasis placed on function, and the related notion of the worthiness and beauty of the ordinary. 'The kitchen in a country farmhouse is most commonly a pleasant and homelike place. The parlour dreary and useless,' he commented in a lecture of 1877. According to the eminent art historian Sir Nikolaus Pevsner, Morris was really campaigning for the democracy of design. Ordinary houses and their furniture should be as worthy of the architect's attention as grand buildings; vases, wallpaper and fabric as worthy of the artist's as fine works of art. As he put it, he believed his duty to be 'to revive a sense of beauty in home life, to restore the dignity of art to ordinary household decoration.'

Morris's most persuasive arguments, however, can be found in his work. The houses he created for himself and his family and his major collaborations with Philip Webb display the essence of what he believed about design and its role in everyday life.

In many ways, Red House was a prototype. All subsequent Arts and Crafts interiors owe a great deal to the basic principles expressed in this building.

RED HOUSE

Red House, so called because of the warm red local bricks used in its construction, is L-shaped in plan, with hipped and gabled roofs, randomly arranged windows and slender chimney stacks. In overall appearance, the house is as vernacular as it is medieval, the entire effect informal and welcoming.

Indoors the same simplified Gothic ornament is evident in the architectural detailing of the open stairway, arches of the upper stair hall and great brick fireplace with its gilded motto: *Ars longa, vita brevis* ('Life is short, art is long'). This repetition of detail, indoors and out, is an important feature of the Arts and Crafts approach.

Structural repetition is emphasized by the use of the same materials and furnishings throughout. Each room, although different in character and function, is related to the whole, as a variation on a theme. This integration is a marked contrast to the Victorian tendency to adopt widely different styles and moods in the various rooms of a house, almost as if each were a stage set for a completely different play.

But it was the honest use of materials which was perhaps the most distinctive characteristic of Red House. Exposed beams, brick arches, contrasting textures of tile and wood, and the plain distempered walls display themselves for what they are, while at the same time revealing the structure of the building itself.

In terms of furnishing and decoration, Red House was the focus of intense communal effort by Morris and his friends. As well as tables and chairs, Webb designed huge cupboards incorporating storage, shelves or seating, fitted with hand-wrought catches and hinges. Much of the furniture was painted by Rossetti and Burne-Jones with narrative scenes inspired by romances and sagas. Morris and Jane embroidered hangings for the bedroom and dining room and frescoed the dining room ceiling. With Burne-Jones,

OPPOSITE The massive settle from Red Lion Square, shown here at Red House. Early furniture designs by Morris, Webb and the Firm were inspired by medieval precedents. This settle, originally decorated by Rossetti and Burne-Jones with scenes from Dante's *Beatrice*, was subsequently painted white.

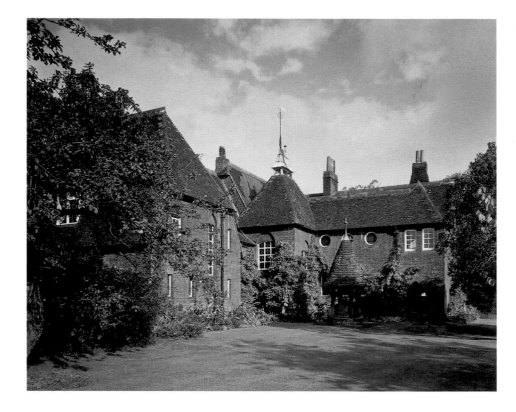

RIGHT Red House, Bexleyheath, Kent, designed by Philip Webb for William Morris. Newly married, Morris and his wife moved here in 1860. The vernacular design, with different roof lines and use of a warm local brick, was very influential.

Morris designed stained glass for the stairway, and Burne-Jones painted the fireplace tiles. Everything, down to the grates, candlesticks and fire-irons (designed by Webb), was created specially for the house and displayed all the vitality of handcrafted work.

In the years to come, Red House was always remembered by Morris and his circle as a happy place, a fulfilment of high ideals. It was enormously influential and helped to change the direction of English domestic building. It was not without its drawbacks, however. Designed during the very hot summer of 1859, the house faced north and proved bitterly cold in winter. There was another minor complaint: Jane found the coal cellar too small.

KELMSCOTT MANOR

Kelmscott Manor was essentially a holiday home, unheated and occupied mainly during the summer months. Nevertheless it held a special place in Morris's affections, eventually inspiring some of his best work. Kelmscott Manor is important as an indication of Morris's approach to old buildings and his general attitude to restoration. The trend in the nineteenth century was for very invasive restoration of ancient

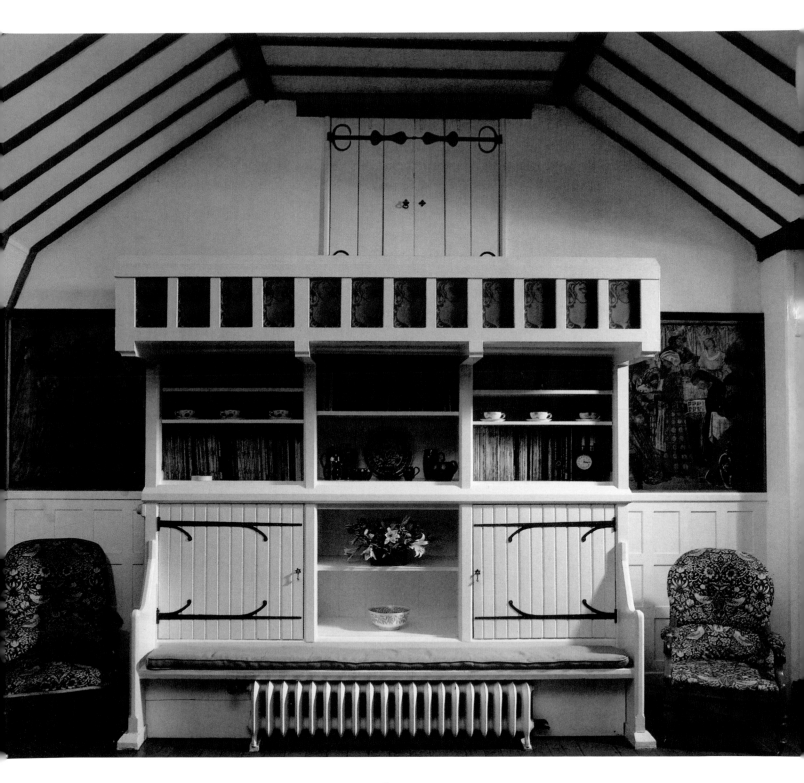

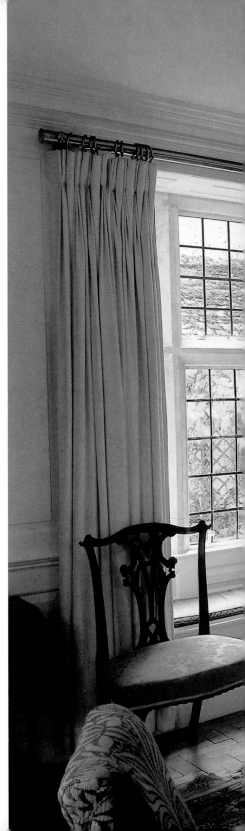

RIGHT The Drawing Room at Kelmscott Manor. White panelled walls and plain white curtains make a simple background for furniture covered in the large scale pattern *Peacock and Dragon*. The simplicity of decoration, perfectly in accord with the setting and architecture of the house, ran counter to Victorian taste. The painting – by Breughal the Younger – over the fireplace, belonged to Morris.

monuments and buildings. In a letter opposing the restoration of St Mark's, Venice, Morris castigates 'those that prefer gilding, glitter, and blankness, to the solemnity of tone and the incident that hundreds of years of wind and weather have given to the marble, always beautiful, but from the first meant to grow more beautiful by the lapse of time'.

To Kelmscott, accordingly, Morris did very little, except replace some rotten floorboards. It contained the minimum of furniture and was uncarpeted. What remained special about the house was its atmosphere, described by Morris as 'the melancholy born of beauty' and this haunting quality is evocatively described at the end of *News from Nowhere* in a fictional account of a very similar house:

Everywhere there was but little furniture, and that only the most necessary, and of the simplest forms. The extravagant love of ornament which I had noted in this people elsewhere seemed here to have given place to the feeling that the house itself and its associations was the ornament of the country life amidst which it had been left stranded from old times, and that to re-ornament it would but take away its use as a piece of natural beauty.

We sat down at last in a room . . . which was still hung with old tapestry, originally of no artistic value, but now faded into pleasant grey tones which harmonised throughout well with the quiet of the place, and which would have been ill supplanted by bright and more striking decoration.

The panelled drawing room at Kelmscott was painted white with plain white curtains hanging at the windows. Armchairs were covered in *Peacock and Dragon*, a woven woollen design by Morris in soft blues and greens. A more striking contrast to the typical Victorian parlour can hardly be imagined. The bedrooms were havens of tranquillity. An attic room was plain and unadorned, with rough whitewashed roof timbers and distempered walls. One bedroom, papered in *Willow*, had a fourposter bed with matching *Willow* hangings, in perfect harmony with the quiet rural setting.

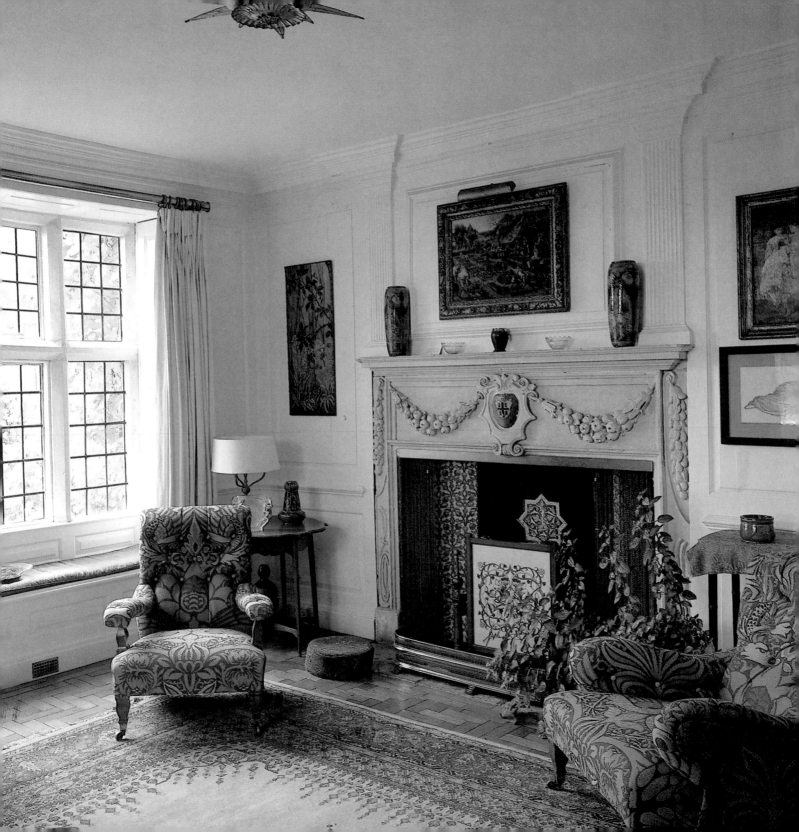

OPPOSITE The Dining Room at Kelmscott House in the late 1890s. The walls were papered in *Pimpernel*, with a fine Persian carpet hung from ceiling to floor. Blue and white crockery was displayed on a white painted dresser.

Morris had a small collection of tapestries which hung in a room at the Manor. This room, known as the 'tapestry room', was used by Rossetti as a study until 1874. Morris loved the faded colours of these tapestries and described them as looking better in their faded state than they would have originally. 'The indigos, greys and "warm yellow browns" of the hangings made the walls a very pleasant background for the living people who haunt the room and in spite of the designer they give an air of romance which nothing else would quite do.'

KELMSCOTT HOUSE

Kelmscott House completes the trio of interiors which Morris decorated for himself and his family. It is the only one of his many London homes which he found at all congenial. This may be due in part to its location, directly on the Thames at Hammersmith, a distance of 130 miles by river from Kelmscott Manor. Morris commemorated this link between his two homes in two summer holidays, journeying by water from Kelmscott House to Manor. In 1880, the whole family with a few friends made the trip in a houseboat called the *Ark*.

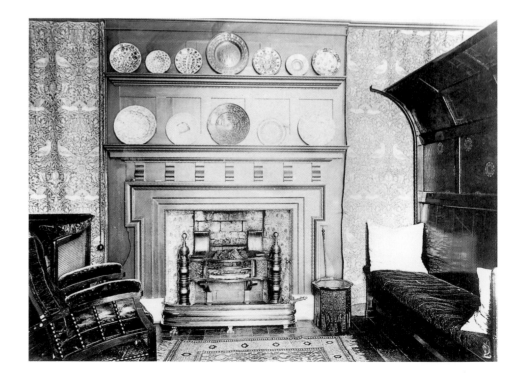

RIGHT The first-floor Drawing Room at Kelmscott House, showing the walls covered in *Bird* hangings lightly caught up. Furniture includes a painted settle by Webb and 'Morris' adjustable chairs.

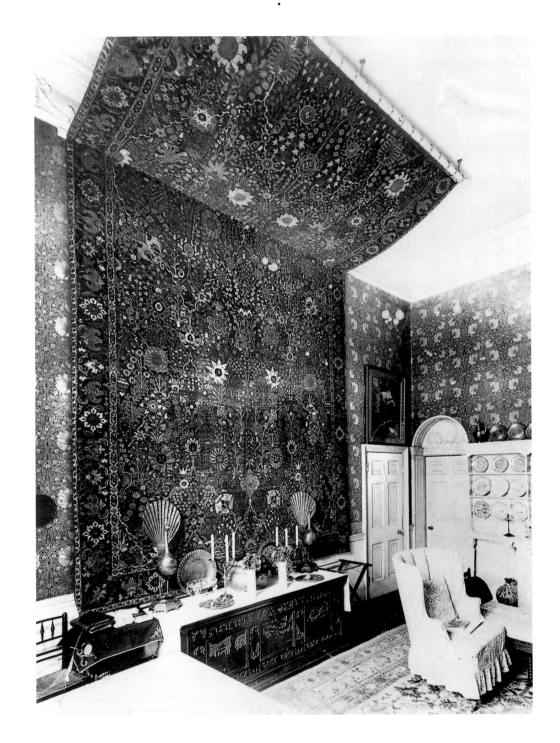

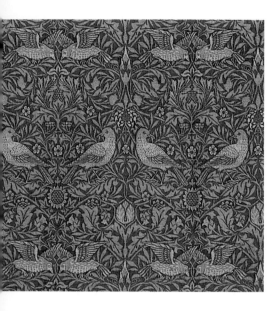

ABOVE *Bird* woollen double cloth, a design of 1878 created especially for Kelmscott House.

Rossetti, househunting himself, had originally discovered Kelmscott House and then tried to dissuade the Morrises from taking it, arguing that the kitchen was too dark and the neighborhood was a slum. Both accusations proved to be true, but the house was spacious and had extensive gardens, which included a kitchen garden and an orchard. There was also a coachhouse with further accommodation above. Morris took the house in 1878, changing its name from the Retreat, which to him suggested an asylum, to Kelmscott House.

Morris worked on the ground floor where he had a study and bedroom. Both, according to an account by his daughter May, were 'frugally bare'. The study had no carpet or curtains, just a trestle table, walls lined with bookshelves and a fine Italian cabinet in one corner. On the floor above, running the whole width of the house, was the long drawing room with five windows overlooking the river.

In a letter to Jane, Morris had commented that the house 'might be made very beautiful with a touch of my art' and, accordingly, the drawing room displays all his decorative skills and sensitivity. May describes it as a 'haven of peace and sweet colour, breathing harmony and simplicity'. The walls were hung with *Bird* woven wool double cloth, designed especially for the room, the soft blues of the fabric echoing the river views. The floor was carpeted with *Tulip and Lily* machine-woven carpet overlaid with oriental rugs. Furniture included the dining room settle by Webb from Red House, and the wardrobe designed by Webb and painted with a scene from *The Prioress's Tale* by Burne-Jones, which had been a wedding present. May described how simple and understated the whole effect was:

> . . . *at right angles to the hearth the Red House settle caught the gleams of the fire on its tawny yellow panels in winter evenings, and in summer the dancing reflections of the river, while lustre plates above the chimney-piece suggested flushed sunsets and dim moonlight nights beyond the elms. At the other end of the room one saw the discreet glimmer of old glass in closed cupboards sunk in the walls, and on a long narrow table lay a few pots and plates from the Far East. No pictures of course . . . no occasional tables, no chairs like feather-beds, no litter of any sort. Plenty of "quarter-deck" in which to march up and down when discussions got animated and ideas needed exercise . . . Without, the waving trees, the shining river with splendid sweep and stretch of sun-lit land, and the blue distance of Richmond and the Surrey hills.*

The dining room was equally lovely, with walls papered in *Pimpernel* and hung with an oriental carpet of outstanding quality. George Bernard Shaw described the carpet as 'so lovely that it would have been a sin to walk on it; consequently it was not on the floor but on the wall and half way across the ceiling.' The dining room also contained a white painted dresser displaying blue and white crockery. Another visitor, Helena Sickert, sister of the painter, noted like Shaw the plain table and the dresser with blue and white crockery. But she was most impressed by the 'deliciously homely' atmosphere and the 'exquisite cleanliness of the whole house'. Jane Morris, as well as being an acknowledged beauty, was an excellent housekeeper.

The interior design work of Morris and Co. ranged from special commissions to redecorate entire houses for important, wealthy clients to simply supplying embroidery, textiles or carpets to more casual customers. But the impact of the retail side of the business should not be underestimated in the development of turn-of-the-century taste. Morris and Co. had an influential and identifiable clientele, mostly drawn from the artistic and intellectual ranks of the upper middle class. No fashionable home in London was without some item from Morris and Co. The firm's work can be even more specifically identified with highbrow Bloomsbury, with the new progressive suburb of Bedford Park designed by Norman Shaw, and with the academic enclave of north Oxford, where the wives of dons (newly allowed to marry) were afficionados of Morris wallpaper and chintz. Although there was little demand for the firm's goods outside London and Oxford, Europeans were also quick to appreciate the quality and originality of the distinctive designs.

By the end of the century a Morris design was synonymous with good taste. Rooms were lighter and emptier. One contemporary writer said that Morris had 'changed the look of half the houses in London and substituted art for ugliness all over the kingdom'. Morris interiors were described in the pages of fashionable novels and satirized in *Punch*. One of *Punch*'s cartoonists, Linley Sambourne, was a client of Morris and Co. His London

INTERIOR DESIGN AND DECORATION BY MORRIS AND CO.

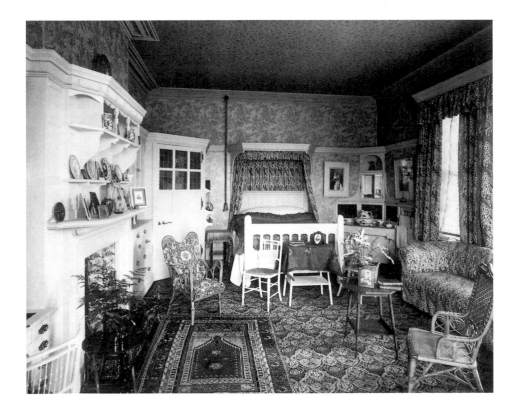

LEFT A nineteenth-century photograph of a bedroom in a house in Edgbaston, Birmingham, showing a Morris carpet and *Daffodil* printed cotton bed hangings, curtains and sofa upholstery. The white woodwork mediates between the areas of different pattern and there is some lightening of the characteristic Victorian clutter.

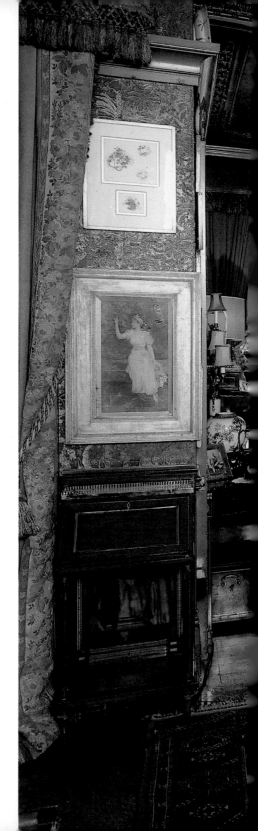

RIGHT The L-shaped Drawing Room in Linley Sambourne's house, 18 Stafford Terrace, London W8. Linley Sambourne (1844-1911), a Punch illustrator, furnished his home in an accepted 'artistic' manner, with Morris patterns, blue and white china and stained glass featuring sunflower motifs, the symbol of the Aesthetic Movement. The house, with furnishings intact, is now the headquarters of the Victorian Society.

house, preserved intact by the Victorian Society, includes a number of Morris designs, including *Pomegranate* paper on the morning-room ceiling and a Dearle carpet in the hall. Sambourne's house, a good example of an 'artistic' interior, is far more cluttered and conventionally decorated than one imagines would have met with Morris's approval. Not all of Morris and Co.'s customers could have been sympathetic to his radical design philosophy. There must have been many who simply added their choice of wallpaper or fabric to the characteristic High Victorian muddle.

More satisfying, at least on one level, was the opportunity to create new interiors from scratch, and much of the best work was produced in collaboration with Webb. For the most part, sympathetic clients gave Morris an element of design control, although he could be very uncomfortable working for what he saw as an privileged élite.

Morris and Co. had a long association with the Howard family. George Howard, later ninth earl of Carlisle, commissioned Webb to build a London house (1868–72). Morris was involved in the decoration of 1 Palace Green and in the decoration of the other family homes, Castle Howard in York and Naworth Castle in Cumberland. For the library at Naworth he designed an immense Hammersmith carpet.

Another important client was Sir Lowthian Bell, a northern industrialist. Webb also built his house, Rounton Grange, Northallerton, Yorkshire (1872–76). Morris and Burne-Jones designed an embroidered frieze for the dining room which was worked by Lady Bell and her daughters. The drawing room had a Hammersmith carpet on the floor and *Flower Garden* fabric stretched on the walls.

Alexander Ionides, a Greek importer, commissioned Morris and Co. to decorate his home in Holland Park, London, in 1880. Well-publicized and highly influential, the house featured a wealth of Morris textiles, carpets, tapestries and wallhangings. The house was one of the best examples of complete Morris decoration at the time.

It is likely that Morris found his work for Wickham Flower even more congenial. Morris had already devised the decorative scheme for Flower's London home when he went to visit his country house, Great Tangley Manor in Surrey, recently enlarged by Webb. A great many textiles were subsequently used in the house, as well as carpets and

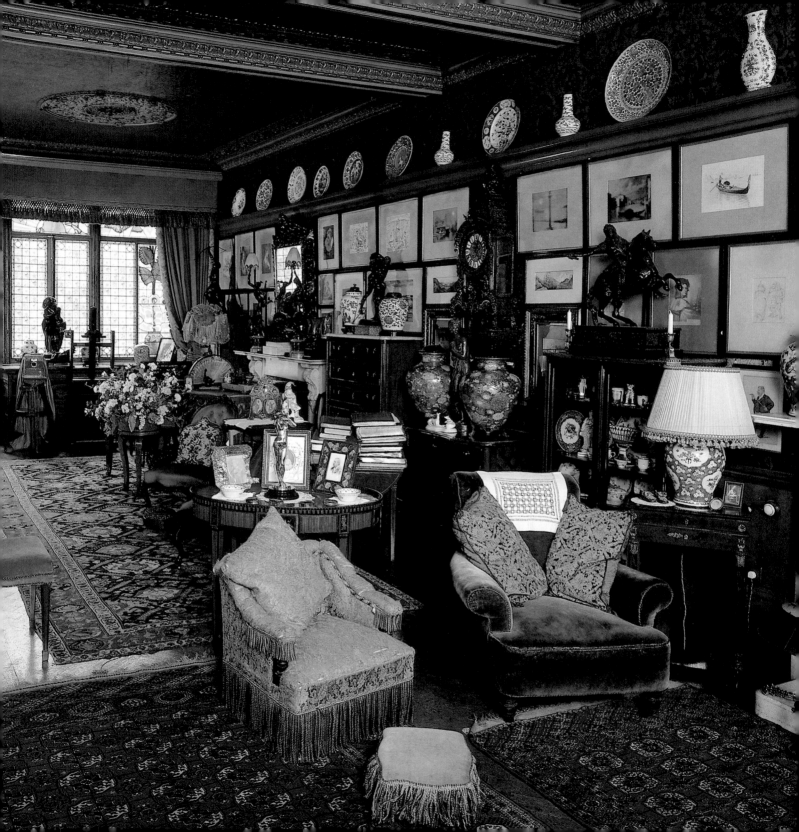

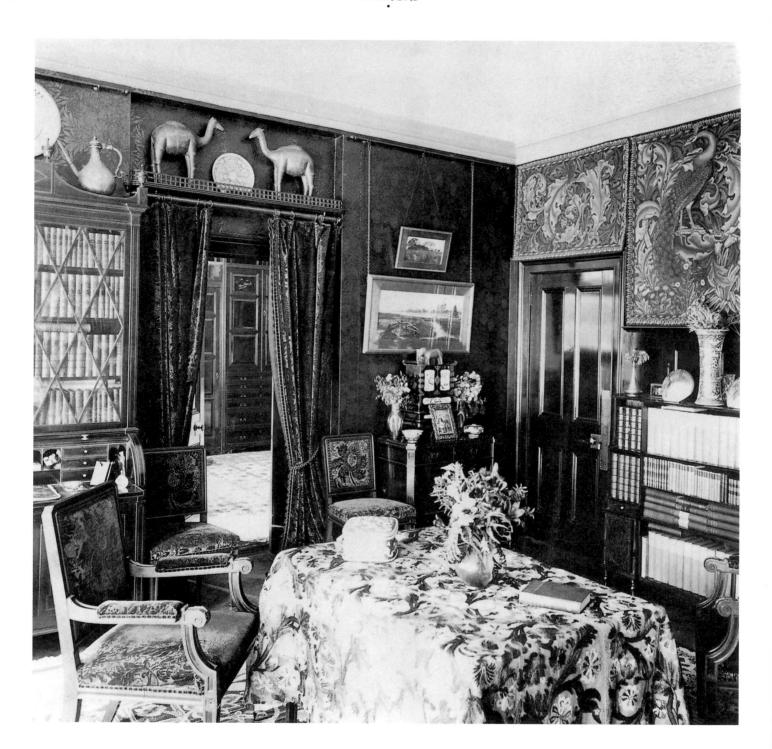

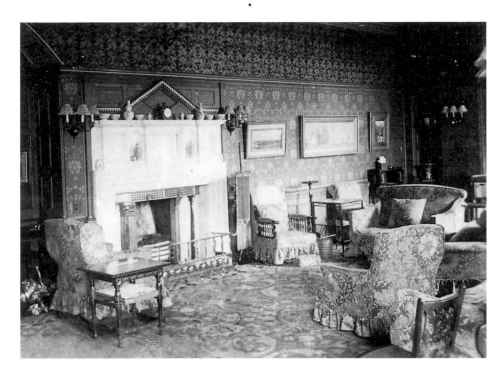

LEFT The Drawing Room at Rounton Grange, Yorkshire, home of northern iron magnate Sir Isaac Lowthian Bell, a Morris and Co commission from the late 1870s. The walls were hung with *Flower Garden*, a woven wool and silk fabric, stretched and battened; the chairs in *Compton*. The carpet was also by Morris.

upholstery fabric. The interior, much admired by Hermann Muthesius in his influential book *Das Englische Haus*, was a good example of Morris's 'country cottage' style, as opposed to the more formal schemes he created for London town houses.

Another house, which virtually on its own was responsible for creating the English country house aesthetic, was Clouds in Wiltshire, built by Webb for the Hon. Percy Wyndham. Walls and ceilings were painted white and wood left unstained, a treatment revolutionary at the time. Against this pure plain background the colours and patterns of Morris tapestries and hangings glowed. The drawing room and hall each featured a large Hammersmith carpet; there were Morris upholstered chairs and loose covers on other furniture.

Wightwick Manor near Wolverhampton is a mock-Elizabethan house built between 1887 and 1893, and now a National Trust property. Many of the Morris textiles in Wightwick's collection were added during the twentieth century by Sir Geoffrey Mander, the son of the original owner, and his wife.

One of Morris's last commissions was the home of the Sanderson family, Bullerswood in Kent. *Bullerswood*, a Hammersmith carpet, was created for the drawing room. Morris apparently supervised the decoration personally.

Standen in Sussex was a weekend home designed by Webb for a solicitor. Much smaller and more intimate in scale, the house is now a National Trust property, and retains something of its original quality. Many of the Morris furnishings are still intact.

OPPOSITE The Study at 1 Holland Park, London, the home of Alexander Ionides, a Greek importer, decorated by Morris and Co 1880-88. *The Forest* tapestry can be seen hanging over the bookshelves to the right. At the time, Ionides' house represented the most complete example of Morris decoration.

RIGHT Great Tangley Manor, Surrey. Morris and Co undertook the furnishing and decoration of the country house of Wickham Flower following Morris's visit of 1887. The sixteenth century house – 'a very beautiful old house' in Morris's estimation – proved to be very influential, its livable quality coming to represent the best of English country life.

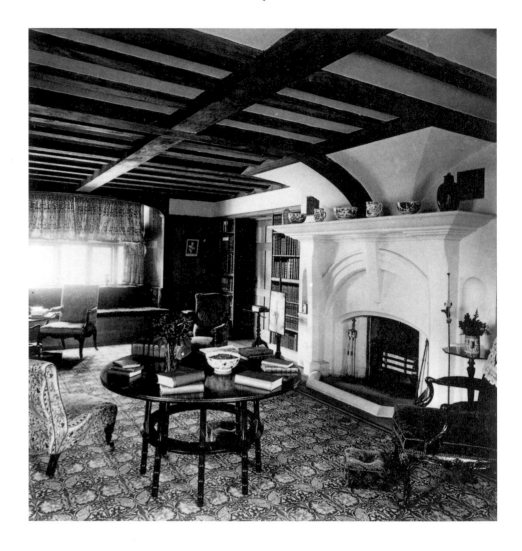

THE ARTS AND CRAFTS INTERIOR: A POSTCRIPT TO MORRIS

William Morris's ideals and principles influenced the Arts and Crafts movement, the last decorative style of the nineteenth century. Forming a bridge between Victorian and modern, Arts and Crafts emphasized individuality and handcrafted work and stressed the importance of responding to the context of local architectural styles and cultural influences. But these very aspects of the movement made it diffuse and quite disparate in its manifestations. There is no one Arts and Crafts interior, no distinctive look, though there are elements of the style which it is possible to identify. It appeals to all those who dislike reproduction interiors of deadening historical accuracy, but who cannot accept the bleakness of more extreme modernism, and to those who cultivate comfort and homeliness and have a positive appreciation of crafts and the decorative arts.

Common characteristics of the Arts and Crafts interior include the display of handcrafted finishes and informal textures – rough-sawn wood, hammered and beaten metal, carved stone, exposed brick. Structure, ornamentation and detail are traditional, rustic and provincial, a kind of 'folk' architecture and decoration which is determinedly simple and unrefined. The window and the fireplace are the most important architectural features, reflecting the priorities of light and warmth. Windows are often smaller and squarer, more randomly placed, with the emphasis on 'cottage' styles and casements. The fireplace, more often than not, is an inglenook, occupying a considerable amount of space, a room within a room.

Arts and Crafts altered the basic proportions of the interior. The ceiling was lower and the wall area was generally divided by a deep frieze, taking up the top third and marked out by a picture rail. Alternatively, there might be a high dado. Ceilings might feature exposed beams or ornamental plasterwork. Wood panelling was common, especially in dining rooms and halls.

The choice of colours and use of textiles varied a great deal, which accounts for many of the differences between individual Arts and Crafts interiors. The English version of the style, which followed on from the work of Morris and was directly inspired by Red House and Webb's other major commissions, was perhaps less extreme than some of the continental or North American versions. In terms of colour, the palette was still sombre: deep indigo blue, warm brown, greens of every hue, creamy white, ochre and purple supplanted the gloomy late Victorian shades. Sharp contrasts and a more extensive use of white helped to lighten the overall effect. For the first time, colour was seen as an important means of generating mood in an interior.

Although there was much less fabric used in the Arts and Crafts interior, textiles still had an important role to play. Plain gathered curtains or casement curtains were usual and there was a general absence of frills, trimming and unnecessary drapery. Embroidery and handwoven fabric were displayed; upholstery was simple, with cotton loose covering used year-round instead of merely in the summer months.

Furniture was honest in construction, largely unadorned and often medieval or traditional in style. Oak refectory tables, farmhouse chairs, massive wooden cupboards and settles and wooden four-poster beds are typical of early Arts and Crafts interiors.

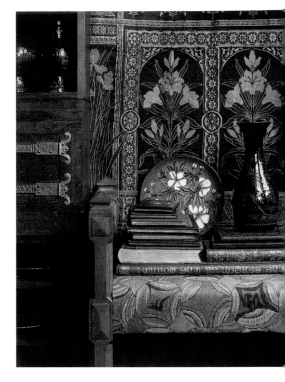

A vibrant-coloured wall hanging sets off the rich dark wood of the Arts and Crafts gothic bench and bookcase.

CHAPTER TWO

I noticed every turn of the banks
of the little brook,
every ripple of its waters over the brown
stones, every line of the
broad-leaved waterflowers;
I went down towards the brook, and,
stooping down, gathered a knot
of lush marsh-marigolds.

Frank's Sealed Letter

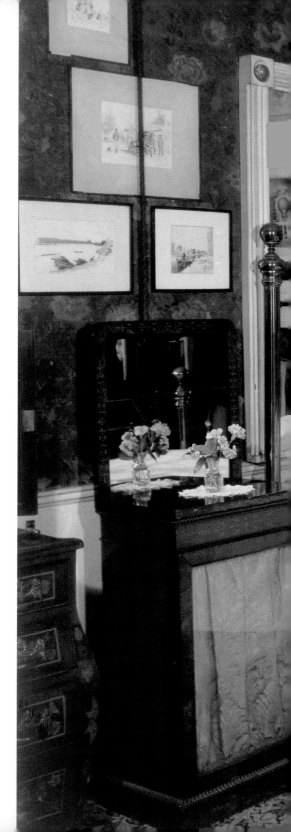

RIGHT Lady Rosse's bedroom, Linley Sambourne House, London. The curtains and bed cover are both in *Golden Lily*.

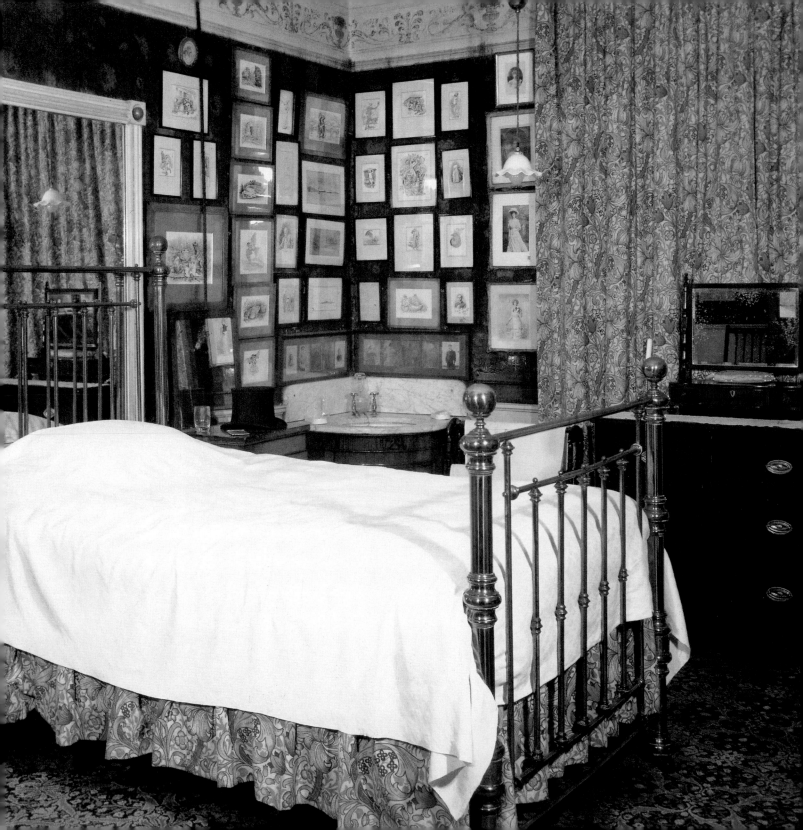

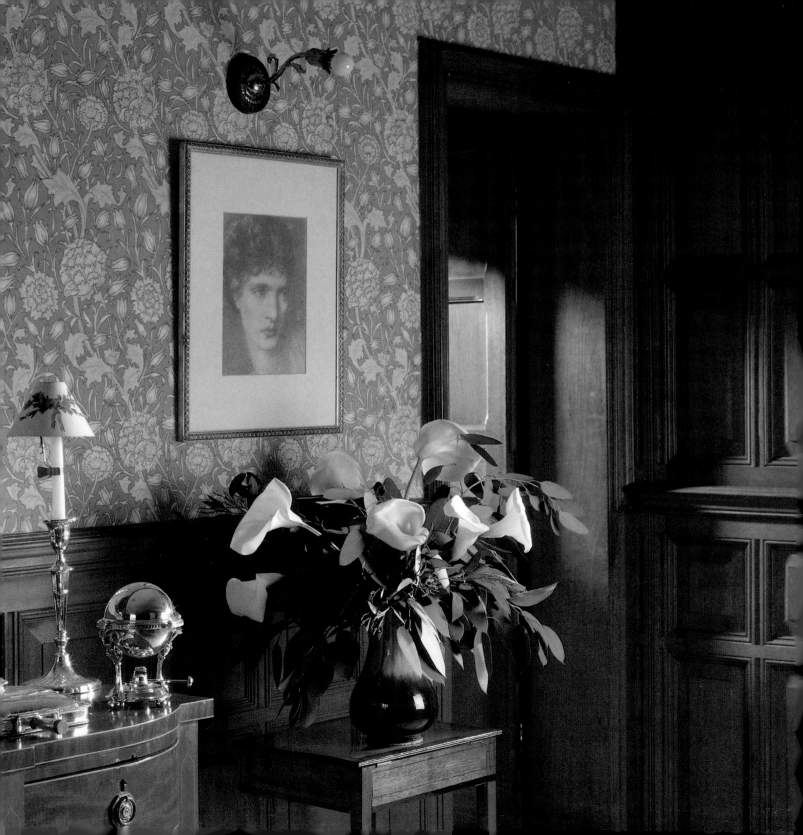

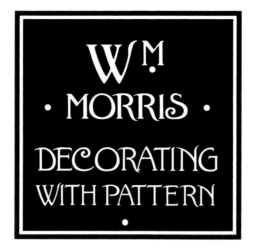

W·M· · MORRIS ·
DECORATING WITH PATTERN
·

'AND FOR YOUR TEACHERS, LET THEM BE NATURE AND HISTORY.' IN ALL SPHERES of his life and work, William Morris derived inspiration from nature and the past, but from nature above all. As a pattern designer, according to some critics one of the finest, his work is as descriptive and evocative of the natural world as the best of his writing: both arise from an intense sympathy for nature and from hours of detailed observation. The quotation at the beginning of this chapter vividly displays Morris's receptiveness to the power of nature and its ability to awaken the senses. But, what is more striking, the style of the description and flowing construction of the writing exactly mirrors the structure and content of his pattern work.

Morris revolutionized the art of pattern-making and altered the course of Western design. In the mid to late nineteenth century, patterns available to the Victorian consumer on wallpaper, fabric and carpeting were often 'naturalistic', which is unfortunately not the same as saying they were inspired by nature. The attempt at realism, with elaborate shading and a wealth of detail, tended to produce awkward three-dimensional effects. The result could be overpowering, almost inspiring a feeling of vertigo if spread underfoot or claustrophobia if displayed on the walls. Challenges to this popular trend in design had already come from a number of directions, notably from the designer Owen Jones. Owen Jones collated and publicized the abstract and geometric designs of cultures all over the world, from Arabia to Polynesia; his own work showed the same interest in flat colour and stylization.

The designs of William Morris, however, display a reaction to both the new formalism and the old naturalism. A century later their power and beauty remains undimmed. A hand-printer, who worked for Arthur Sanderson and Sons, the English firm which still produces Morris's designs, recalled researching old designs, leafing through a logbook from Jeffrey and Co., Morris's original wallpaper printer: '. . . you run through

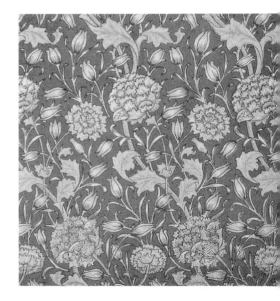

ABOVE *Wild Tulip*, a wallpaper design from 1884, based on an Italian cut velvet acquired by the Victoria and Albert Museum in 1883.

OPPOSITE The Dining Room at Wightwick Manor, with walls papered in *Wild Tulip*. The chalk drawing is by Burne-Jones.

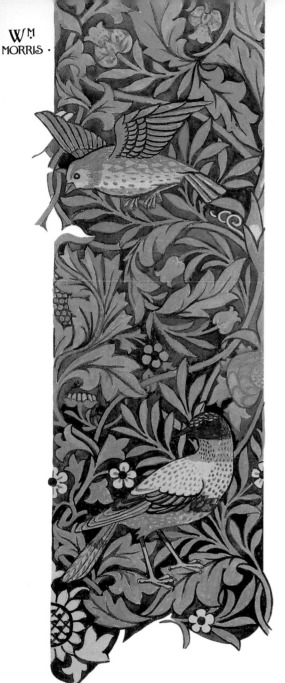

ABOVE Design for *Bird*, woven wool double cloth, 1878.

THE PATTERNS OF WILLIAM MORRIS

page after page after page of lovely old designs of that period . . . you suddenly come to the Morris section of about six or seven pages and it's just like lighting up a light.'

Many factors can be identified as contributing to the luminosity of these patterns, their ability to convey the inspiration which Morris felt and remain beautiful and meaningful after so long a time. The effect, although difficult to analyse, did not ever occur merely by accident.

Morris, unlike contemporary pattern designers, always retained an awareness of 'surface'. His great strength as a designer was his ability to enrich a surface, giving it depth, vitality and a sense of movement, without succumbing to the faked realism he despised. In all his work, he had an instinctive appreciation for the qualities of each material – whether it was glass, paper or fabric – and an understanding of what it could do best. Added to this was his determination to learn thoroughly the intricacies of each related craft. His fabric designs, therefore, were not conceived in the abstract, but were informed by his mastery of printing, dyeing, weaving and so on. Morris himself wrote: 'The special limitations of the material should be a pleasure to you, not a hindrance: a designer, therefore, should always thoroughly understand the process of the special manufacture he is dealing with or the result will be a mere "tour de force".' (From *Textiles*, 1893).

Like the best designers in any field, Morris was naturally gifted with a 'good eye'. Extremely retentive and with an excellent visual memory, according to Burne-Jones 'he never at any time needed books of reference or anything.' As a draughtsman, however, he knew his limitations. He was always unhappy with his figure drawing, an area left largely to Burne-Jones. Webb contributed the animals which inhabit some of his most delightful patterns, including *Strawberry Thief* and *Brer Rabbit*. Webb's talent for drawing wildlife arose out of his natural sympathy with animals, which complemented Morris's feelings about nature so well. Webb is quoted as saying: 'To draw animals you must sympathize with them; you must know what it feels like to be an animal.' Morris was also extremely particular about colour and the colour balance and composition of his patterns is both refined and challenging. He used colour in a way that was both imaginative and highly disciplined.

Ultimately, however, what makes these patterns so memorable is something apart, which could perhaps be described as Morris's ability to communicate his particular vision of the natural world. The English architect Ted Cullinan has described Morris's 'unique way of using plants, abstracting from them both a poignant summary of their own nature and a series of overlaid rhythms and events that are far more than skin deep.' Morris put it another way: 'Any decoration is futile if it does not remind you of something beyond itself, craftsmanship involving not only the mastery of technique, but the evocation of the spiritual qualities of breadth, imagination and order.'

William Morris patterns for wallpaper and printed textiles have immortalized the wildflowers of the watermeadows and country gardens of southern England. This section concentrates on the designs he produced for printed papers and fabrics (about forty in

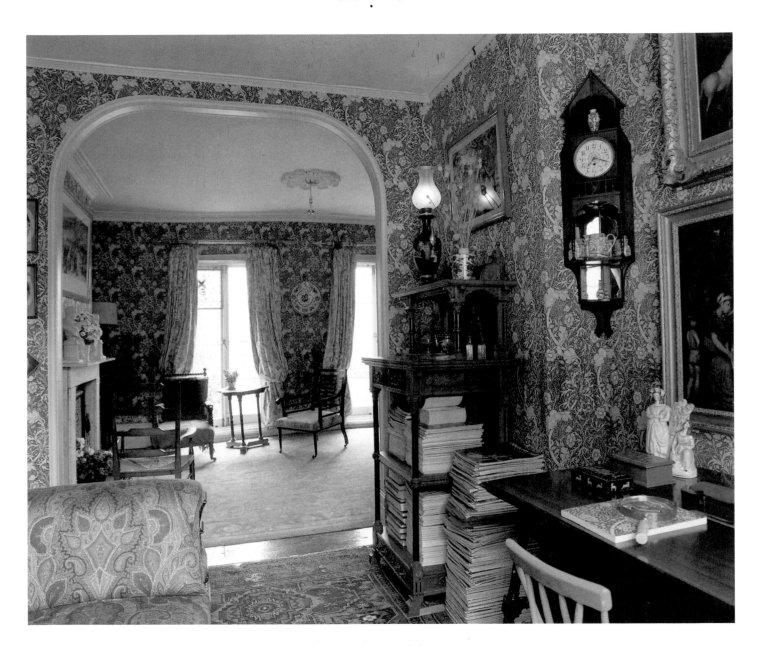

ABOVE A sympathetic and harmonious
mingling of pattern. The walls are papered
with Dearle's *Seaweed* design, one of the
most popular he created. Blue and white
china, the paisley print of the sofa upholstery and patterned rugs blend comfortably.

RIGHT Many of Morris's patterns work well
in modern rooms: *Willow* wallpaper, *Willow* chintz (top left), *Strawberry Thief* (left)
and *Lodden* chintz (right).

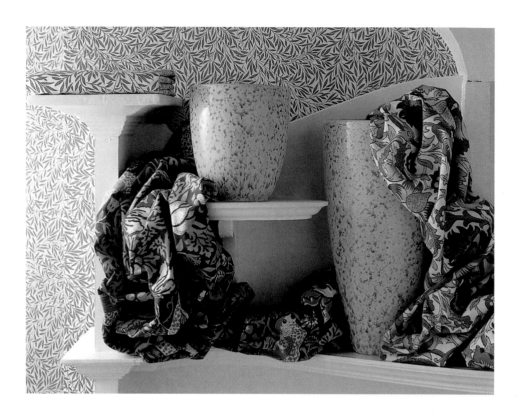

each case), largely excluding embroidery, tapestry, carpets and, to some extent, woven fabrics, since these are no longer in production.

The English firm Arthur Sanderson and Sons Ltd, which took over the printing of Morris wallpapers from Jeffrey and Co., Morris's original printers, also produces fabrics in Morris designs. Some of these patterns have been recoloured or reduced in scale to suit the proportions of modern rooms. Occasionally paper designs have been converted to fabric to satisfy the demand for coordinated ranges. Although Sanderson holds all the original printing blocks, enabling special commissions to be undertaken to order, only a limited number of designs are currently in production and these vary from year to year. A full list of Morris designs in current production is given on page 188.

Morris's design work falls into four main periods. His first wallpaper patterns, however, published in the year 1864, stand alone. *Daisy*, *Fruit* or *Pomegranate* and *Trellis* were not successful when they were first produced and the lack of an enthusiastic reception may have discouraged Morris at this stage. Ironically, *Daisy* later grew in popularity to become one of the bestsellers. All three designs are naive and simple compared to the mature work, and represent an attack on both full-blown naturalism and the flat formalism of Owen Jones. *Daisy* features one of Morris's favourite motifs. *Fruit* is perhaps the most sophisticated of the three designs and approaches the naturalism of the

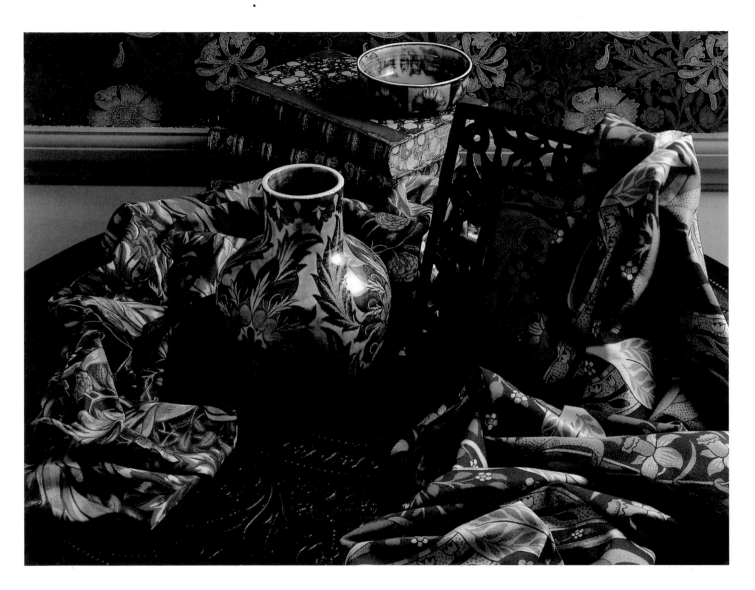

later patterns. *Trellis* is said to have been inspired by the rose trellises which bordered the quadrangle at Red House. Red House's architect, Webb, designed the birds which feature prominently in the design. *Trellis* remained a favourite design of Webb's and he used it over thirty years later at Standen.

The first true period of design comprises the four years between 1872 and 1876, when Morris produced over seventeen patterns, stimulated by his visits to Iceland and the move to Kelmscott Manor. Full of life and never tiring, the designs from this period

ABOVE Morris chintzes in rich jewel colours: *African Marigold* (left) and *Daffodil* (right). The wallpaper is *Compton* and the vases are by de Morgan.

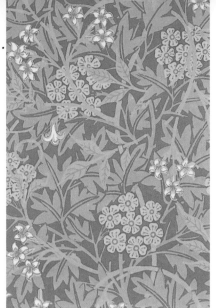

ABOVE *Jasmine*, a wallpaper design from 1872.

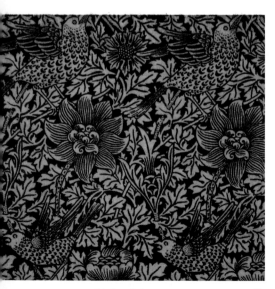

ABOVE Bird and Anemone, 1882, originally designed as printed cotton, but also used as a wallpaper.

include some of the best known and loved of all, such as *Jasmine, Willow, Vine, Scroll, Acanthus* and *Larkspur*. Loose and meandering in structure, the patterns realistically simulated natural growth and represent Morris's naturalism at its height. *Jasmine* is particularly sophisticated and mature, setting up major and minor rhythms in the structure as dark foreground elements cross over and under light background ones. In an analysis of the pattern, the architect Ted Cullinan wrote: 'This crossing of darker by lighter, from behind, when combined with the intermediate background, creates a great sense of "depth of surface".' *Willow*, informal and fresh, was a favourite pattern of Morris's and has remained popular with the public. *Acanthus*, which was also very popular in its day, features a subtle colour gradation achieved by the use of thirty different printing blocks. The undulating, scrolling design challenges the flatness of the surface without ever becoming too insistent.

In the second period, from 1876 to 1882, the emphasis shifted slightly towards fabric design, with sixteen patterns created for papers and twenty-two for textiles. At this time Morris was much preoccupied with learning the craft of weaving and many of these patterns display the type of symmetry and structure common to woven designs. The 'turnover' or mirror repeat is displayed in the wallpaper *Acorn* where the motifs are mirrored on a vertical axis. *Sunflower* of 1879 is another example of the turnover structure. These designs show full naturalism being abandoned for more formal patterning, with plant forms arranged symmetrically.

In the fabric designs, the turnover structure was also evident. *Honeysuckle* of 1876 was May Morris's favourite: 'the most mysterious and poetic – the very symbol of a garden tangle'. *Snakeshead*, reputedly Morris's own favourite design, commemorates the fritillary, a wildflower native to the watermeadows of Oxford. *Bird and Anemone* dates from 1882, as does *Brer Rabbit*, a tribute to the Uncle Remus stories, which enthralled the Morris family at this time. In 1883 Morris designed the colourful *Strawberry Thief*, drawn from life and based on the behaviour of thrushes in the garden at Kelmscott Manor. May Morris recalled: 'You can picture my Father going out in the early morning and watching the rascally thrushes at work on the fruitbeds and telling the gardener who growls, "I'd like to wring their necks!" that no bird in the garden must be touched.'

This direct observation of nature gave way to another source of inspiration for Morris during the third period, from 1883 to 1890. 'Perhaps I have used the museum as much as any man living,' Morris said of the South Kensington (Victoria and Albert) Museum in 1882. An Italian cut velvet acquired by the museum at this time, together with other historic textiles studied by Morris, inspired almost half of the 17 patterns designed in this period. The diagonal structure of the cut velvet, displayed in the *Wild Tulip* paper, was typically expressed by continuous stems whose offshoots stray towards the horizontal. The 'river' chintzes, including *Kennet, Wandle, Evenlode* and *Cray*, were also diagonally structured.

The final period of design, from 1890 to 1896, saw little direct involvement from Morris, increasingly preoccupied as he was with the Kelmscott Press. The patterns which date from this time display a softening of structure and a partial return to naturalism. Many 'Morris' patterns of this date were designed by his former assistant, now the

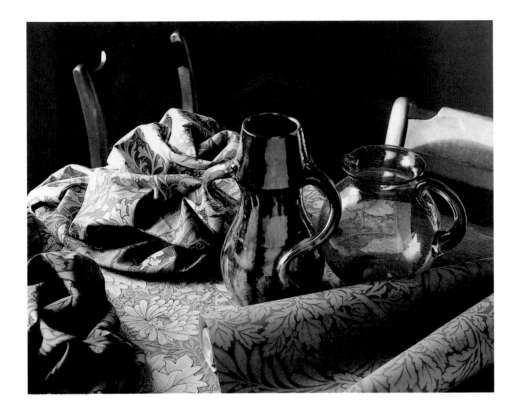

workshop manager, J. H. Dearle, who was responsible for *Compton*, a design once considered to be Morris's last repeating pattern.

Morris wrote and lectured a great deal about pattern-making. 'No pattern should be without some sort of meaning,' he declared, adding that the meaning had to be communicated properly so that it was understood. He believed that a geometric structure was the basis for all repeating patterns: the interest lay in how far this underlying structure was concealed or expressed. Morris was generally in favour of expressing the structure of a pattern clearly, particularly in the case of large designs. At the same time, as he wrote in *Making the Best of It* he believed, '. . . there should be a certain mystery. We should not be able to read the whole thing at once, nor desire to do so, nor be impelled by that desire to go on tracing line after line to find out how the pattern is made . . .' The role of geometry, therefore, was to prevent the feeling of restlessness. Then the ground had to be covered 'equably and richly' which was the real test of a skilled designer. And he acknowledged the demands on draughtsmanship: '. . . a pattern is either right or wrong . . . it is no stronger than its weakest point.' No amount of detail could cure a design whose main structure and 'leading lines' were badly formed.

As far as wallpaper design was concerned, Morris was more specific. He advised that the best way of tackling patterns for papers was 'to accept their mechanical nature

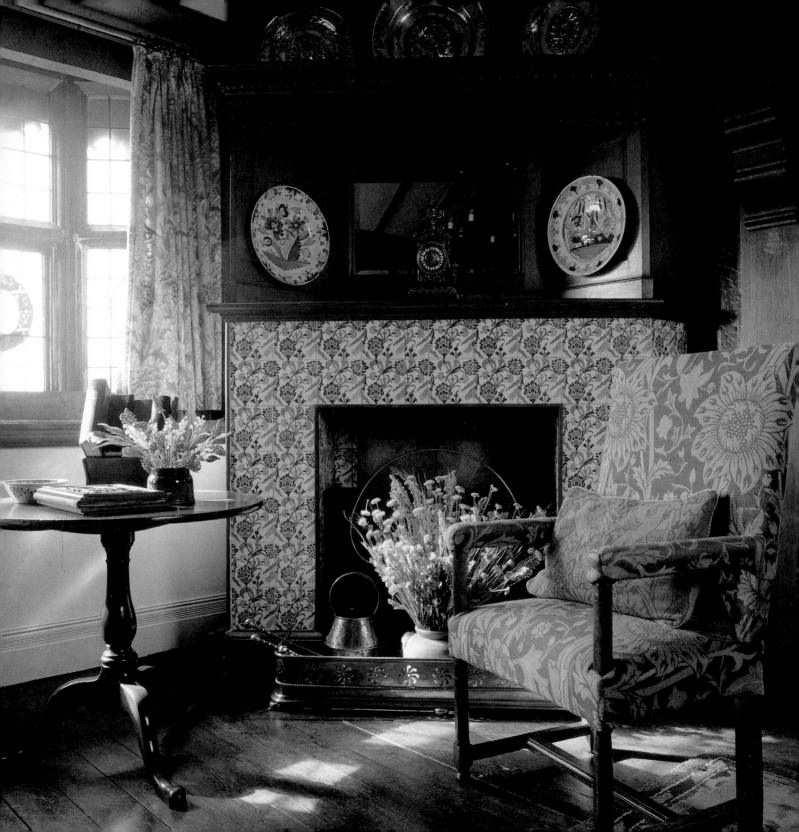

frankly, to avoid falling into the trap of trying to make your paper look as if it were painted by hand'. He welcomed 'mechanical enrichment' – dots, lines and hatching – to give a sense of depth. For the same reason, 'the more mysteriously you interweave your sprays and stems the better for your purpose, as the whole thing has to be pasted flat on a wall . . .'. The lack of inherent interest in the basic material – the paper – had to be compensated for by the art of the designer who, having observed some 'beautiful piece of nature' was driven to express his pleasure to others.

There are no Morris patterns – even those which derive most closely from his study of historic textiles – which are abstract. Every design makes some reference to nature. Nature, particularly the sense of spontaneous growth, allowed Morris the freedom to cover the entire ground of the design in continuous, flowing lines. Compared to other floral patterns, Morris's flowers are still growing, not picked and static.

The flatness of paper demands the introduction of depth in wallpaper design, whereas fabric, which is inherently textured and can be gathered in soft folds, contributes a sense of movement. Small breaks in the pattern where the fabric pleats or folds only emphasize the undulating nature of the design.

Morris believed that all pattern could be categorized in terms of two basic elements: the 'branch' or diagonal line and the 'diaper' or net. All of his patterns can be classified in this way. What sets his work apart, however, is his sensitivity to the techniques of production. He worked not only with the special characteristics of the material in mind – the flatness of paper, the fluidity of cloth – but also with the processes to which it would be subjected. For this reason, it is not possible to consider his pattern-making without going on to look at the way the designs were made.

Morris designed a total of forty-one wallpapers and five ceiling papers. Although he attempted to print his own designs himself, the technical problems which he encountered were too great and a high quality hand-printing firm, Jeffrey and Co. of Essex Road, Islington, was chosen for the work. Morris continued to inspect the tracings of the designs prepared for transferral to the wood blocks and chose all the colours, sometimes changing his mind at the last minute.

All the wallpapers were handprinted from pearwood blocks, using distemper colours. Each colour in a design required a separate block, which made printing a highly skilled and time-consuming business, and hence contributed to the relatively high cost of the finished product. Today, the contrast between hand and machine printing is even more marked. In a day, a handprinter can complete approximately thirty rolls of wallpaper, printing a single colour. During the same period of time a machine can complete twenty *miles*.

The first printing of a Morris paper was typically the outline of the design, which contributed to the crispness and legibility of the final result. Each subsequent printing then had to be correctly registered. There was skill also in the way the printing block was dipped into the colour blanket to produce an even distribution of colour from front to

WALLPAPER PRODUCTION

OPPOSITE The Oak Room at Wightwick Manor. *Golden Stem* (1890), a large scale pattern in woven wool by Dearle, is used to cover the chair. The curtains are *Cray* (1884), one of the most complex of all Morris's patterns. The soft rose of the cushion cover is echoed in the curtain fabric. Much of the decoration by Morris and Co was done after 1893.

OPPOSITE An Arts and Crafts sideboard is displayed against Indian wallpaper. The glowing green of the glazed ceramics is an evocative Arts and Crafts colour.

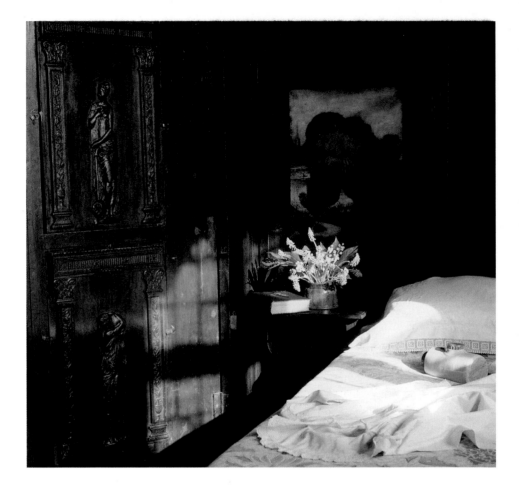

RIGHT The Oak Room at Wightwick Manor. The cupboard, which encloses a folding bed, is decorated with painted panels after pictures by Rossetti and carved decoration by Treffry Dunn. Cray is the fabric used as the bed cover.

back and side to side. These variables in the process and the contribution of the individual craftsman helped the work retain its individuality.

Pearwood blocks have a fine grain which is both easy to work and absorbent. The wood is also extremely durable, as evidenced by the fact that some of the original blocks, now 120 years old, are still used.

PRINTED TEXTILES

'What a difficult matter it is to translate a painter's design into material.' Morris became involved in the production of printed cottons (or chintzes) in the early years of Morris and Co. when there was a clear need for affordable products to expand the retail side of the business. His spectacular success with these patterns was a direct result, however, of his

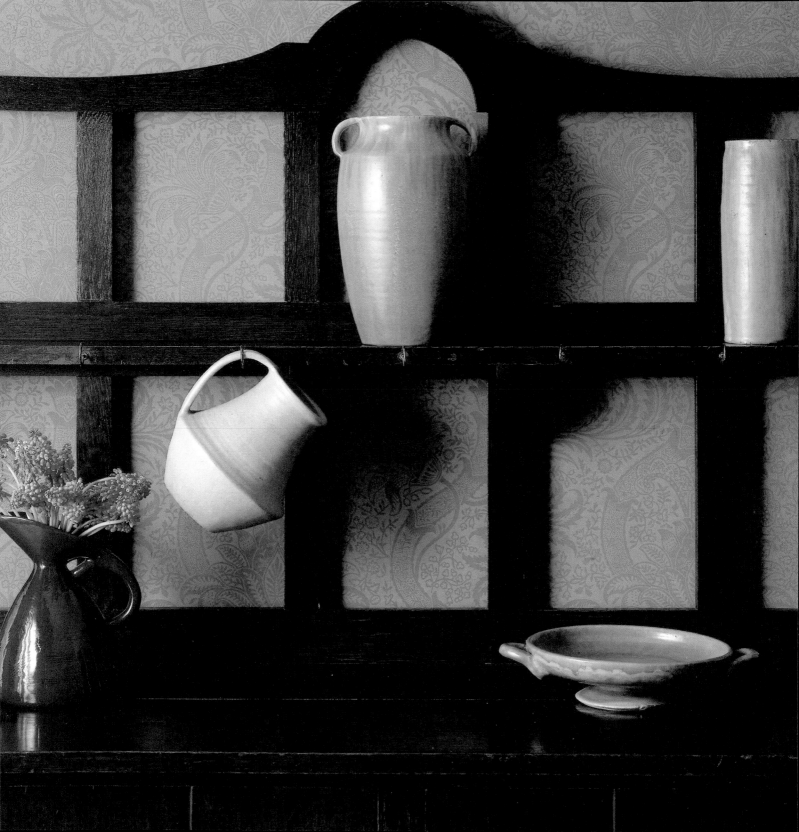

OPPOSITE *Acorn* wallpaper forms the back-
drop to a Sussex three-seater. The grey-
green colourway of the paper combines well
with light mint green woodwork.

experiments with natural dyeing methods, a study he first pursued when he was trying to
produce brilliant colourfast silks and wools for embroidery.

The craft of dyeing, which Morris revived from near-obscurity, is entirely bound up
with his textile production. At one difficult stage, when he was unsure of success, he
declared that he would give up the production of textiles altogether if he could not
achieve the results he wanted with natural dyes.

Chemical dyes, also known as aniline and made from coal tar, came into use during
the nineteenth century. The colours these dyes produced were harsh and overbright,
rather crude. They had technical faults as well, being prone to fading, discolouration and
bleeding. When these chemically produced colours faded, they did so in such a way as to
upset the original tonal balance in a design, fading out of synchronization with each
other. Morris, who particularly admired the old faded colours of medieval tapestries, the
soft greens, greys and blues which subtly and gently harmonized with each other, was
horrified when one of his early textile designs was commercially printed with chemical
dyes. 'Prussian blue' was no substitute for the particular soft indigo he sought. Fabric
dyed with indigo, Morris noted, kept its colour by candlelight.

The brother of Morris's business manager, Thomas Wardle, owned a dyeworks at
Leek, Staffordshire, and the collaboration between Wardle and Morris marks the

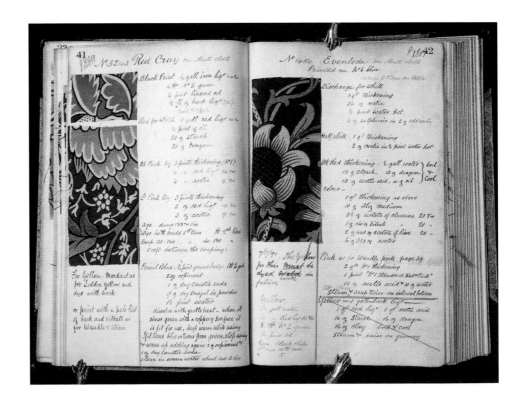

RIGHT Recipes for dyes given in Merton
Abbey dye book, 1882-91. The pages shown
refer to *Cray* and *Evenlode*. *Cray* was the
most complicated fabric of all to print,
requiring 34 blocks; hence its expense.

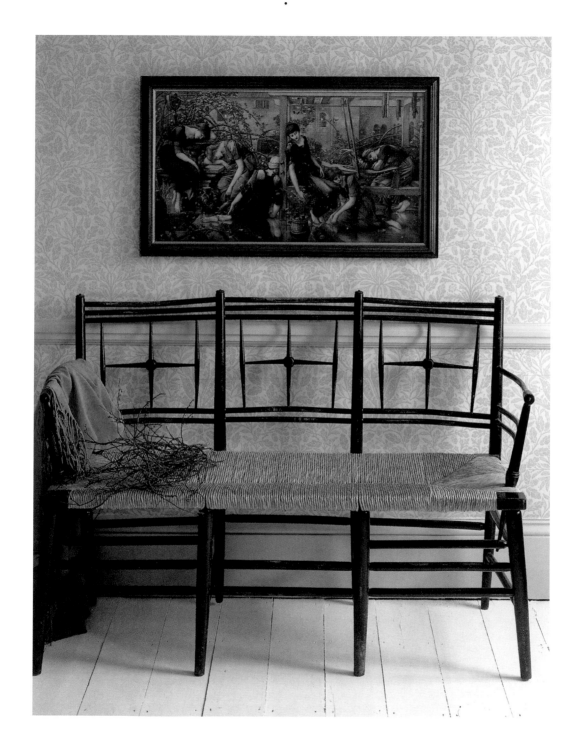

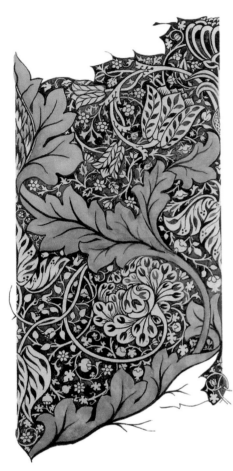

beginning of Morris's first successes in reviving the old craft. Consulting medieval herbals (Gerard's *Herball or Generall Historie of Plants*, in particular) and French dyers' manuals, Morris devised formulae using materials from natural sources, plants, bark, insects and so on. Unlike his contemporaries, Morris loved primary colours and believed that all the shades he needed could be made from various combinations of red, blue, yellow and brown. Blue was derived from indigo and woad. Red came from madder, cochineal and kermes, the latter two being insect dyes. Yellow came from weld, a plant, from the bark of the American black oak and from a whole range of plant sources including broom, heather, birch and poplar twigs. Brown was made with walnut roots and shells. From these, black, green, purple and orange could be achieved using various combinations and strengths of the basic colour dyes.

The most complex and demanding process was indigo-discharge printing, which Morris finally perfected when dyeing transferred from Wardle's to the new workshops at Merton Abbey. To obtain a solid even blue, fabric or yarn had to be submerged in a deep vat (often sunk into the ground). When the material was taken from the vat and exposed to air, the dye oxidized, becoming fixed. In order to print subsequent colours, it was necessary to have a system of resist or discharge using a bleaching reagent which reduced or removed colour in areas required by the design, ready for the next dyeing. In the 1880s it became Morris's custom to display the technique to Merton Abbey visitors, as described by an American guest in 1886:

In the first outhouse that we entered stood great vats of liquid dye into which some skeins of unbleached wool were dipped for our amusement; as they were brought dripping forth, they appeared of a sea-green colour, but after a few minutes' exposure to the air, they settled into a fast, dusky blue.

The sudden transformation of colour from green to blue was evidently a favourite spectacle. The visitor went on to record the orderly atmosphere in the dye-house and how the smell of dried herbs from the vegetable dyes blended with the fresh country air.

'The art of dyeing leads me naturally to the humble but useful art of printing on cloth,' Morris said. Standard commercial printing at that time involved the use of engraved rollers operated mechanically. Yard upon yard of cheap cottons were churned out from mills in Lancashire and elsewhere. Hand-printing, by contrast, was an individual process which added distinction and variety. Thomas Wardle printed Morris's early designs until the move to Merton Abbey where a print shop was established. By this time Wardle's output had become somewhat inconsistent and there had been a general slackening off in the standard of dyeing.

The first step in hand-printing was the transferral of the design to wooden blocks. The cutting of the pearwood had to be matched to the pattern exactly; each block, corresponding to a colour of the design, also had to match up so that the final print was in register. Then the cloth was stretched along the printing tables and the printer set to work, pressing the block on to a dye-pad and then laying it in position on the fabric. Hitting the block with a mallet helped the print to take. This was repeated down the length of the cloth and then the whole process was begun again using a different block

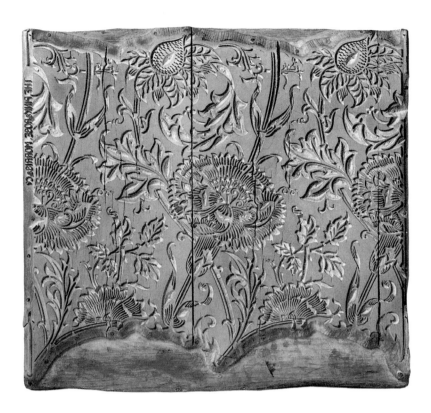

LEFT Fruitwood block used for printing *Pink and Rose* wallpaper, designed by Morris in 1890.

and different colour. After all the colours were printed, the cloth was usually washed in the river and dried in the open air on the meadows. Baths of soap or bran were used to clean up the white areas in a design or help fix the colours.

Although the entire production of chintzes, from the making of the dye to the actual printing process, was difficult and time-consuming, Morris mistrusted the ease of mechanization and the lack of discipline in design which resulted from it. What he called 'the natural and healthy difficulties' of the old techniques made designers work in sympathy with their craft. From this arose 'that character which you so easily recognize in India palampores, or in the faded curtains of our grandmothers' time, which still, in spite of many and many a strenuous washing, retain at least their reds and blues.' In cylinder printing, where there are no obstacles to be overcome, the designer was limited only by the size of the roller and the number of colours required. The result was 'ornament on the cotton, which might just as well have been printed or drawn on paper . . .', designs which Morris believed were invariably 'dull, hard, unsympathetic'.

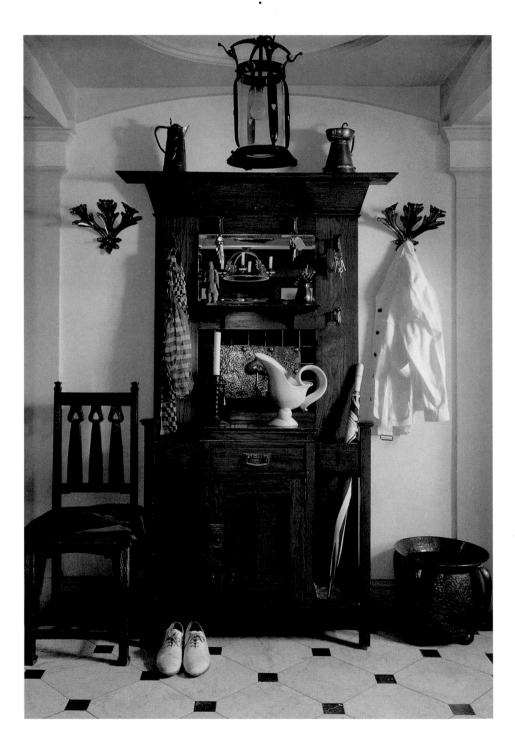

RIGHT A late Arts and Crafts oak hallstand, incorporating characteristic details: tiling, beaten copper panel and individually designed catches and hooks. Tones of light green accentuate the crisp architectural detail of the hall, set off by a traditional black and white marble floor.

Not surprisingly, he came to the conclusion that '. . . there is nothing for it but the trouble and the simplicity of the earlier craft, if you are to have any beauty in cloth-printing at all.'

Having examined in detail how Morris's patterns evolved and the techniques used in their production, it is useful to look at how the end product can be applied in the interior. After years of living in relatively plain rooms the instinctive handling of pattern is something of a lost art today. The legacy of modern design is a reticence about decoration which Morris would probably have found congenial, if a little extreme. Nowadays most people are simply not accustomed to seeing a combination of patterns or confident about using large-scale designs.

There are a variety of ways of using pattern, just as there are a variety of ways in which pattern can enliven a decorative scheme. Broadly speaking, pattern can be used singly as a focal point; as a coordinating element; or in a combination of related patterns to create a sympathetic mixture.

Pattern on its own – as a focal point – is a decorative strategy seen quite often in modern rooms. Here pattern is treated as a feature to be emphasized by contrast with plain surfaces and finishes: a beautiful Oriental rug, a woven wall hanging, or richly patterned curtain fabric supplying all the decorative detail in an otherwise understated room. Many Morris designs, as might be expected, stand up quite well to this level of attention, particularly the large-scale repeats and the more intricate patterns. Morris himself used patterns in this way, displaying fine Eastern rugs on the wall, hanging tapestries and so on. And it is notable that at Clouds, one of Morris's most influential interiors, crisp white walls were used to set off tapestries and upholstery. For this strategy to be effective, the pattern on display must have real quality and there must be enough of it. One chair upholstered in a patterned fabric does not provide enough surface area to create the required dramatic effect: you must be fairly generous with the amount. And a room can look unbalanced or even unfinished if the strength of the pattern is not counterweighted by colour or texture. If there is no other pattern in the room, variations of natural textures in weaves and finishes are needed to supply the necessary sense of depth and interest. Similarly, the background colour should be a shade which complements the main tones of the design.

Coordinated pattern schemes have become a cliché of contemporary decorating, aided and abetted by coordinated ranges of paper and fabric marketed as 'total' looks. Coordination usually involves taking a design and repeating it on a different scale or in a different application. Occasionally a motif is abstracted from the main pattern to create a simplified complementary design or the pattern may be reversed out. Or there might be matching plain shades, trimmed with patterned bands. In this way an entire room might be kitted out with curtains, wallpaper, paper borders, upholstery, table coverings, all in the same basic pattern with its variants. The strength of this strategy – aside from its appeal as a way of reducing decision-making in decorating – is that it can give warmth

USING PATTERN IN THE INTERIOR

ABOVE *Sunflower*, a wallpaper design, adapted by Dearle for woven wool in 1890.

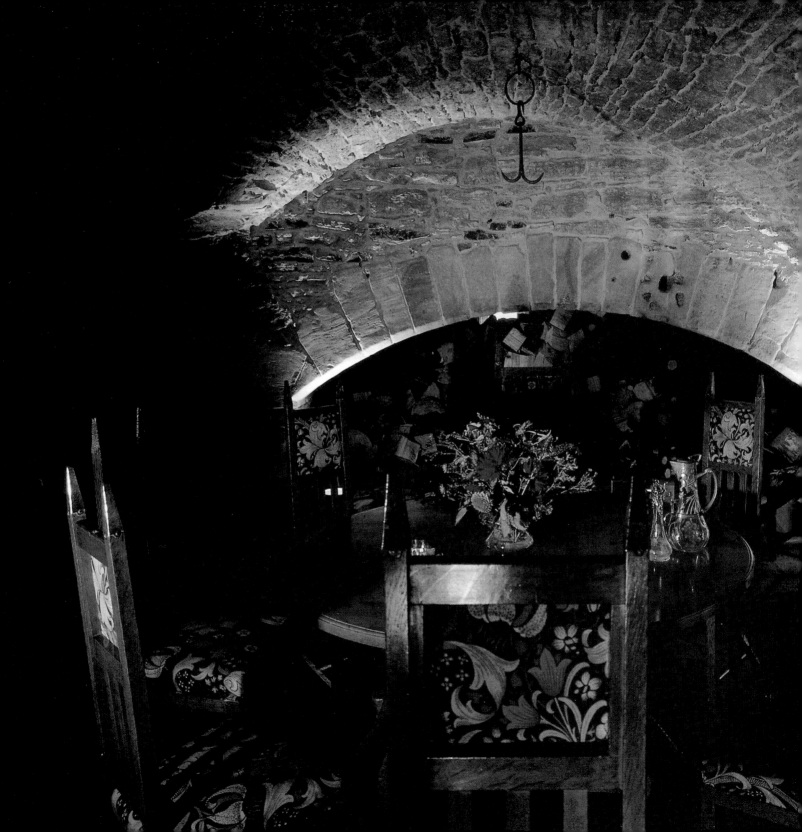

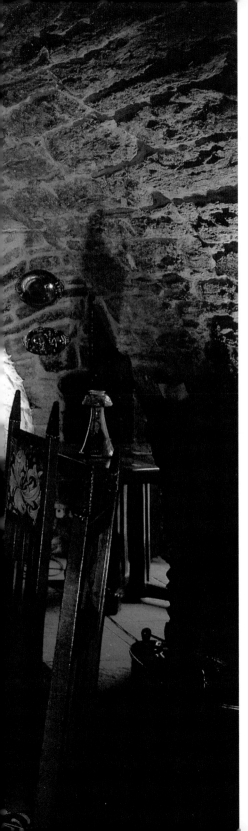

OPPOSITE A dark vaulted room with a
romantic medieval atmosphere. Arts and
Crafts chairs are upholstered in *Golden Lily*
in a strong colourway.

and intimacy to a room, creating a sense of unity. Its weakness, as Morris was aware, is
that the same designs do not always work as well displayed flat on wallpaper as they do
on fabric which drapes and gathers (and vice versa).

Few of Morris's patterns during his lifetime were translated from one medium to
another for the reason that they were each conceived with a particular application in
mind. Some designs, however, were. At Kelmscott Manor, for example, there is a
bedroom papered in *Willow* furnished with a bed featuring *Willow* hangings. The overall
effect is the same type of enveloping coordination sought by decorators today. Where this
strategy is adopted, appropriateness is important. The *Willow* bedroom at Kelmscott is
sympathetic because of its rural setting and the associations the design provokes. (*Willow
Bough* was a favourite of May Morris because of 'the pleasant river-scenes it recalls'.)
Coordination is often most successful in simpler, country-style interiors or in rooms
such as bedrooms where the sense of enclosure is desirable. Choice of pattern is also
critical. In the case of coordination, the simpler the design the better, which is another
reason why *Willow* is successful. Intricate or bold patterns are very overpowering and
visually tiring repeated from surface to surface in the same room.

The third way of using pattern requires the most skill and confidence but is
ultimately the most rewarding. Combining or mixing patterns is an unrivalled way of
providing depth and interest in an interior, creating rooms that are harmonious, restful
and pleasant. In this case, the risk is not brashness, as with focal-point schemes, or
lifelessness as with certain relentlessly coordinated looks, but confusion and muddle. To
some extent, advice can be given on assembling sympathetic mixtures of pattern but
practice and knowing what looks right also count for a great deal. Morris warned that
'Pattern choosing, like pattern making, is an architectural art,' adding that 'personal
liking' is 'not an infallible guide'.

When it comes to choosing a selection of patterns to work together in one room,
what you are looking for is some sense of affinity between different designs. It can be an
affinity of colour, mood or type, but it is often a good idea not to have patterns all of the

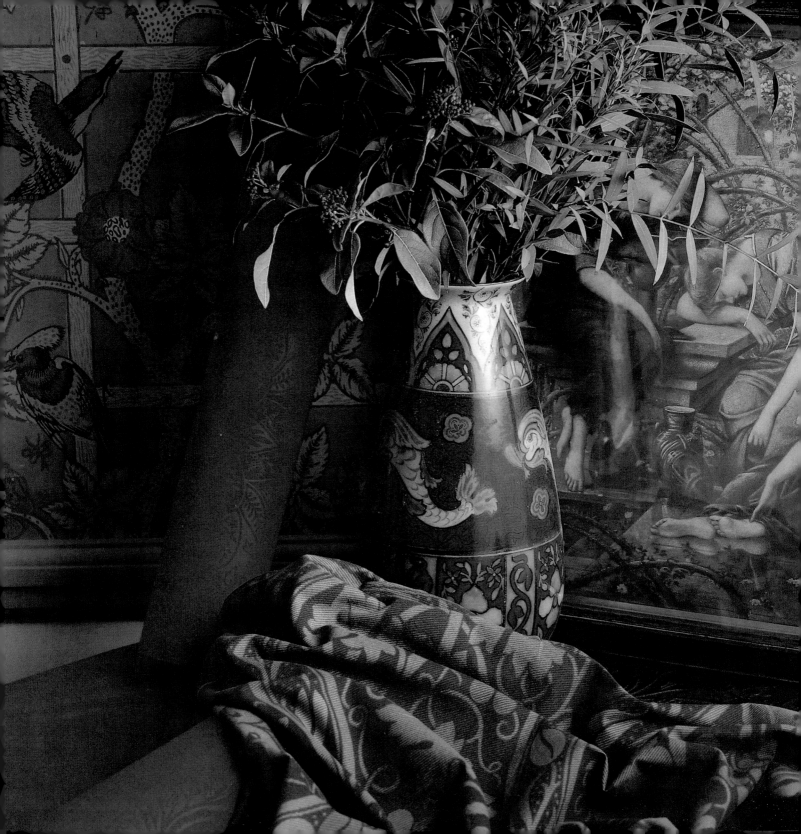

same scale. Morris was all in favour of large patterns, even in small rooms, feeling that they were more 'restful' than small designs. *Peacock and Dragon*, a fairly large repeat, was used to cover chairs in the drawing room at Kelmscott Manor; at Kelmscott House it was used in combination with *Bird* and *Swivel*, as well as patterned carpets, Oriental rugs and wall hangings. At Standen, *Willow Bough* wallpaper is effortlessly combined with *Tulip* curtains. Morris designs naturally harmonize well with each other, providing subtle variations of tone and rhythm.

To gain some idea how different patterns will work together it is often useful to assemble samples of wallpaper or swatches of fabric and try out your proposed combination on a small scale before committing yourself to what will inevitably be a considerable outlay. Experiment with a variety of different colourways: many Morris designs take on a radically different appearance in different colours. View the samples by natural and artificial light to see if there are significant changes in tone. Try to obtain large enough samples so that you can see how fabric looks draped, for example, or appreciate the extent and directional stress of a repeat in a wallpaper. To assess whether the mixture of patterns is successful, look first at the range of colours. There should be some kind of link between all the designs in terms of colour and tone. One pattern may be multicoloured, another feature a dominant colour from the first together with white, a third display a combination of two toning shades. Many Morris patterns blend well together even though they are composed of many different shades. The subtle variety of the original vegetable dyes promoted this kind of affinity.

The next step is to look at the combination of patterns from the point of view of scale. Two big patterns will work together only if they are similar in content; otherwise the clash of imagery will be tiring. Geometric and floral patterns work perfectly well together, provided there is a difference in scale: a small check with a larger floral pattern, for example.

The last point to consider is the question of proportion. If you are only covering a small chair and a few cushions in a pattern the impact will be very different to that gained from papering an entire room in the same design.

With a degree of practice, hesitancy in using pattern can be overcome. A beautiful pattern, in Morris's view, was an acceptable substitute if you could not afford to hang a fine painting or a wonderful tapestry on the wall. The patterns he designed for printed papers and textiles were produced in that spirit.

ABOVE *Kelmscott Vine*, a design for woven wool by Dearle, 1890.

OPPOSITE A William de Morgan fish vase is the centrepiece for patterns in soft reds and greens. On the wall is *Trellis*, hand-printed paper; the rolls of paper are *Indian*, another hand-printed paper. The fabric is *Kelmscott Vine*.

CHAPTER THREE

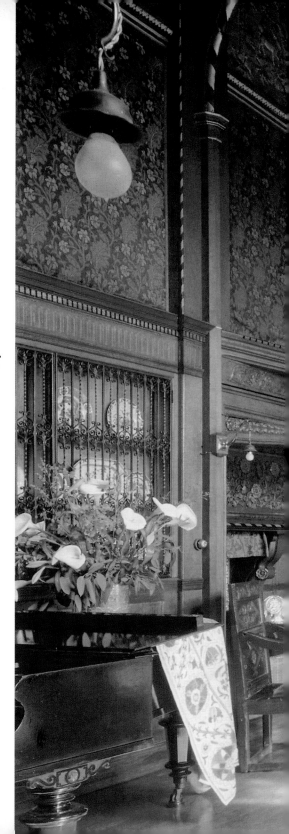

. . . You may hang your walls
with tapestry instead of whitewash or
paper; or you may cover them
with mosaic; or have them frescoed
by a great painter:
all this is not luxury, if it be done
for beauty's sake, and not for show:
it does not break our golden rule:
Have nothing in your houses
which you do not know to be useful
or believe to be beautiful.

From *The Beauty of Life*, 1880

RIGHT The Great Parlour at Wightwick
Manor, with decorated timber roof and
gallery. The chandeliers are by Benson; the
electric light brackets by George Jack.
Diagonal Trail, a woven wool, is the wall
covering.

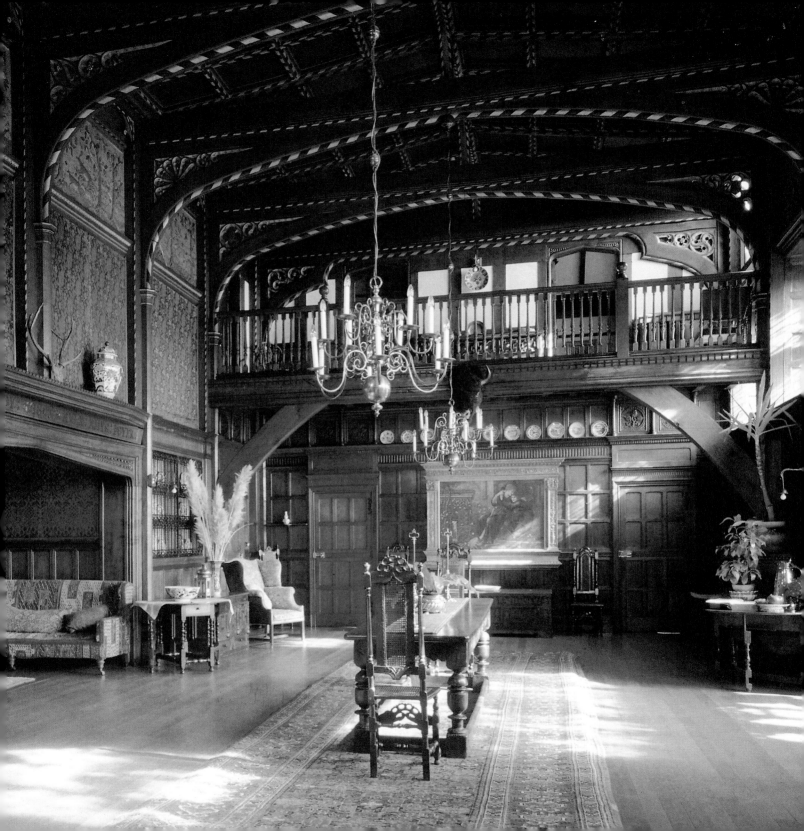

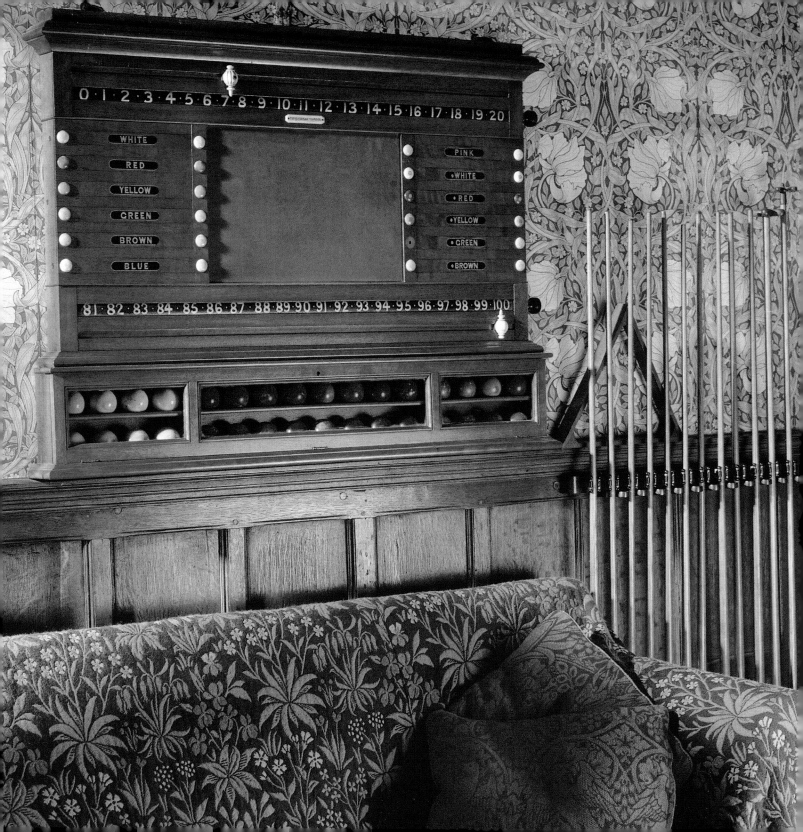

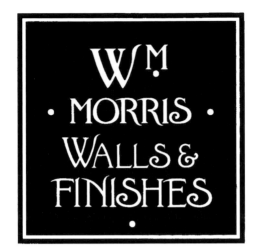

Wᴹ · MORRIS · WALLS & FINISHES

WHAT GOES ON THE WALL — PAINT, PAPER, FABRIC — HAS A TREMENDOUS IMPACT on the overall atmosphere and style of a room. In terms of surface area alone, any wall treatment must exert a considerable and critical influence on a decorative scheme. But how the treatment is applied can also affect the more architectural qualities of apparent size, proportion and quality of light.

Morris's one stipulation for the decoration of walls was that any finish should be beautiful of its kind. A handsome wallpaper was an acceptable substitute for an artist's fresco; printed cloth hangings could stand in for antique tapestry. And there was nothing wrong at all with simple well-executed whitewash, a treatment he himself adopted on numerous occasions.

It was important to consider the decoration of walls very carefully. In *The Lesser Arts of Life*, Morris insisted: 'Whatever you have in your rooms, think first of the walls; for they are that which makes your house and home; and if you don't make some sacrifice in their favour, you will find your chambers have a kind of makeshift, lodging-house look about them, however rich and handsome your movables may be.'

Today we have a far wider choice of alternatives than was common one hundred or more years ago and a better tolerance of different approaches. But it is unlikely that Morris would have approved of a recent decorating fashion, the trend for paint finishes simulating another material. Honesty and natural beauty were qualities he prized above all others: mock or *faux* anything was simply not his style. He called trying to make stone look like ironwork or wood like silk 'the last resource of the decrepitude of art.' On one occasion, he became greatly distressed and angered when he discovered that Rossetti had painted over an old fire-place at Kelmscott Manor. Rosetti had applied a *faux* marble finish in deep green, and this artificial treatment had obliterated the beauty of the original stonework.

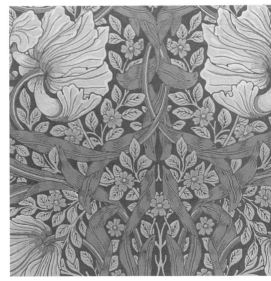

ABOVE *Pimernel*, a wallpaper design of 1875.

OPPOSITE The Billiard Room, Wightwick Manor. The walls are papered in *Pimpernel*; the sofa upholstery is *Millefleurs*, a woven wool designed by Dearle 1912-14.

PROPORTION AND DETAILING

The Arts and Crafts interior represents a transition from Victorian to modern in terms of the architectural proportions and detailing of rooms. Victorian rooms were still essentially based on classical models as interpreted by architects of the seventeenth and eighteenth centuries. The ceiling was typically high and often decorated with a central plasterwork 'rose'.

The wall area was subdivided by a deep skirting board, a chair rail at about waist height, a picture rail, a frieze and a cornice in classically approved ratios which had altered little over two hundred years. If any element was missing, which more often was the chair rail, these basic proportions were still implicit. The division of wall was further emphasized by choice of coverings. The area below the chair rail – the dado – might be panelled or papered with an embossed design subsequently painted a dark colour. The area above the chair rail was used to display the 'filling paper', a design of higher quality. Cornices were elaborate. As the century progressed, the area of the frieze (between picture rail and cornice) became slightly deeper and might be decorated with stencilling.

The architects of the Arts and Crafts movement adjusted these proportions and subdivisions; in some cases they were abandoned altogether. Generally rooms became lower or seemed lower, with the ceiling made to extend visually down by means of a

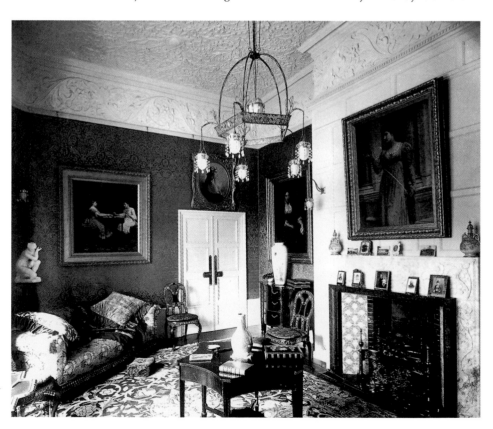

RIGHT The Small Drawing Room at Stanmore Hall, decorated by Morris and Co 1888-96. The walls are covered in *St James's* damask, a woven silk (1881); the carpet is a specially woven design featuring a lotus motif.

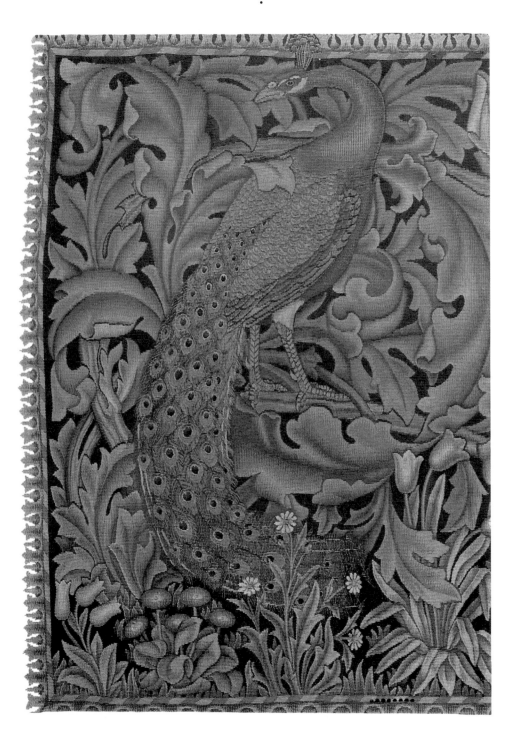

LEFT A detail from *The Forest* tapestry, designed by Morris in 1887, with animals – a peacock, hare, lion, fox and raven – by Webb arranged on an acanthus ground. The tapestry was bought by Alexander Ionides and hung at 1 Holland Park.

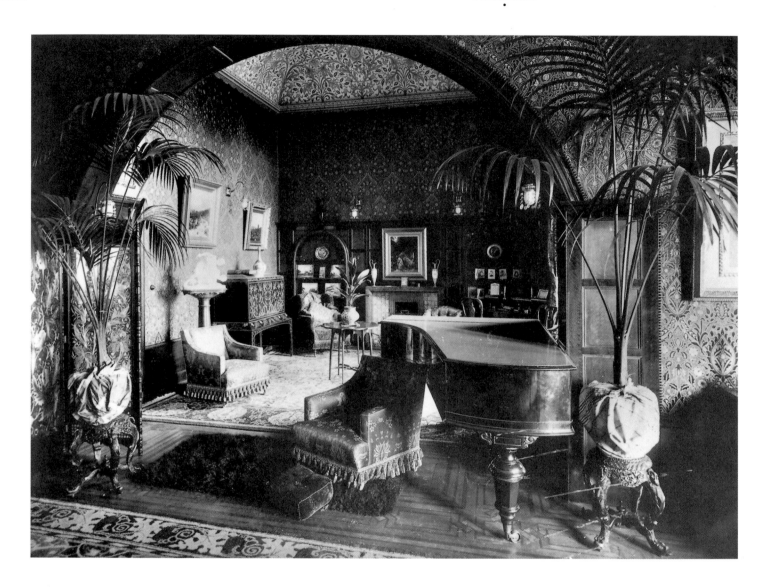

ABOVE The Drawing Room, Stanmore Hall. The commission to decorate the interior of this mansion was largely the responsibility of Dearle, as Morris disapproved of the ostentation and extravagance of the client, William Knox D'Arcy. Morris did, however, design the *Holy Grail* tapestries for the Dining Room, perhaps his most influential work in that medium.

frieze of up to four feet in depth, marked by a picture rail aligning with the top of the door. Alternatively, the dado or wainscoting was extended upwards to about shoulder height. There was a general simplification of detail and a move away from decorative plasterwork in favour of plainer wood mouldings, exposed beams and other elements that suggested rusticity. Exposed brick hearths and fireplaces were other radical departures. References to classicism were gone and there was often a strong horizontal emphasis. There are also examples of rooms where the entire wall surface is treated as a single unity, which naturally look exceptionally modern to our eyes.

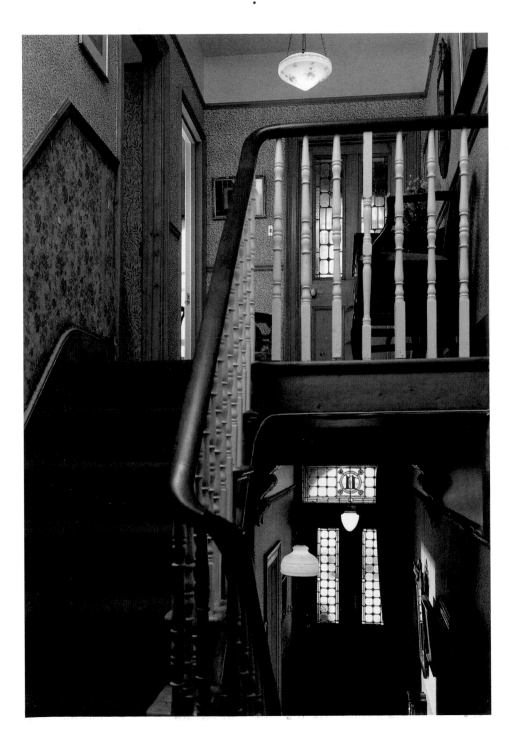

LEFT *Willow Bough* paper decorates the stairway of a Victorian terraced house. The trailing design is well suited to changes in level and, like all Morris designs, combines easily with other patterns, such as the bedroom wallpaper, *Sweet Briar*.

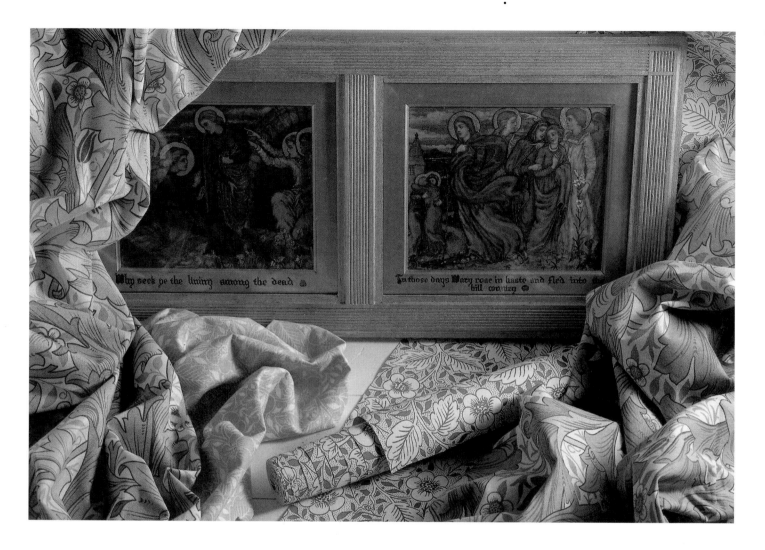

ABOVE Light fresh colours mean that Morris patterns readily adapt for use in modern rooms. The wallpaper is *Christchurch*; the fabrics (left to right) are *Granville* and *Christchurch*. The diptych was painted in 1888 by Phoebe Tracquair.

Because Arts and Crafts is such a transitional style, it can be adapted to suit a wide range of applications today. Typical nineteenth-century terraced houses with their architectural detail intact are as suitable as more modern rooms whose proportions were anticipated by the Arts and Crafts practitioners.

COLOUR SCHEMES

It is ironic that a designer whose name is so strongly associated with richly patterned paper and fabric should have been so influential in establishing plain white walls as an acceptable interior feature. From our perspective, it is difficult to imagine just how radical a notion this must have been to the Victorians. Accustomed to a degree of detail and a richness of design and ornament most people today would find difficult to live with, nineteenth-century families would have found the idea of bare whitewash disconcerting to say the least. Only on the fringes of society – as in the religious communities of the American Shakers – was such a lack of elaboration a common and welcome sight.

Morris was a strong advocate of the plain white wall, counting it infinitely preferable to anything makeshift, shoddy or commonplace: '. . . if we really care about art we shall not put up with "something or other", but shall choose honest whitewash instead, on which sun and shadow play so pleasantly . . .' Pale distempered walls were an often remarked feature of Red House, as were the plain white panelled walls at Kelmscott Manor. Few of the clients of Morris and Co. shared these radical ideas. The outstanding exception was the Wyndhams family, whose country house Clouds, built by Philip Webb, proved to be such an influential landmark in English interior design. The house had already been decorated by Morris and Co. when a housemaid started a fire by leaving a lighted candle in a cupboard. Much of the inside was gutted, but a full insurance settlement paid for the restoration. Walls and ceilings were white-washed, setting off the colour and patterns of Morris fabrics and tapestries. As Webb commented to his client,

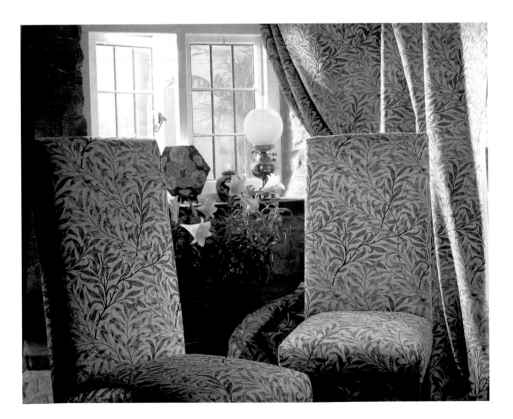

LEFT *Willow Bough*, a wallpaper design of 1887, was adapted for use as a fabric in 1895. A perennial favourite, it works as well flat on the wall or upholstering plain upright pieces as it does draped or gathered into simple curtians. The pattern has a timeless vitality and freshness.

the Hon. Percy Wyndham, 'when you decide on doing any white-washing as advised by William Morris, let me know; there is a way of doing even this properly.' Many contemporary critics were scathing. White, after all, to most Victorians was utilitarian or 'low-class', a colour you would paint a cowshed or a privy.

Morris also advised painting woodwork white. In typical Victorian homes all the woodwork, including skirting boards, doorcases and panelling, would have been painted a dark mahogany brown, perhaps also grained to restore the impression of wood. Many artistic or aesthetic interiors, by contrast, had adopted a particular shade of dull green for woodwork and wainscoting, a much lighter treatment which gave rise to the common term 'greenery-yallery' for this particular style.

Some of Morris's concern about wall colours had to do with a general lack of skill on the part of decorators. This was a time, it must be remembered, when present-day ranges of commercially produced paints in every conceivable shade were unknown. The following comments come from a brochure produced for the Boston Foreign Fair of 1883, where Morris and Co. took a stand:

> The use of positive colour is very difficult, and house-painters are peculiarly ignorant of it. Their incapacity may have led to the use of the dull, gray, even dirty shades, which have become so general since house decoration began to interest educated people. The revolt against crude, inharmonious colouring has pushed things to the other extreme, and instead of over-bright colours, we now have the dirty no-colours. The aim was to get sobriety and tenderness, but the inherent difficulty was not less great than before. It is not more easy to paint grays that shall have colour, than to paint colour that shall be gray; and whichever it be, colour is still the essential. In this difficulty, the use of white paint is the only way of safety. White is perfectly neutral; it is a perfect foil to most colours, and by judicious toning may be assimilated with any.

Morris also took pains to dissociate himself from the yellowish green which became the trademark of the Aesthetes. In 1881 Gilbert and Sullivan satirized the movement in *Patience*. A year later, in *Making the Best of It*, Morris warned his audience not to:

> fall into the trap of a dingy bilious looking yellow-green, a colour to which I have special and personal hatred, because (if you will excuse my mentioning personal matters) I have been supposed to have somewhat brought it into vogue. I assure you I am not really responsible for it.

Nowadays it can be surprisingly difficult to find a good shade of white. The distemper or white-wash which would have been used in Morris's day continued in general production right up to the Second World War when modern paints began to come in. Today's commercial whites are considerably brighter and do not age as sympathetically as the traditional recipes. Many have blue tints added to produce the 'brilliance' promoted so enthusiastically by manufacturers. Plain white paint without any added tints is still produced and can often be found at specialist trade outlets; this is sometimes known as

OPPOSITE The Upper Landing at Red House. The ceiling was stencilled by Morris in a way which recalls the medieval practice of painting patterns between ceiling beams and joists. The exposed brick arch and plain whitewashed walls show a delight in the rugged beauty of natural materials, revolutionary at a time when Italianate villas crammed with decoration were the height of architectural fashion.

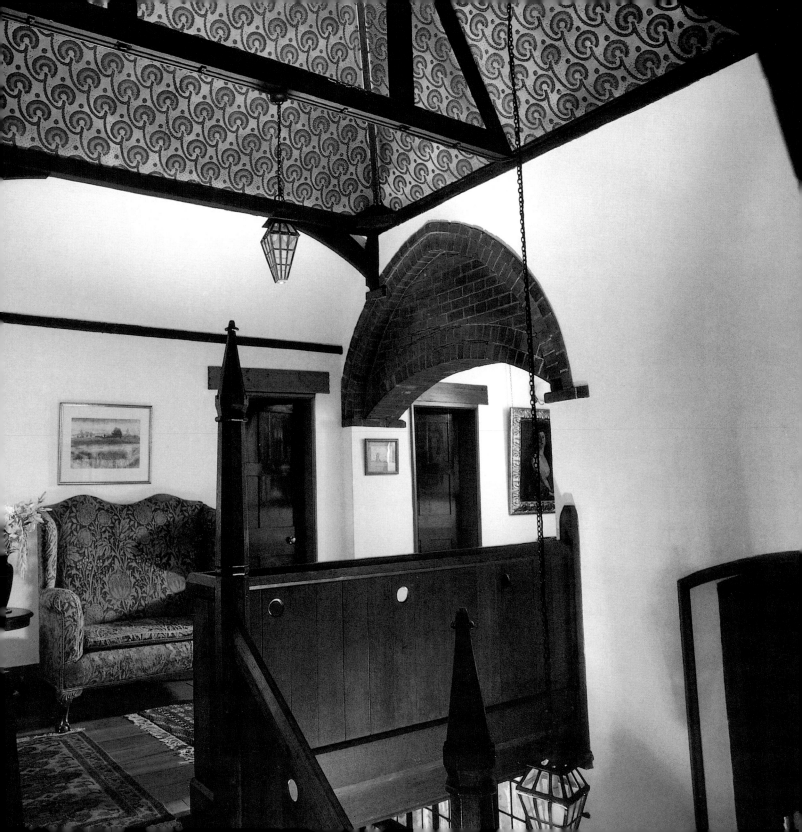

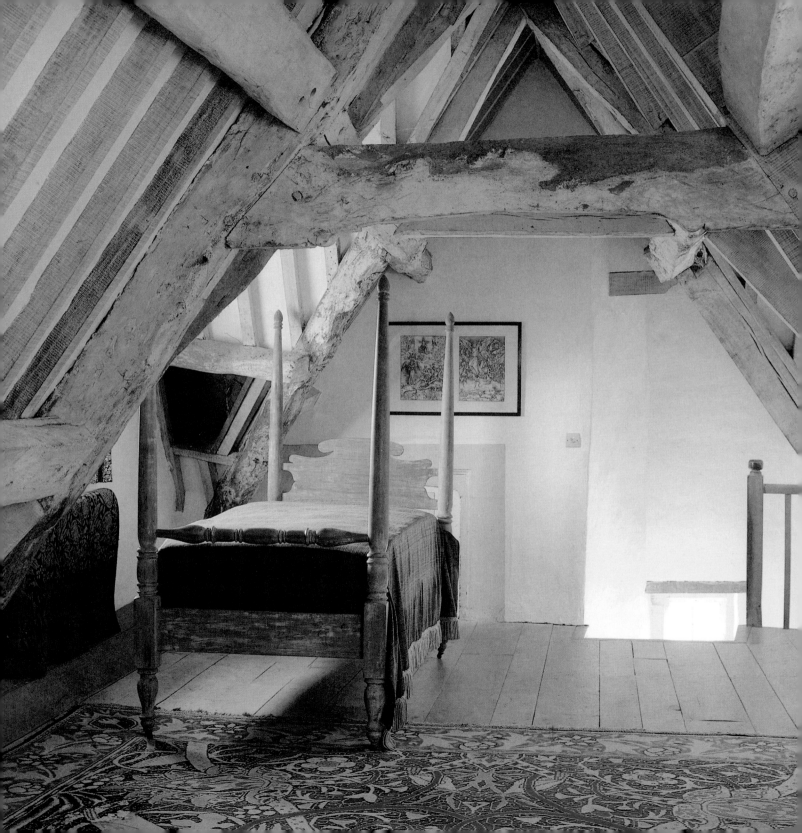

'pastel base' or 'decorator's white' because it is used by professional decorators as a base for mixing up individual tints. Distemper, with its unique chalky finish which mellows attractively with age, can be reconstructed using a recipe and ingredients available from a trade supplier, but it is chemically incompatible with modern paints and would have to be applied to a surface which has been completely stripped of any previous coats.

Morris worked at a time of increasing awareness and sophistication in interior design. One new idea was the use of colour to generate mood and atmosphere. Aside from that aesthetic dull green, rather muddy colours – mauve, dark blue, ochre, even black – were adopted in reaction to the virulent shades in fashion around mid-century; it is possibly these off-shades to which Morris was referring when he spoke of 'dirty no-colours'. In progressive circles lighter, more natural colours began to come in at the end of the 1880s; by the turn of the century, forty years after Morris had first used it at Red House, white was the height of fashion. No longer utilitarian or 'lower class', white was part of the general desire for more light and air in the interior, some of the impetus for which came from Sweden and the work of the artist Carl Larsson, whose domestic and affectionate watercolours inspired a whole new attitude to interior design and furnishing.

Constructing a sympathetic colour scheme to accompany Morris fabrics or paper is far less difficult today: there is no need to rely on the colour mixing skills of a professional housepainter when practically every conceivable tint is supplied commercially by modern paint manufacturers. This makes it a fairly simple proposition to pick

OPPOSITE The Attic Room, Kelmscott Manor. The integrity of old surfaces and finishes was an aspect of interior decoration championed by Morris, who believed that much of so-called 'restoration' was no less than architectural vandalism.

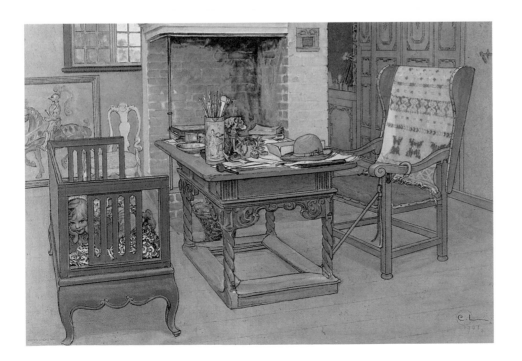

LEFT *Hide and Seek*, by Carl Larsson (1855-1919). The paintings of Swedish artist Carl Larsson, many of which depicted his domestic life, had an impact on taste at the turn of the century. His interiors, which displayed fresh colours, such as orange and green, together with a liberal use of white, pale wood tones and plenty of natural light, helped to divert the course of popular taste away from the gloomy, draped and overstuffed rooms of High Victoriana in favour of the lighter approach, which came in during the Edwardian period.

OPPOSITE Bedroom at Kelmscott Manor. *Willow Bough*, used on the walls and as hangings for the bed, has an enveloping, restful quality perfectly in tune with the riverside setting. The bed hangings are softly gathered in an informal heading and lined in plain white cotton.

out a shade from a swatch of fabric or paper and match it in eggshell for woodwork or emulsion for walls. Any of the soft grey-blues, grey-greens, creams, and of course white would make a good foil to many of the designs.

If a greater degree of depth and luminosity of finish is required, it may well be necessary to try some of the old techniques. Although illusory paint finishes are at odds with everything Morris believed about decoration, some of the 'broken colour' methods can be very effective, supplying an extra dimension of subtlety which complements the patterns very well. Most of these techniques involve applying successive thin washes of water-based paint (or thin glazes of oil-based paint) in such a way that the underlying or background colour is modified. The top coat can be 'broken' by distressing with a tool such as a rag or sponge when the paint is still wet, lifting it off in patches, or by applying the paint in an uneven fashion to begin with, or the top coat can be applied in a translucent enough layer that the basic colour shows through. A thin glaze of pink over a base coat of pale grey, for example, results in a warmer, more saturated colour than the flat grey on its own. It must be stressed, however, that overt sponging and ragging, where the marks of the tool are obvious and insistent, would not be compatible and could all too easily look crude.

☙

WALLPAPER

Compared to wallhangings, tapestry and embroidery, Morris considered wallpaper 'makeshift'. He rarely used it in his own houses, although May later recorded her delight in the *Willow Bough* paper which covered the walls of her bedroom. But although Morris himself would always prefer the fluidity of cloth to the flat surface of wallpaper, this did

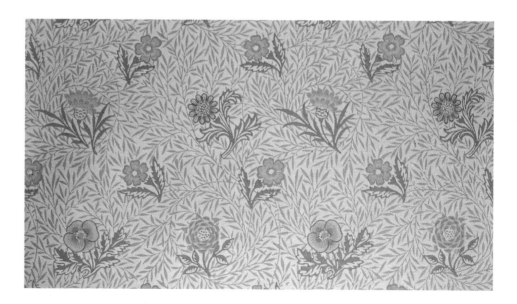

RIGHT *Powdered*, an uncharacteristically naïve design from 1874. The background of the pattern was abstracted and used as the fabric *Little Scroll* or *Willow*.

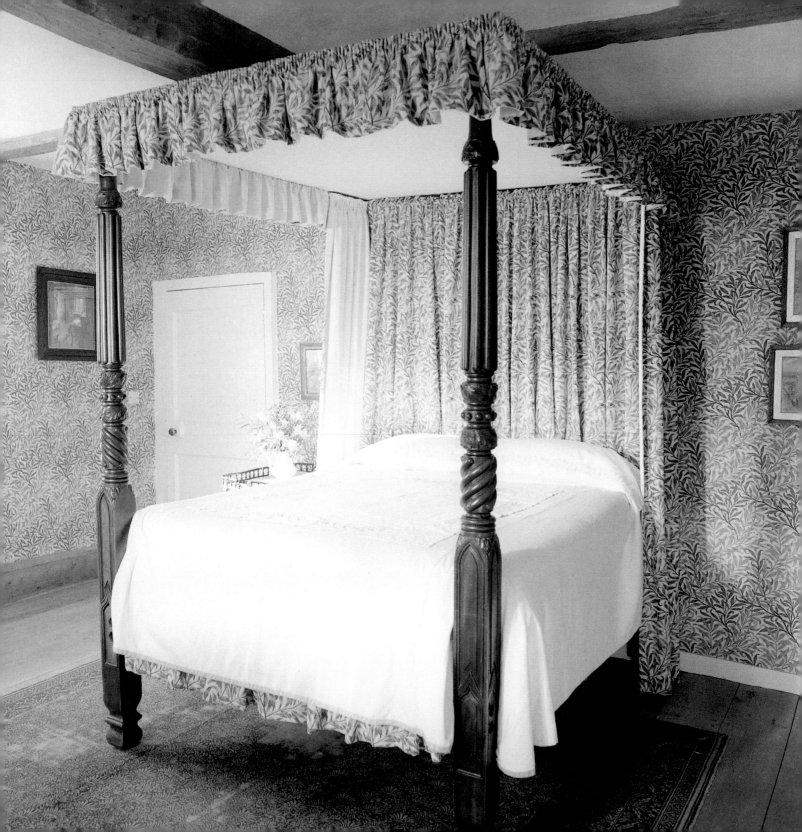

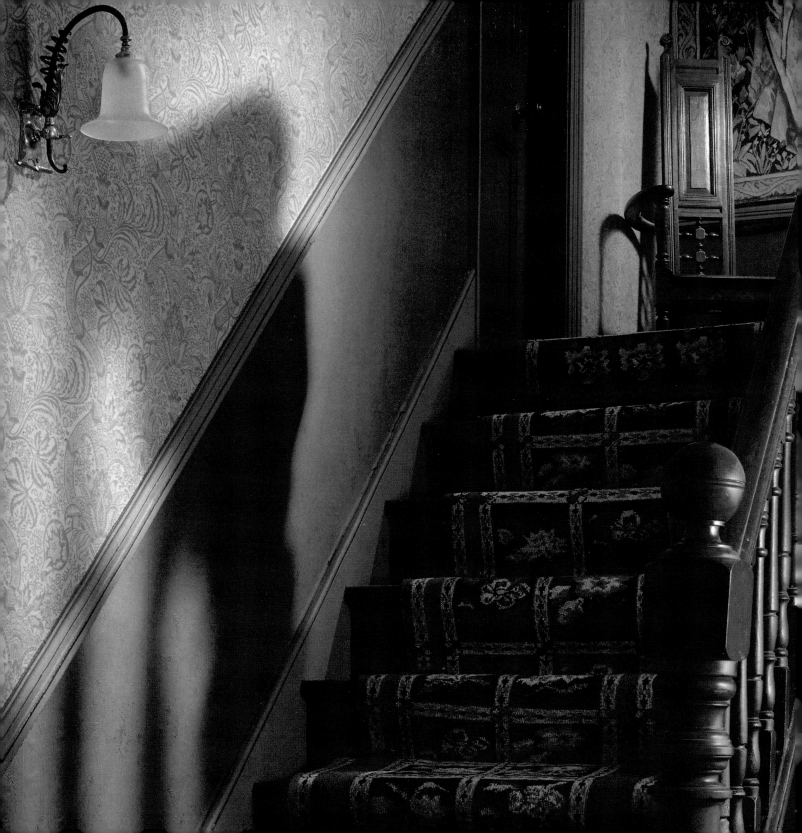

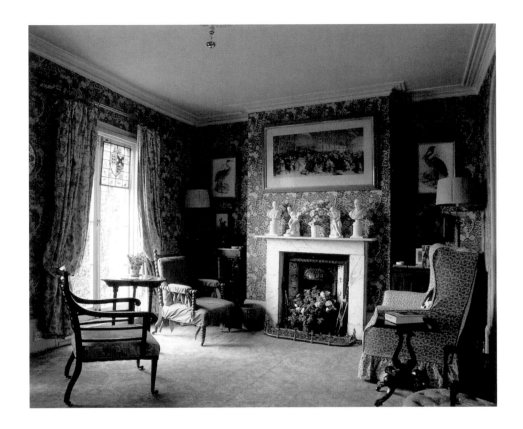

LEFT 'All rooms ought to look as if they were lived in, and to have, so to say, a friendly welcome ready for the incomer', wrote Morris in *Making the Best of It*. The wallpaper is *Seaweed* by Dearle, a design which looks forward to the sinuous curves of Art Nouveau.

not prevent him from designing patterns which enlarged and defined the medium, nor from considering, in detail, the effect the use his papers would have on the decoration of a room. The Boston Foreign Fair brochure sets out Morris's views on the choice of pattern, stressing that wallpaper is only part of a decorative scheme and must be looked at in the context of the other colours and forms. The advice was specific and it is worth quoting it in its entirety.

> *If there is a reason for keeping the wall very quiet, choose a pattern that works all over without pronounced lines, such as the* Diapers, Mallows, Venetians, Poppy, Scroll, Jasmine, *etc.*
>
> *If you may venture on more decided patterning, and you ought always to go for positive patterns when they may be had, choose the* Daisy, Trellis, Vine, Chrysanthemum, Lily, Honeysuckle, Larkspur, Rose, Acanthus, *or such. In deciding between those whose direction or set is horizontal, and those which have more obviously vertical or oblique lines, you must be guided entirely by the look of the room. Put very succinctly, architectural effect depends upon a nice balance of horizontal, vertical and oblique. No rules can say how much*

OPPOSITE *Indian* paper combined with a relief paper painted a dull olive used as a dado. Papering the lower portion of the wall in a heavily embossed paper was a Victorian convention; such an arrangement protected surfaces from wear.

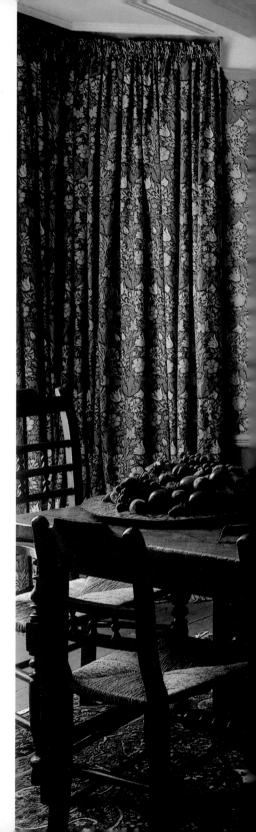

RIGHT *Compton* fabric and wallpaper coordinate in this contemporary dining room, creating a warm but lively background for an oak refectory table and rush seated chairs. The paint colours – claret for the dado, olive for woodwork and a biscuit shade for the frieze and ceiling – pick out colours from *Compton*.

of each; so nothing can really take the place of feeling and good judgement. If you have no professional aid, you must decide for yourself whether the room most wants stability and repose, or if it is too stiff and formal. If repose be wanted, choose the pattern, other things being considered, which has horizontal arrangement of its parts. If too great a rigidity be the fault, choose a pattern with soft easy lines, either boldly circular or oblique-wavy – say Scroll, Vine, Pimpernel, Fruit. *If the fault lie in the too great predominance of horizontal lines, without any marked stiffness in the parts, as when the walls are very low and long, choose one of the columnar patterns, as* Larkspur, Spray, *or* Indian; *or better still, hang the walls with chintz, or cloth, in folds. . . .*

Wallpaper, as is demonstrated in this passage, can go a long way to correct a room's inherent architectural defects as well as emphasize its strengths. The directional stress of the pattern literally dissolves the flat surface of the wall and takes the eye beyond. Morris envisaged his designs turning a room into a kind of bower.

In the nineteenth century it was not that common for a single design to cover the whole wall. The division of the wall by the dado and picture rail, especially in reception rooms, meant that the wallpaper was displayed in a much smaller area. Although the horizontal emphasis of many Arts and Crafts interiors did little to change this, there were also instances, particularly in country bedrooms, where Morris paper was used from floor to ceiling uninterrupted by panelling, chair or picture rail, in a fashion more typical of today's usage. There were also occasions where paper extended from the skirting board to a deep picture rail.

Wallpaper generally acquired a poor stylistic reputation in the twentieth century as the standards of design and manufacture plummeted and the plain painted plastered wall became universal. But for those who wish to reacquaint themselves with the decorative potential of wallpaper, Morris designs are an excellent place to begin. A printer who once worked for Sanderson's attested to their unique qualities of restfulness and timelessness.

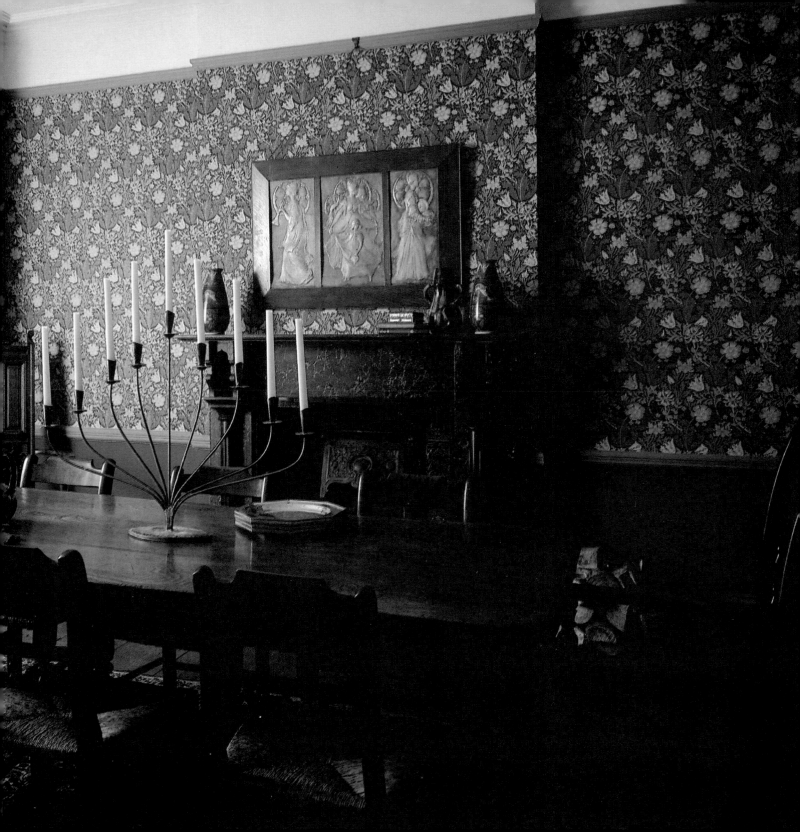

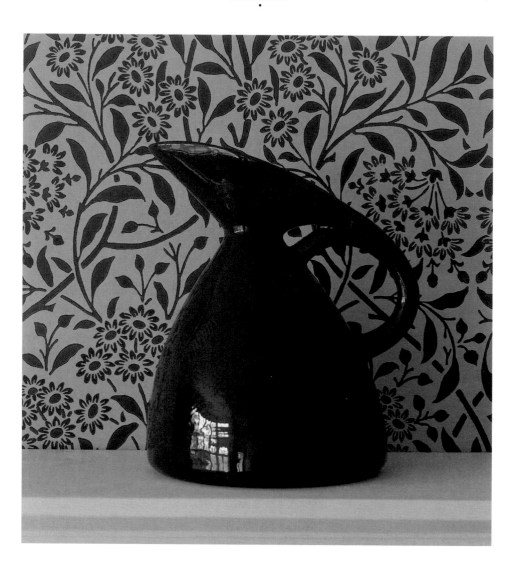

RIGHT *Michaelmas Daisy*, a 1912 design by Dearle, is available as a hand-printed paper. Its simple, graphic quality would make it a good choice for a bedroom or study.

It was not unknown during his time as a hand-printer for customers to reorder the same pattern after thirty years of living with it.

Today adjustments have been made to the production process and to some of the designs themselves to accommodate the needs of the market. Many are machine-printed, which brings down the price considerably and designs have been simplified accordingly. Machine-printing, however, gives a far higher quality result today than it did in the nineteenth century. At the top end of the market, hand-printed papers are still available and designs not in stock can be ordered on request. Some papers have been adjusted to account for the smaller proportions of today's rooms.

Many of Morris's most successful papers were large and bold; there is often a concern that, however beautiful a pattern may be, it must prove overpowering and claustrophobic in practice. A similar reservation was expressed by Morris's contemporary, the architect Richard Norman Shaw, when he declared: 'William Morris was a great man who somehow delighted in glaring wallpapers.' It is true that some of the designs work best in large high-ceilinged rooms where there is adequate space to appreciate the intricacies of the design. However, as Morris himself advised, large patterns, with all their vitality, can work just as well in small rooms and need not be oppressive. Many Morris papers look vastly different in different colourways; a lighter combination of colours can make a large pattern much less insistent in a small space. Combining wallpaper with half panelling in the form of a dado is another solution.

If Morris designs are timeless, they are also adaptable and suit many different locations in the house as well as many different periods. Branching, diagonal patterns, such as the late design *Compton*, are well suited to stairways and halls, where the eye is naturally led upwards. *Acorn*, a classically sedate mirror repeat, in a single colour on a coloured ground, would be equally at home in a Georgian interior as a contemporary living room. The charming rusticity of *Willow* has a freshness and enveloping quality which makes it a good choice for a country bedroom.

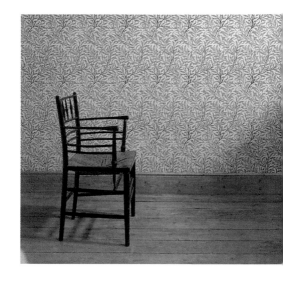

ABOVE A Sussex chair in front of *Willow Bough* paper. Original pieces of Morris furniture, particularly Sussex chairs in their various forms, can still be found.

FABRIC HANGING

'People dressed themselves in his wallhangings, covered books with them, did this or that with them according to their fancy, but hang walls with them they would not,' commented Mackail. When the *Daisy* hanging, worked by Jane Morris to her husband's design, won a medal at the 1862 exhibition, the *Clerical Journal* was dismissive:

> *Middle class people do not use hangings of any kind upon their walls and are not likely to furnish their drawing rooms, or even their bedrooms, with such a homely-looking material as this . . . we should be a little surprised to see the material in actual use anywhere except in the quaintly-furnished bachelor rooms of an artist, or the private snuggery of a medievalist.*

William Morris was alone in his enthusiasm for covering walls with fabric. Wallhangings of various kinds, however, have a long history, dating back to the great medieval halls hung with tapestries and fine embroidered cloths. Fabric as a means of declaring status and decorating a wall was a practical choice for the peripatetic households of the Middle Ages, since it could easily be packed and transported, along with other valuables, from place to place; wallhangings must also have considerably increased comfort, insulating against draughts, damp and cold. Another kind of fabric covering, where the material was stretched flat against the wall, was common in wealthier households from the seventeenth right up to the nineteenth century and it was as a means of simulating the effect of these fine damask or silk coverings, but at a fraction of their cost, that machine-made wallpaper found its first decorative role.

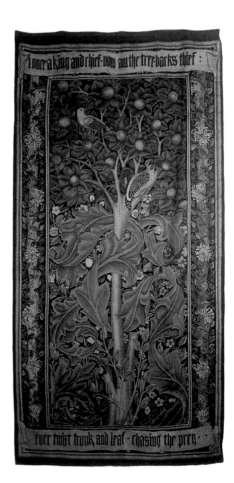

ABOVE *The Woodpecker* tapestry, designed by Morris in 1885. The inscription was embroidered by May and assistants.

Morris was an advocate of all these forms of fabric covering: the display of richly embroidered hangings or tapestries; the use of woven cloth to enclose a room; and fine fabric stretched over a wall to provide a background for pictures or a foil for panelling. The *Daisy* hanging, which attracted as much scorn as praise, was worked for the bedroom at Red House. More ambitious were twelve figure panels, designed to imitate tapestry and intended for the dining room. But perhaps the most famous example of Morris's use of fabric coverings were the *Bird* hangings which he designed for the drawing room at Kelmscott House. This heavy woven wool double cloth was hung from a picture rail, two feet below the ceiling and extended to the skirting board. The hangings went right around the perimeter of the room, their soft blues emphasizing the river views from the drawing room windows. On the end wall, the fabric was cut out to accommodate the fireplace opening. The cloth was simply hooked to the rail and gathered only slightly: 'only just enough modulation of the surface being allowed to just break the pattern here and there'. The Boston Foreign Fair brochure asserted: 'The beautiful effect of a long wall hung in this way is quite inconceivable.'

In Kelmscott House there was also a Persian carpet of outstanding beauty hung on the dining room wall like a tapestry; and at Kelmscott Manor an entire room was hung with Morris's own collection of tapestries.

Another woven fabric which Morris may have intended to be made into hangings was *Peacock and Dragon*. This design, with its repeat of 43 by 35 inches (109 by 90cm), needed to be displayed in a large enough quantity for the full extent of the pattern to be appreciated. The 'dragon' of the pattern is thought to have been inspired by phoenixes in Chinese textiles. Many of Morris's woven fabrics, including *Bird* and *Peacock and Dragon*, found more favour as material for upholstery or curtains than as wallhangings. The silk damasks, *Oak* and *St James's*, designed as part of the 1881 St James's commission, were intended as flat wall coverings and were used as such at the Palace. Their muted patterns, based on leaf forms, were designed to provide a sympathetic background for paintings. The brochure for the Boston Foreign Fair commented about a similar silk and wool damask: '. . . an admirable wall covering, even where pictures are hung; though the pattern is large and full of variety, a tone of warm, broken greyness is the prevailing effect. It is quite warm enough to harmonize with the gold of picture frames, and gray enough not to hurt the colour of a picture. The introduction of the fine wool through the pattern is the main cause of the subdued splendour.' Needless to say, these damasks were extremely expensive and proved more popular for curtains and upholstery. May Morris recorded how her mother had a dress made of *Oak* silk in green, shot through with 'moon-beam lights'.

But for Morris, 'the noblest of all the weaving arts' was tapestry. It was 'a mosaic of pieces of colour made up of dyed threads' and 'special excellencies can be expected of it', including 'depth of tone, richness of colour and exquisite gradation of tints'; at the same time, it demanded 'crispness and abundance of beautiful detail'. In the late nineteenth century, tapestries were a more popular and acceptable form of wallhanging than lengths of woven cloth. By the end of the century, small tapestry panels, often featuring female figures, became a popular art form, produced at a reasonable cost and size to suit the ordinary domestic interior.

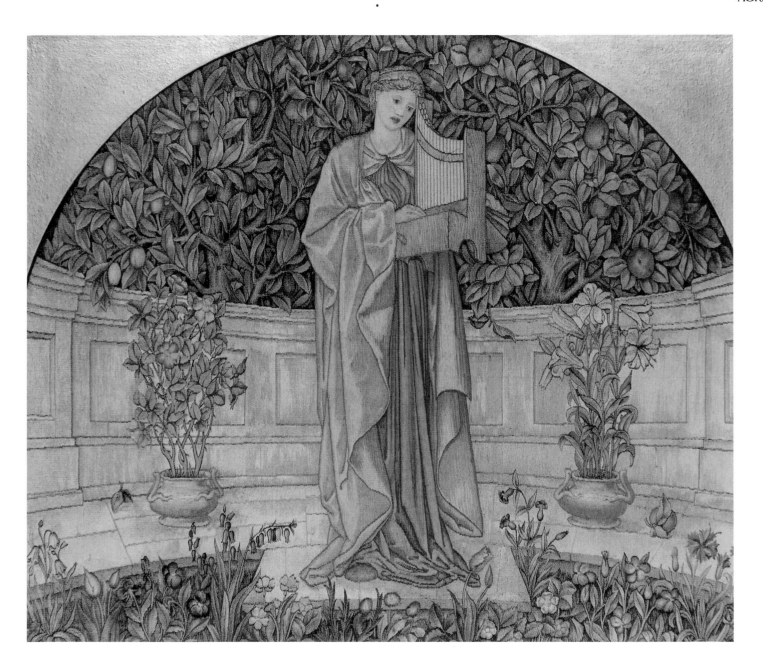

ABOVE *Minstrel Figure*, 1890, the only
figurative tapestry designed by Morris. It
was intended to hang over a fireplace. The
fruit trees and balustrade are by Dearle.

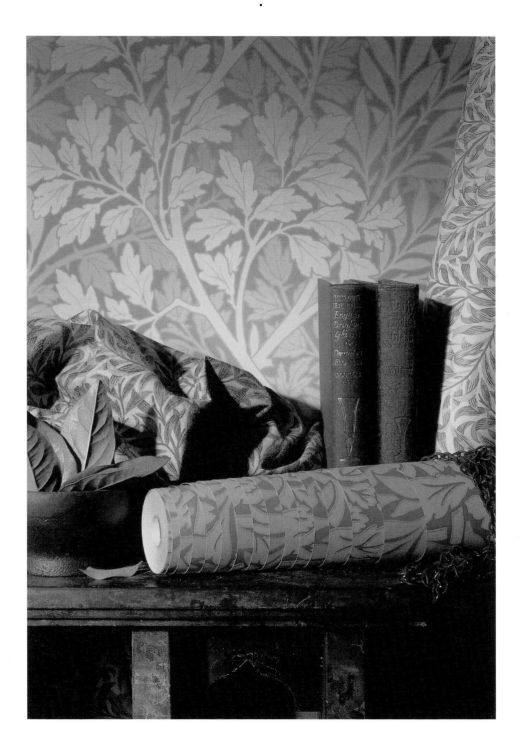

RIGHT Subtle tonalities – greys, grey-browns and grey-greens – harmonize beautifully with old wood. In the background is *Foliage* wallpaper; on the table *Willow Bough* fabric and paper.

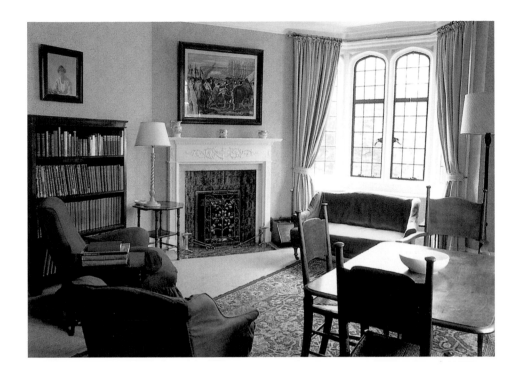

LEFT 'A drawing room ought to look as if some kind of work could be done in it less toilsome than being bored', wrote Morris in *Making the Best of It*. The informal nature of today's living rooms, with their accommodation of different activities, as in this Oxford sitting room, would have met with Morris's approval.

Morris wove his first tapestry panel in 1879, teaching himself the technique on a loom he had set up in his bedroom at Kelmscott House. The panel was called *Acanthus and Vine*, which he nicknamed *Cabbage and Vine*. Morris's finest tapestries, however, were the result of a collaboration between himself and J. H. Dearle as designers of backgrounds and borders, with Edward Burne-Jones as the figure designer and Webb who, as usual, drew the animals. Notable examples include *The Orchard* (1890) where Morris designed the figures and *The Forest*, commissioned by Alexander Ionides for his house at 1 Holland Park. Another famous series of panels were the six *Holy Grail* tapestries, designed for the dining room of Stanmore Hall in 1890, and acknowledged to be the finest of all nineteenth-century work of this kind. Following the usual practice, the wall area was divided into two, with figurative panels hung above eye level. The design of these panels was cleverly distorted as they were to be viewed from below. In place of a dado or chair rail were inscriptions and below were 'verdures' depicting deer, trees and heraldic shields. The tapestries were highly influential. Furniture shown in the first panel appears to have inspired designs by Charles Rennie Mackintosh, among other Art Nouveau practitioners.

For all of Morris's enthusiasm and skill, fabric hangings of any description remain a rarity in the ordinary interior, largely due to cost. But while draping hand-printed material around the entire perimeter of a room is extremely expensive, there are other ways of gaining the same effect at a fraction of the cost. Morris was not advocating lavish

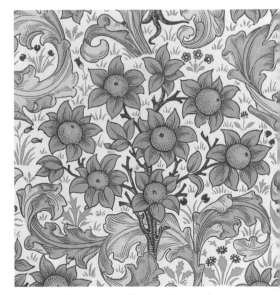

ABOVE *Orchard*, a wallpaper design by Dearle, 1899.

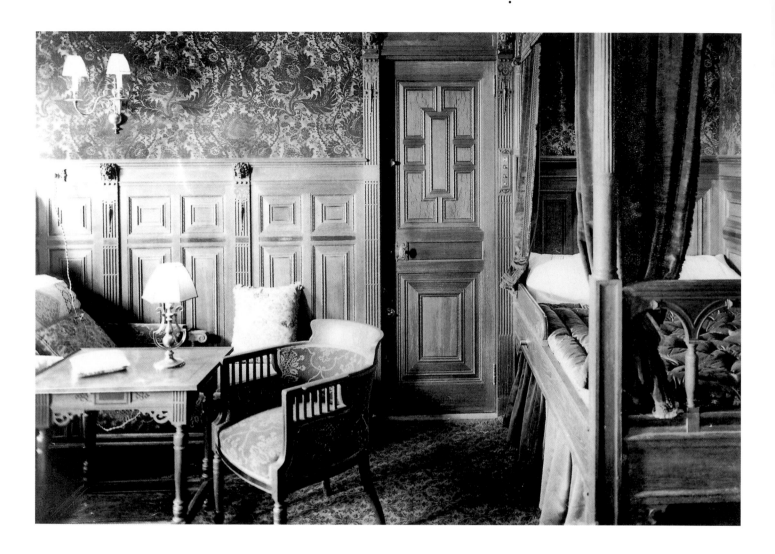

ABOVE A first class suite on the *Titanic*, with walls covered in *Utrecht Velvet*, a plush fabric of 1871 whose design derived from seventeenth-century velvets.

pleated wall hangings or tented ceilings in any case; his solution was to gather the fabric only slightly so that the full beauty of its pattern could be displayed. One solution might be to limit the scale of application, so that only one wall is treated in this way. Fabric could be hung behind a headboard, for example, or on one wall of a living or dining room. An advantage of this treatment, aside from the sheer visual impact, is the extra warmth and sense of comfort it provides. If the fabric is simply hooked over a picture rail or strip of moulding, it can be easily removed for cleaning or taken down during the summer if a lighter decorative scheme is desired.

Covering a wall with fabric displayed flat like wallpaper is another matter. Again, this is often an expensive option unless you choose plain dyed cotton; most printed fabrics will be more expensive than wallpaper, as they were in Morris's day. The fabric is usually stretched tight over battens nailed around the perimeter of the wall and stapled in position; unless you are exceptionally practical, this is really not a job for an amateur. The particular advantage of fabric-covered walls is the softness and depth of colour you can achieve; a muted pattern is also very effective, suggesting the richness of early damask coverings.

Similarly, few people today are in a position to display medieval tapestries on their walls. But this is an area where there are a number of acceptable alternatives. Any length of handwoven, embroidered or worked fabric can be displayed in this way, from South American appliqué pictures to Indian dhurrie rugs. There is a wealth of textile artistry available at reasonable cost, both traditional designs from around the world and modern work from young designers at home. The best has all the vitality, textural interest and delight in decoration that Morris found such attractive features of medieval work.

OTHER FINISHES

Morris adopted a whole range of other decorative wall treatments to complement his wallpapers and hangings – many for a portion of the wall rather than the entire area – that could be attempted today.

Some of these consist of a form of special embellishment for the top-most part of the wall, between the picture rail and the cornice. The 'frieze', as this narrow band is correctly termed, became increasingly the focus of decorative attention in the nineteenth century; by the end of the century special frieze papers, featuring large horizontal patterns of landscapes or trees were produced. Morris and Co. produced no frieze papers but often treated this part of the wall in a highly elaborate way. One of the most famous examples was the painted frieze executed by Burne-Jones (and completed by Walter Crane) for the Howards' London house, I Palace Green in Kensington. The thirteen panels featured scenes from the Cupid and Psyche myth, taken from Morris's telling of the story in the *Earthly Paradise*. The frieze, which ran around the perimeter of the dining room above panelling, was highly praised at the time and was said to glow like the pages of an illuminated manuscript.

An earlier example of wallpainting, some of which was also by Burne-Jones, were the seven frescoes which enlivened the drawing room walls at Red House. Painted in tempera and featuring scenes from an Arthurian myth, the decoration included designs of birds and trees by Morris.

Hand-painted tiles were an early part of the Firm's production. Morris bought plain blank tiles which were then painted and fired in the workshop. Many of the Firm's original members contributed either to the design or painting of the tiles.

Tiled fireplace surrounds were a common feature of late nineteenth-century interiors and some of the tiles produced by the Firm were used in this way. Other tile panels were designed to cover a larger wall area. A tile panel intended as an overmantel was produced for the Victorian watercolourist Miles Birket Foster in 1863. The design, by Burne-Jones, featured scenes from Beauty and the Beast and was painted by Lucy

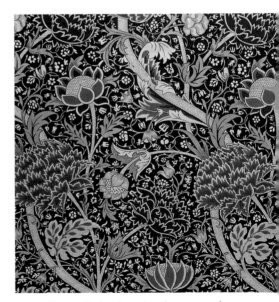

ABOVE *Cray*, a design for printed cotton and linen, 1884.

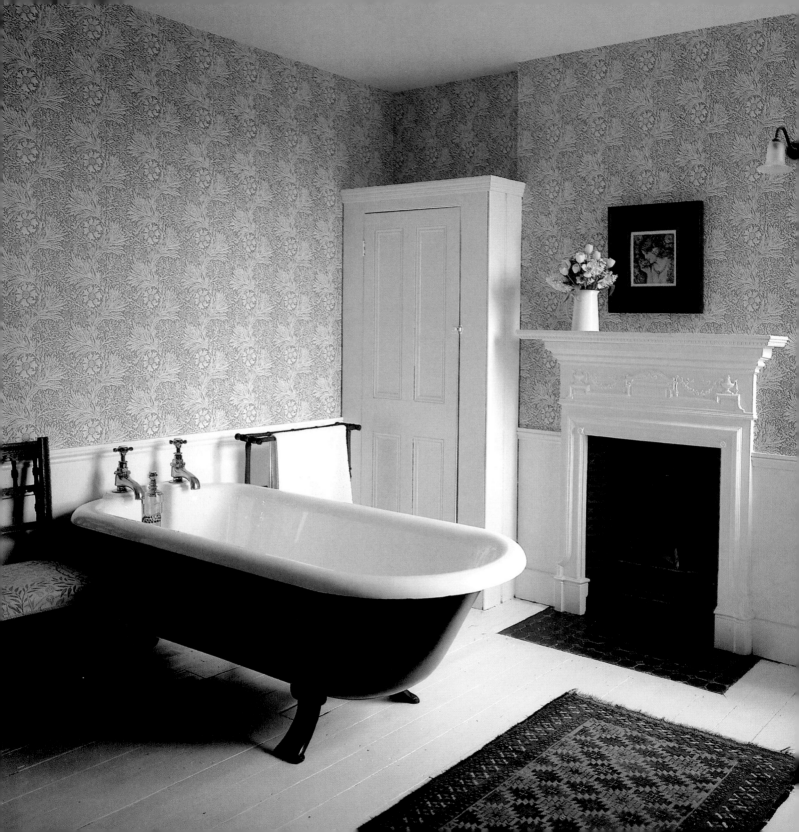

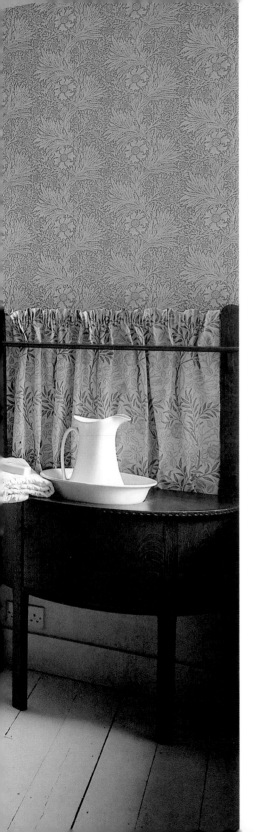

Morris promoted the beauty of useful things. In this functional setting, his patterns are just as enriching as in a drawing room or dining room. Beautifully detailed *Marigold* is the wallpaper; the oak washstand is curtained with *Sweet Briar*, a 1912 Dearle design. Pure white woodwork, painted boards and towels make an effective counterpoint.

Faulkner, sister of Charles Faulkner. Lucy Faulkner also painted another panel for Birket Foster depicting the story of Cinderella. A large fireplace panel was produced for Queen's College Hall in Cambridge, with designs illustrating every month of the year.

Webb designed a sixteen-square tile border of alternating swans and foliage, which was very popular as a fireplace surround. It can be seen on the fireplace in the Green Room at Kelmscott Manor.

William de Morgan (1839–1917) was an early associate of Morris who became interested in the decoration of tiles and went on to become a leading ceramicist, producing pottery which in design and conception was the equivalent of Morris's work in fabric. He is best known for his revival of lustreglaze, his interest in Islamic decoration and his affinity with the natural forms of birds, animals and plants.

The success of the Morris and Co. decorative wall painting was largely dependent on the talent of accomplished artists like Burne-Jones. Mural painting, as a way of decorating a wall, is simply not available to everyone. Morris, of course, was well aware of this and intended his wallpaper and fabric designs to be acceptable substitutes. As an alternative, but by no means as a substitute for these realistic, narrative wall paintings, stencilled decoration might be adopted instead. A stencilled frieze of twining leaf shapes or flower forms, daisies, roses or sprays of berries could complement a Morris pattern very well. Birds or stylized animals might also be effective. Part of the appeal of stencilling is the contrast between the rhythm of the repeating pattern and the liveliness of the execution with all of its variety; such a quality is very sympathetic to the basic principles of Morris and Co. Stencilling is also a way of emphasizing both horizontal and vertical elements. As a frieze or dado decoration, it stresses the horizontal; outlining a doorframe or fireplace, it draws attention to the vertical. There is a wide range of precut stencils by talented designers on the market. The technique itself is relatively easy to master and quick to do.

Similarly, tiled panels or portions of a wall can also be readily accomplished today. Morris was particularly fond of blue and white tiles; basic designs in blue and white often

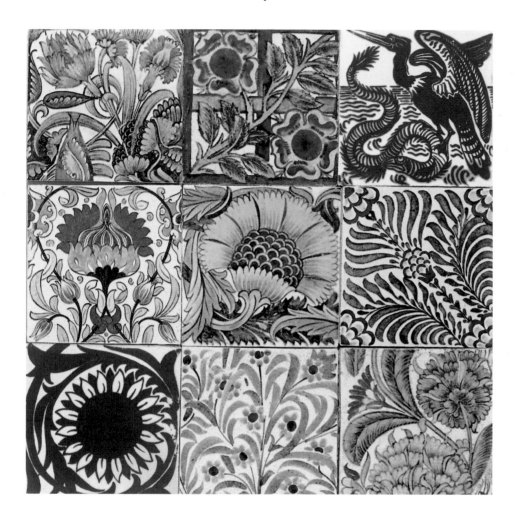

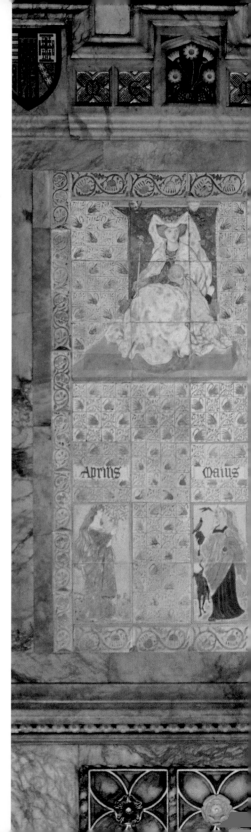

ABOVE Earthenware tiles by William de Morgan, 1882-1907. De Morgan (1839-1917), who worked alongside Morris from the early days of the Firm, moved to Merton Abbey in 1882 before establishing his own factory in London. Tiles were a speciality, although he also made plates, vases and other ceramic pieces.

LEFT Fireplace tile panel at Queen's College, Old Hall, Cambridge, 1862-4. The architect Bodley, who restored the hall, commissioned the Firm to produce the panel; it depicts the months of the year. The blue and white background tiles are by Webb.

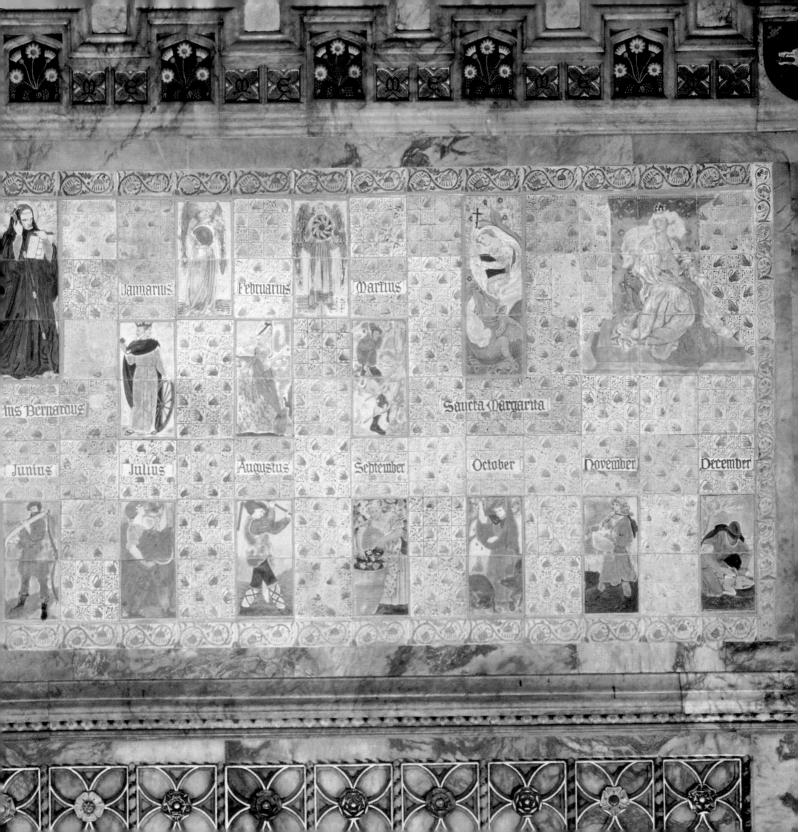

Jannarius Februarius Martius

ius Bernardus

Sancta Margarita

Junius Julius Augustus September October November December

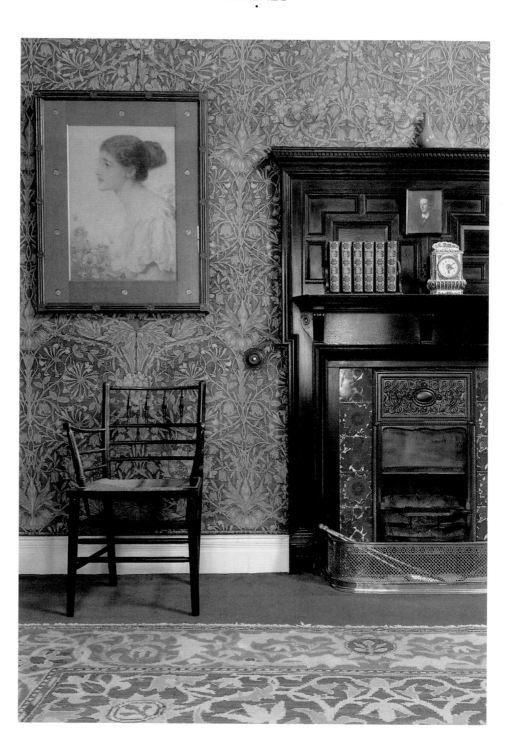

RIGHT Wightwick Manor, showing *Honey-suckle* (1876), printed on linen, used to cover the walls. The portrait by Frederick Sandys is in a frame by Rossetti.

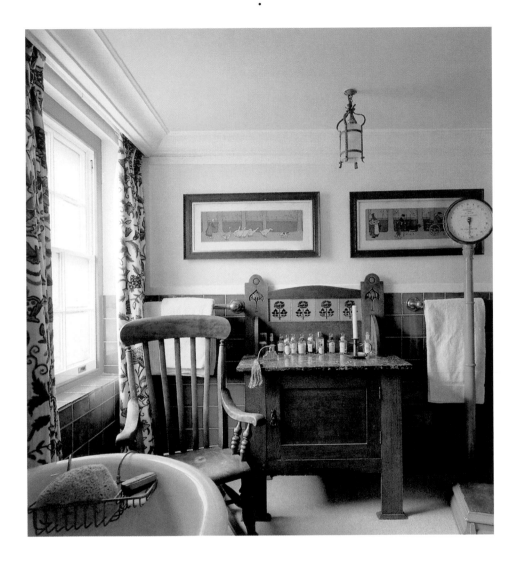

LEFT An Arts and Crafts bathroom, accented with shades of sharp green and turquoise. The oak washstand, with its marble top and tiling, antique weighing machine and Victorian rocking chair have their own distinctive characters but work well together. The wall tiling, extending from the floor two-thirds of the way up the wall, divides the wall in typical Arts and crafts proportions.

formed the background to the more highly coloured and realized inset panels. With the recent revival of craft skills, handpainted tiles are easily available at a fairly reasonable cost. Tiled walls or parts of a wall are practical choices for kitchens and bathrooms, where water is splashed or frequent cleaning is necessary. The utilitarian blandness this type of finish normally offers can be overcome by searching out good examples of hand-decorated tile. For the sake of economy, plain coloured tiles or simple repeat designs could be used as a background, with the more pictorial tiles inset along the wall.

CHAPTER FOUR

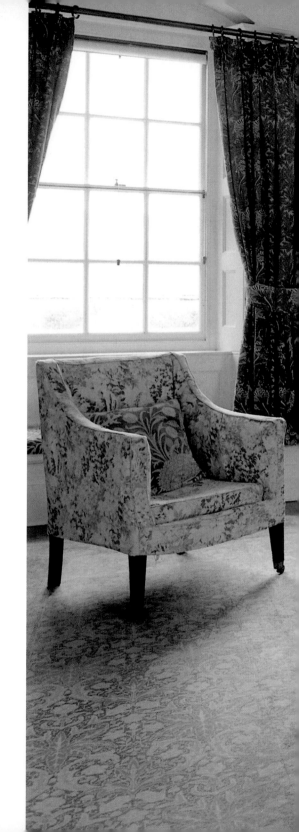

Midways of a walled garden,
  In the happy poplar land,
  Did an ancient castle stand,
With an old knight for a warden.

Many scarlet bricks there were
  In its walls, and old grey stone;
  Over which red apples shone
At the right time of the year.

On the bricks the green moss grew,
  Yellow lichen on the stone,
  Over which red apples shone;
Little war that castle knew.

Golden Wings

RIGHT The *Willow* Bedroom, Standen, Sussex, a house designed by Philip Webb. The walls are papered in *Willow Bough*; the curtains are *Tulip* chintz.

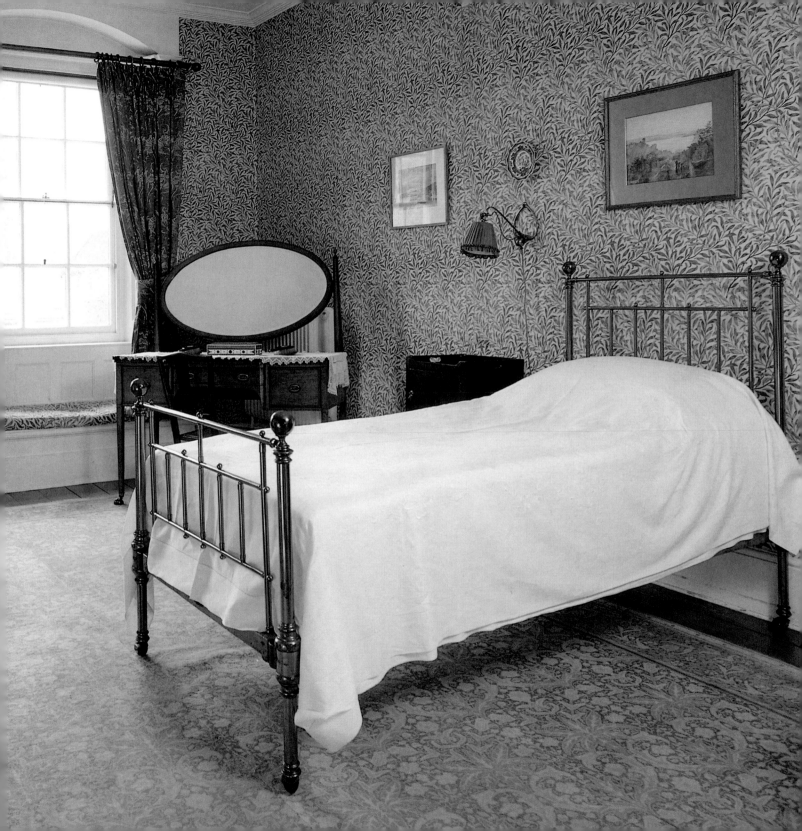

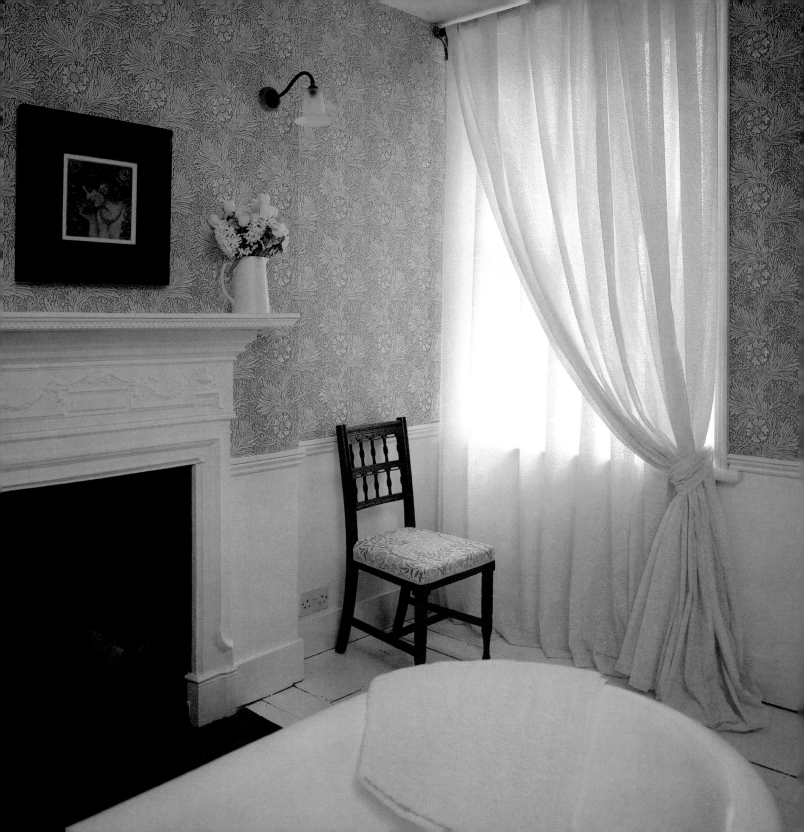

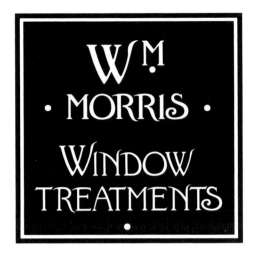

Wm · MORRIS · WINDOW TREATMENTS

WINDOWS HAVE ALWAYS BEEN FOCAL POINTS IN INTERIOR DESIGN, JUST AS THEY are expressive elements architecturally. Before central heating and electric light, the window and the fireplace were the two most important features of any room – for practical reasons as well as aesthetic ones. Window glass radically improved around the beginning of the nineteenth century; technical developments meant that glass was more transparent than formerly and the size of the individual panes also increased, making windows altogether more effective.

Windows admit light and air, frame views and generally create a sense of expansion and freedom, connecting with the world outside. How they are decorated has an enormous impact on the mood of a room. A window treatment can alter the quality of light, enhance architectural detail, add relatively large blocks of colour, pattern and texture. And in modern rooms, window treatments consist of the single most important use of fabric, often contrasting with plain painted walls and simple upholstery.

The way houses are decorated today is essentially much simpler than the fashion of one hundred years ago. Even the most elaborate contemporary interior barely approaches the full-blown upholstered, tasselled, fringed and draped stuffiness of High Victoriana, with its clutter of mementoes, occasional tables, whatnots and curios. This trend for simplification, of surfaces, content and finishes, would certainly have met with Morris's full approval.

Relatively plain rooms, with few layers and minimal trimming, might seem an unlikely setting for patterns conceived in the last century, but, in some ways, Morris designs actually work better in modern homes than they did in the homes of his contemporaries. Few Victorians embraced the Arts and Crafts aesthetic with anything like the rigour its designers would have liked and Morris fabrics and papers were often simply added to the general *mélange* so characteristic of late Victorian decorating.

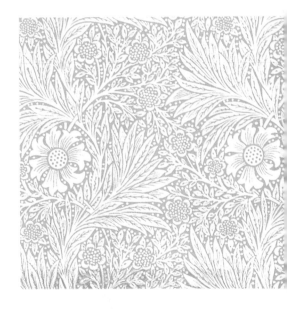

ABOVE *Marigold*, originally a paper design (1875), but also available in silk, cotton and linen union.

LEFT *Willow Bough Minor* voile, a semi-transparent fabric allows light to filter through to reveal a tracery of pattern.

WILLIAM MORRIS AND TEXTILE DESIGN

'Never forget the material you are working with and try always to use it for what it can do best.' This advice, given by Morris in an article entitled *Textiles* published in 1893, summarizes his entire approach. Morris was acutely aware of the properties of different fabrics, the way they draped, hung and printed, and never designed a textile without considering its eventual use in furnishing. His designs for fabric were conceived, not as exercises in flat patterning, but always with their specific end in mind. Wallpaper designs were different, intended to be displayed flat. Fabric, which folded, draped and moved, had a distinct quality of its own which Morris always acknowledged. During his lifetime, patterns originally intended for use as flat wallpaper were never transferred to textiles.

There were also differences from fabric to fabric, particularly differences in texture and tactility. In the nineteenth century, before artificial fibres were developed, the range of available furnishing fabrics was somewhat limited. Silk, the most luxurious, with its

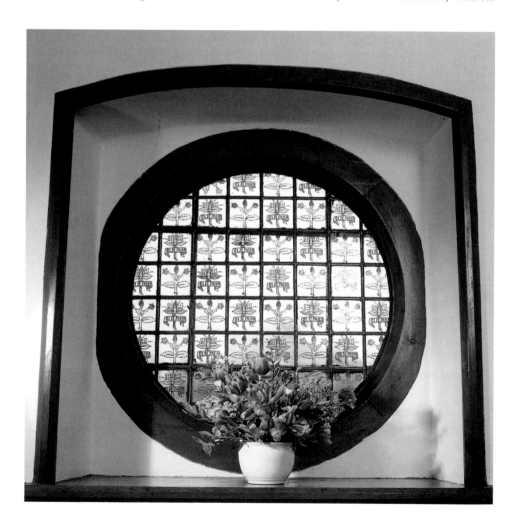

RIGHT The window on the upper landing at Red House. Stained glass panes display Morris's motto *Si je puis* ('if I can'), apposite for a life notable for creative endeavour in almost every field of the applied arts. The beauty of the glass and the framing of the window in its recess make curtaining an irrelevance.

shimmering reflective sheen, was too expensive for the majority of people; woven textiles, chiefly composed of wool, were almost universal. There were also cotton and hardwearing cotton and linen mixtures, but these were almost exclusively reserved for informal summer use. Most nineteenth-century households, for reasons of economy and insulation, adopted the practice of changing loose covers and curtains according to the season. In the summer, the heavy, dark winter drapery would be replaced by lighter summer curtains and the dark plush upholstery covered up with lighter washable cotton covers in cheerful floral prints. One of the specific influences that Morris had on nineteenth-century domestic decoration was to popularize cotton as a year-round furnishing material, a direct result of the success of his printed chintzes.

In addition to cotton and 'glazed' chintz (cotton treated to give it a surface shine), Morris designed patterns for a number of mixtures of cotton, linen, wool and silk. He also experimented with hand-weaving. Contrasting fibres – silk and linen, woven silk and wool, velveteen, woven linen and silk, woven wool and mohair, cotton and silk gauze – led to a richness of surface and depth of texture which gave Morris textiles great versatility. More than any other textile designer of his day, he exploited the range of fibres available and enjoyed their distinct characteristics, trying to make 'woollen substances as woollen as possible, cotton as cotton as possible'.

In his capacity as a decorator, choosing fabrics of his own design for clients' houses, Morris was especially sensitive to subtleties of colour and texture. An early commission was the London home of George Howard, later the ninth Earl of Carlisle. The house, built by Philip Webb in 1868–72, was decorated over a period of ten years. For the boudoir, Morris suggested drapery in 'shades of red that would brighten all up without fighting with the wall-hangings'. In 1881, he chose curtains of *St James* silk damask for the drawing room: 'I suggest a dullish pink shot with amber like some of the chrysanthemums we see just now.' However, for his own house, Kelmscott Manor, Morris chose white wool curtains in the drawing room, at that time a treatment revolutionary in its simplicity but perfectly in keeping with the house's tranquil setting on the banks of the Thames.

As described in the previous chapter, one of Morris's great contributions to textile design was the rediscovery of traditional working methods, particularly the revival of natural or vegetable dyeing, a technique which had almost completely disappeared in the nineteenth century. Victorian chemical or aniline dyes produced harsh, violent and rather lurid shades which were 'fugitive' (prone to fading), apt to discolour, bleed and fade out of synchronization with each other. By contrast, vegetable dyes produced true, clear colours which blended beautifully, and meant that a number of different patterns could be combined successfully in one room. With age, these natural colours faded evenly across the tonal range, preserving the original colour relationships of the pattern. Vegetable dyes perfectly complemented the natural designs of the fabric. W. R. Lethaby, a leading figure in the Arts and Crafts movement, described the material looking as if it were 'stained through and through with the juices of flowers'. Morris was just as concerned, however, with the practical consequences of dyeing, taking particular interest in colour-fastness, a critical consideration for fabrics which were intended to be used in upholstery.

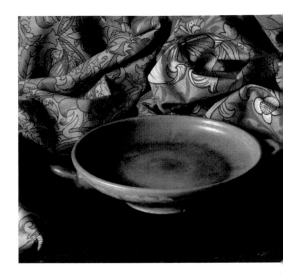

ABOVE *Granville* (left), originally a wallpaper design by Dearle from 1896 and *Golden Lily* (right), also a wallpaper design transferred to fabric, a Dearle pattern from 1897.

As far as pattern was concerned, Morris held predictably strong views. 'Do not be afraid of large patterns,' he told an audience in a lecture of 1888, 'if properly designed they are more restful to the eye than small ones: on the whole, a pattern where the structure is large and the details much broken up is the most useful . . . very small rooms, as well as very large ones, look better ornamented with large patterns.' Indeed, one of the joys of decorating with Morris designs is the scale of the patterns and the sense of movement and rhythm they impart to a room.

USING WILLIAM MORRIS FABRICS

During the latter part of the nineteenth century, the vogue for draping interiors with layers of fabric was at its peak. It is hard to appreciate today just how dark and oppressive many of these rooms must have been and what a challenge to received notions of taste and propriety the ideas of Morris and other Arts and Crafts practitioners must have represented. A typical late Victorian drawing room window might be covered with anything up to four layers of fabric: a pelmet, main curtains, lace undercurtains, and short muslin or net 'glass' curtains set against the lower panes of the window. All would be trimmed with tassels, cords, braid and fringing. Windows were not the only features sporting drapery: doors, fireplaces, mantlepieces, cupboards, alcoves and mirrors might all have draw curtains and swagged pelmets. Gloom was fashionable.

RIGHT The Family of Alfrederick Smith Hatch, 1871, by J. Eastman (1824-1906). Mid- to late Victorian interiors were re-markable for their gloom as much as their clutter. Natural light was all but excluded. This window treatment – heavy crimson drapery, a deep pelmet or lambrequin and lace undercurtains – is fairly typical of the kind of lavish use of fabric in well-to-do homes.

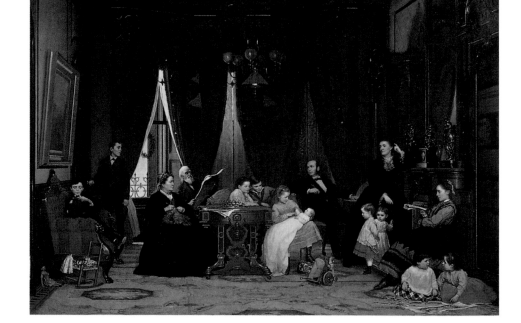

Although Morris naturally would not stipulate the way his customers used the fabric they bought, among the educated middle classes the ideas of the Arts and Crafts movement gradually took hold and there was a general lightening effect in the interior. Window treatments became much simpler, with plain gathered headings, shaped or soft pleated pelmets and plain rods and poles, a style we would generally recognize and appreciate today.

The fact that Morris designed such characteristic patterns, which bear such a strong family resemblance and which are so readily distinguished from the work of other nineteenth-century designers, might be expected to limit their application. Morris fabrics, like his papers, embroidery, carpets and everything else to which he turned his attention, are specific: they largely depict nature and in such a way as to constitute almost a signature. Yet, instead of being tied to a particular period in time – the late nineteenth century – or to a particular style or vision – such as the Arts and Crafts movement – these patterns have proved to be exceptionally enduring and versatile in their application.

In *The Lesser Arts of Life*, which Morris wrote in 1882, he specifies the type of pattern one should choose for furnishings. The qualities he sought included beauty, and 'something that will not drive us either to unrest or into callousness', but 'reminds us of life beyond itself, and which has the impress of human imagination strong on it'.

Morris fabrics are as at home in modern rooms as they are in more historical interiors. Although they are perhaps at their best when used simply, they can be effective in a whole range of different window treatments, from tailored fabric blinds to full-length traditional curtains. It is perfectly possible, of course, to use Morris fabric to make up elaborate fanciful drapery, with tiers of swags and fringed tails, or to create a frilly, ruched festoon blind which pulls up in deep, blowsy flounces. However, neither approach is at all sympathetic. The flowing natural forms of these designs need little further embellishment. They are best displayed in soft, full folds, with understated trimming. This still leaves considerable scope for a wide variety of different decorative looks and practical applications.

Morris fabrics are a natural choice for rooms with a strong historical flavour. But this needs some qualification. Morris had particularly harsh things to say about reproduction. In *Making the Best of It*, he stated: 'It is no longer tradition if it is servilely copied, without change, [which is] the token of life.' Here he was no doubt attacking the epidemic of reproduction furniture, furnishings, decoration and architecture which raged in the late nineteenth century. Every style from Louis Quinze to Jacobean was copied by manufacturers and offered to a growing market eager to give their homes some borrowed status and distinction. Such historical fakery was the opposite of everything Morris stood for, but he was a passionate supporter of maintaining traditions and keeping alive a sense of continuity.

Perhaps because of underlying respect for the past, Morris designs work well in many different types of 'period' interiors. If you avoid slavish recreations of period drapery and opt for classic, traditional curtain styles, you will find Morris patterns suit anything from oak-beamed cottages to nineteenth-century terraces. Even Georgian townhouses, a style of architecture Morris richly detested, could have windows covered in one of the statelier

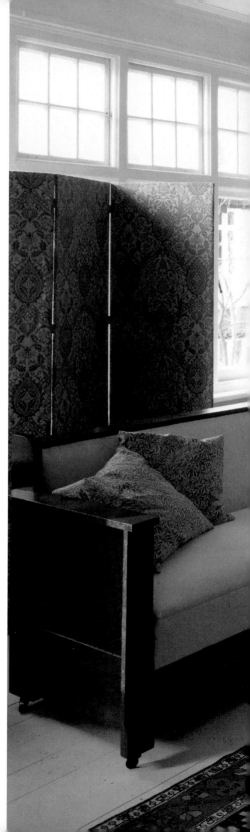

RIGHT A contemporary living room furnished with a selection of Arts and Crafts
furniture and Morris patterns. This light
airy scheme well illustrates Morris's belief
that furniture and ornament should be
limited to allow the decorative interest
to arise from the mixing of sympathetic
patterns.

brocade-like patterns such as *Iris* or *Larkspur*. Dense naturalistic designs like *Honey-suckle* have an unmistakeable Victorian appeal, while the fresh, trailing diagonal patterns such as *Trellis* suit the informality of country cottages or relaxed, Edwardian-style drawing rooms.

Coming up to date, in modern rooms Morris fabrics really display their versatility. The crispness and rhythm of *Willow* has a timeless quality which makes it perfectly at home with contemporary furniture. Many of the denser, richer designs combine well with ethnic furnishings, with oriental rugs, kelims and Indian prints. And in rooms where pattern is kept to a minimum, a Morris fabric has such a degree of quality and interest that it can sustain the attention as a single focus of interest, displayed against plain walls. Morris fabric does not look out of place made up into Roman blinds, an elegant, tailored treatment that works particularly well in modern interiors.

The full range of Morris designs is no longer in production, but there are still a substantial number from which to choose. The British-based firm of Sanderson and Sons maintains a stock of some twenty designs which are produced in the traditional hand-blocked manner, as well as a number of others which are machine-printed on cotton. (The glossary at the back of the book (starting on page 167) contains examples of sixty of the most popular Morris designs. These have been arranged alphabetically by pattern name, rather than by date, to make pattern identification simpler.) Although purists may frown, there are also a number of fabric patterns which have been taken from original wallpaper designs, to satisfy the popular demand for coordinated paper and fabric. Some machine-printed fabrics have been recoloured, but the hand-blocked prints are as true to the originals as possible.

Although Morris fabrics today are not available in as wide a variety of different weaves as the original examples, there are still important distinctions to be made between the standard furnishing fabrics of cotton, cotton sateen, linen union and wool.

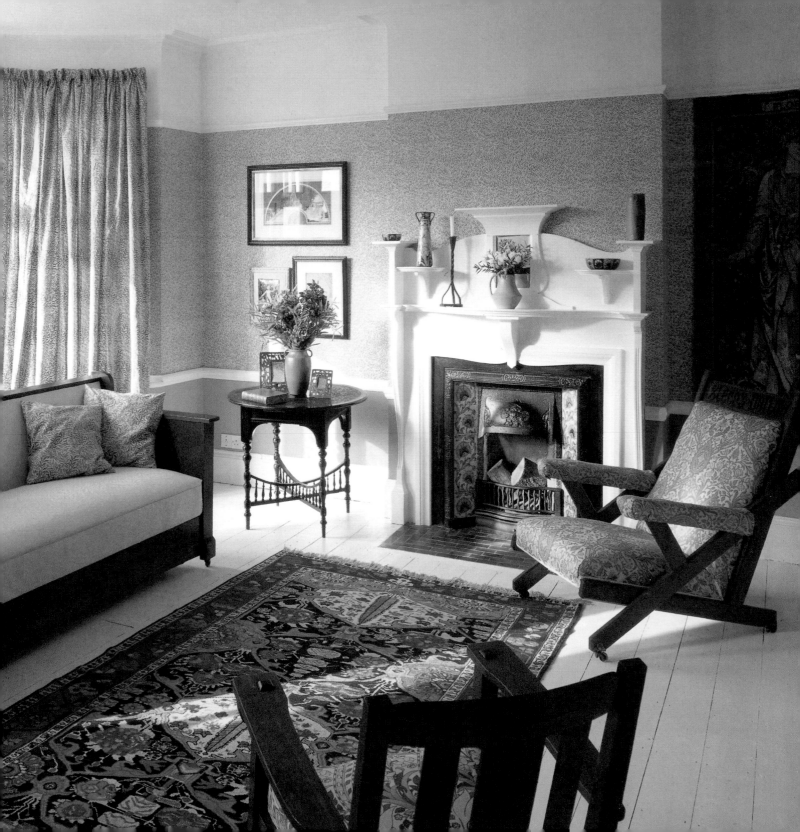

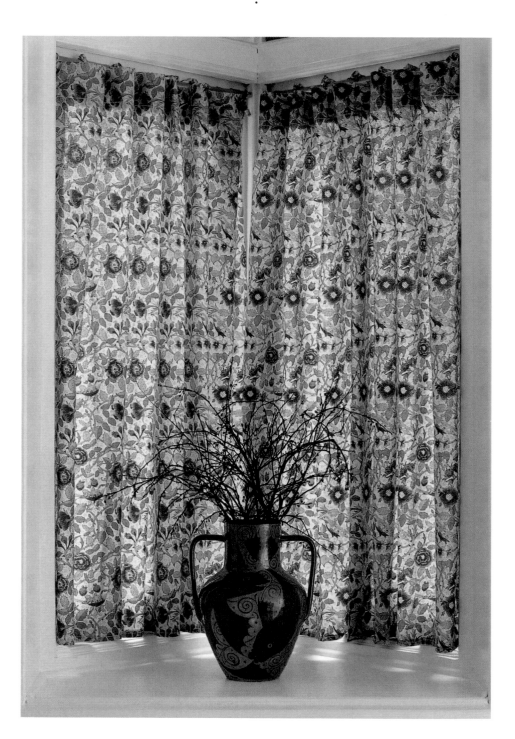

RIGHT This recessed, angled window is simply curtained in a Liberty print, *Briar-wood*, tied onto rods set into the window frames. The fabric has been left unlined to let light shine through, intensifying pattern and colour.

Cotton on its own is generally less formal than the heavier drape of wool, with its depth of colour. Glazed chintz is exceptionally crisp and luminous; cotton sateen has a certain weight and richness. Linen union is a popular hardwearing blend of linen and cotton.

Fabric is relatively expensive; properly lined and finished curtains can represent quite an outlay. To avoid costly mistakes, it is a good idea to plan the whole of the room, its decoration, furnishing and function, as well as considering the window, its size, shape and position. Think about practical matters as well as style and appearance.

WINDOW DRESSING

The degree to which you screen light or views is an important factor. If you need privacy, you may wish to consider lightweight under-curtains or plain roller blinds as well as outer curtains. Semi-transparent fabric such as muslin or lace makes attractive screening without sacrificing too much light if there is an ugly view that needs to be hidden. If you want to block light completely, for example in a bedroom, blackout lining can be added to curtains or fabric blinds.

The shape, position or design of the window can pose problems. A window set high up a wall often looks better covered with a blind rather than curtains. A series of windows along one wall can be visually unified by extending a pelmet along the tops of all the windows. A window which has awkward proportions can also be adjusted to a certain extent. A long narrow window can be visually widened by adding full curtains that extend past the frame at either side. You can give a window height by adding a pelmet to cover the margin of wall above the window, or 'lower' a tall window by hanging a pelmet to cover the upper portion of glass. Some windows, and this is particularly true of very fine examples, may not need to be covered at all.

Occasionally, the function of the room imposes conditions. Blinds may be a better choice in dining rooms, where heavy drapery can hold the smell of cooking. Blinds which pull up out of the way are often better in the kitchen, too, where trailing curtains can be a fire hazard. And you must bear in mind the effects of steam when choosing material for bathroom windows.

Morris and Co. offered a curtain-making service to its customers, based in a rambling gaslit building located just off Oxford Street. Curtains were made up with 'Morris' headings, sewn in by hand as was the custom for all quality work. These headings resembled the 'rufflette' tape available commercially today.

CURTAINS

The curtain heading, or the means by which the fabric is drawn up and attached to the track or pole, determines the way the curtain looks: how full it is, the way it hangs, its basic proportion and style. Headings are rarely hand-sewn today, as they were in Morris's time, but are achieved by means of heading tape, narrow strips of fabric which are available in a range of weights, fabrics and types, to suit different materials and

OPPOSITE A strong, rich effect for a dining room. Dining rooms, which tend to be used in the evening and are seen by artificial light and candlelight, can take deeper and more dramatic colour schemes than rooms largely used during the day. *Acanthus Damask* curtain fabric picks up on the deep warm reds in the *Compton* paper.

achieve a variety of effects. The tape is attached to the curtain fabric and cords running through the tape are drawn up to pleat or gather the fabric in the required style. In another version, pleater hooks are inserted in the tape to gather the fabric. The heading can be hidden by a pelmet, but more often today it remains on view.

Shallow headings, which are soft and unstructured, include standard gathering and cluster pleats. The essential simplicity of these headings means that they are well suited to curtains for bedrooms, kitchen or other informal locations. The gentle gathering suits lighter fabrics in simple patterns and soft colours, as well as curtains which are not lined. For heavier, more densely patterned or woven fabric, lined curtains, period treatments or formal styles in general, it is better to choose a deeper heading with a degree of tailoring. Pencil pleats, box pleats, triple and pinch pleats all fall into this category and help the fabric to hang in full, straight folds, emphasizing its weight and richness.

The other main type of heading suitable for Morris fabrics is the cased heading, a sewn style which consists of a channel of fabric made at the top of a curtain which is then gathered or shirred by a wire or rod passed through it. Cased headings are more usually adopted for extremely lightweight or semi-transparent fabrics, such as muslin, lace, net and voile, but they can also be used to make half-curtains, also known as café curtains, which hang against the lower portion of a window, a style often seen in Arts and Crafts interiors in combination with stained glass.

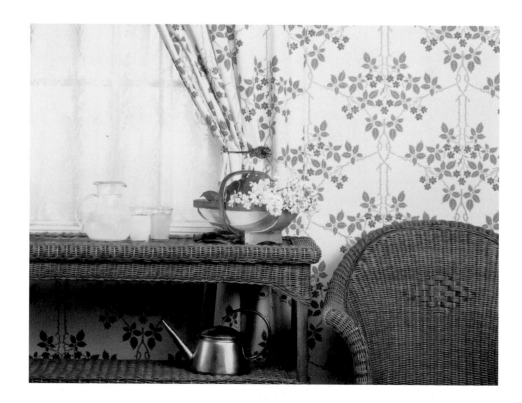

RIGHT In some situations, coordinating fabric and wallpaper can be very effective, especially if the pattern is light and open rather than dense and enclosing. Here the small scale green and red floral motif of *Blackberry* by Dearle suggests a garden room.

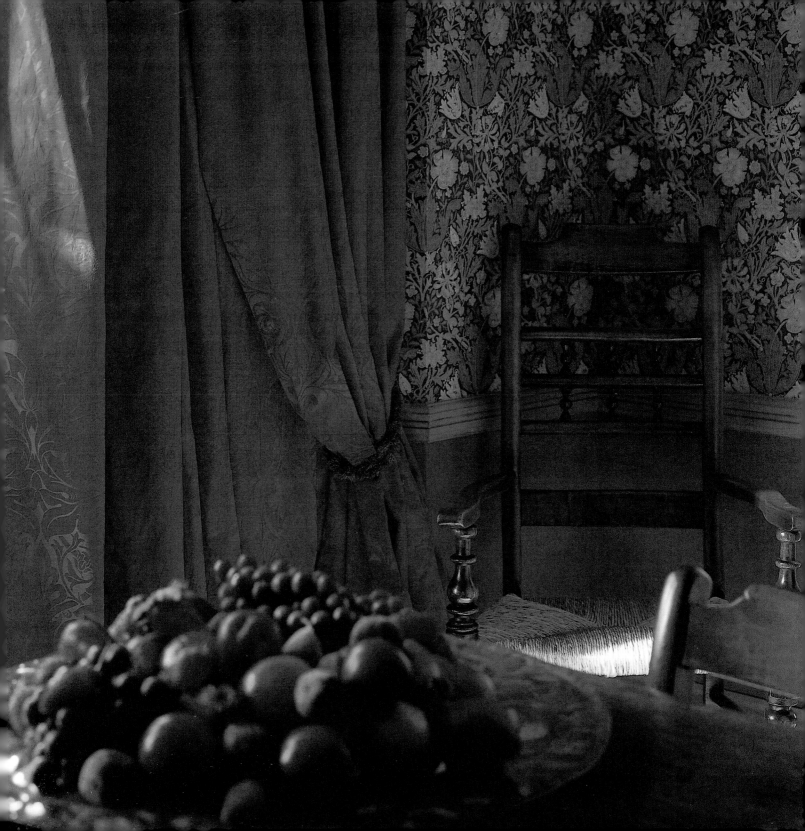

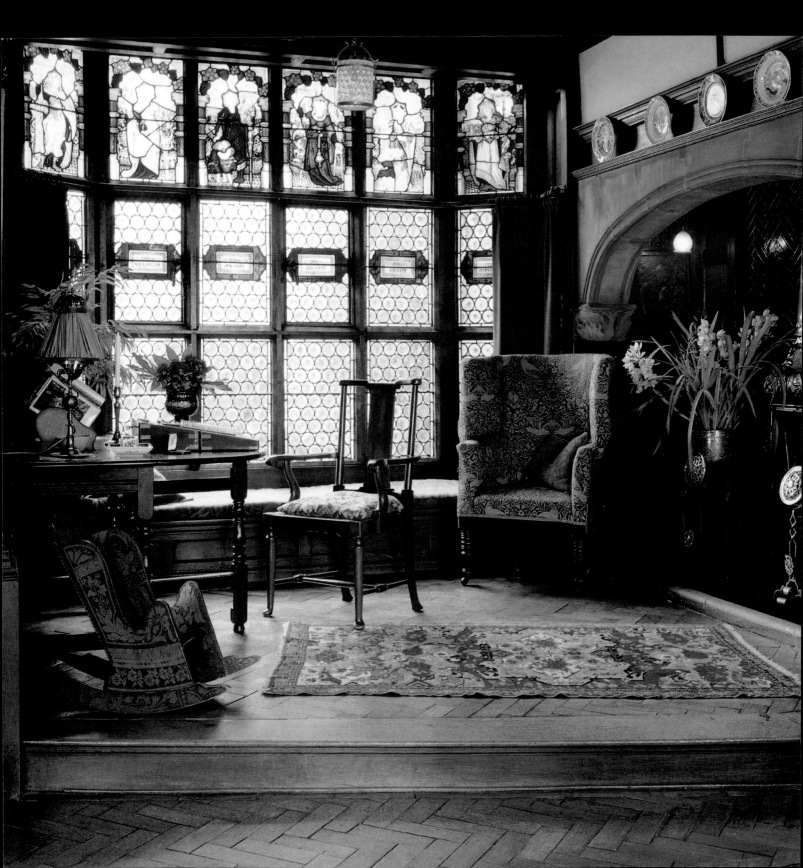

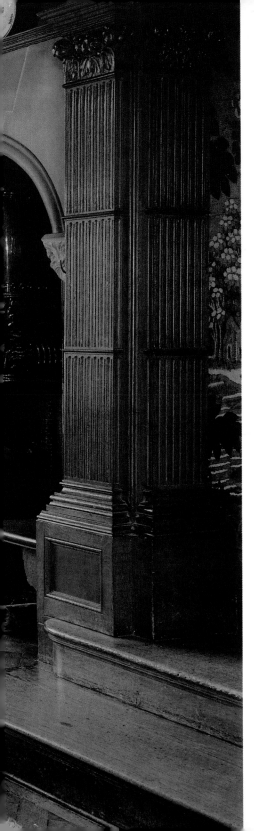

LEFT An alcove in the Hall at Wightwick. The painted glass windows are by C Kempe (1888). The inglenook fireplace was a feature of many Arts and Crafts interiors. Morris believed that in fireplace design one should avoid 'mean, miserable, uncomfortable and showy' surrounds with 'wretched sham ornament'.

Length is another important variable which contributes to curtain style. Most formal curtains in living rooms and dining rooms need to be full length. Sill length or some indeterminate place midway between sill and floor – perhaps skimming a radiator – tends to look ungenerous and visually awkward. But sill length is perfectly acceptable in kitchens (where it is also safer), bathrooms and bedrooms, and for cottage or casement windows, dormers or any window design which has essentially horizontal proportions. Morris fabrics do not really lend themselves to the type of dramatic treatment where fabric is allowed to tumble over the floor in deep luxurious folds – this extravagant style is not compatible with the aesthetic.

Tracks, poles, rods, hooks and rings – the means by which a curtain is suspended – can be obvious or discreet, decorative or disguised, depending on the style you wish to adopt. The first decision is where you want the track or pole to go. You can attach fittings to the window frame, to the wall extending beyond the frame to widen the appearance of the window, to the wall above the window or to the underside of the window reveal. Tracks can be bent and shaped to follow curved or angled windows; wooden and metal poles can be mitred to fit around a bay, but cannot usually be fitted to a bow window.

A classic and traditional look for Morris fabric would be to adopt the style often seen in the nineteenth century and hang curtains on wooden rings threaded along a polished wooden pole. Wooden poles can be painted, stained or varnished and are available new in a variety of designs, or secondhand from antique shops. They usually come with supporting brackets and matching rings; alternatively, some modern versions may be fitted with inset runners and hooks which enable you to combine poles easily with modern heading tapes.

Metal poles – often brass, or metal of a similar appearance – look more formal than wooden poles and may have decorative flourishes. Reproduction antique styles have elaborate finials shaped like acorns, feathers and the like. On the whole, it is better to avoid the fussier styles or those most reminiscent of the Regency or Georgian periods and restrict your choice to restrained 'classical' designs which are more versatile and sympathetic to the Morris style.

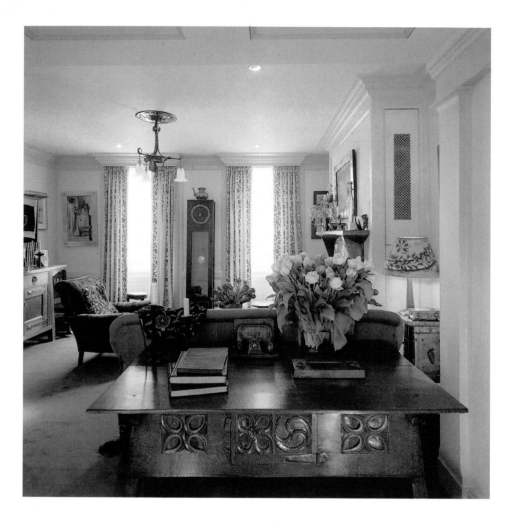

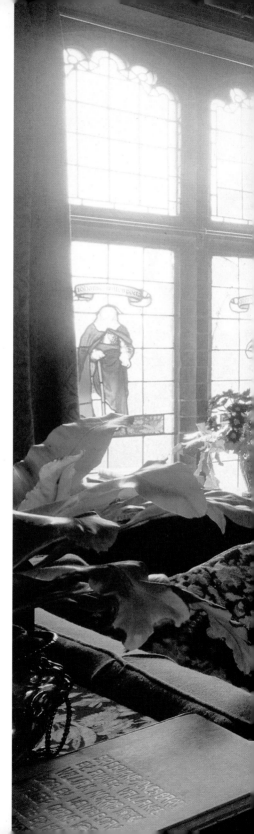

ABOVE An Arts and Crafts drawing room, with subtly articulated architectural detail, expressed in cool shades of light green. At the windows, columns of fabric hang from solid wooden pelmets, extensions of the deep cornice. Brilliant blue carpeting provides a jolt of contrasting colour, setting off the mellow tones of the oak furniture.

OPPOSITE The Library at Wightwick. Gothic windows with stained glass figures by Burne-Jones and Ford Madox Brown are simply framed with curtains hung from a plain brass rod and rings on a shallow gathered heading.

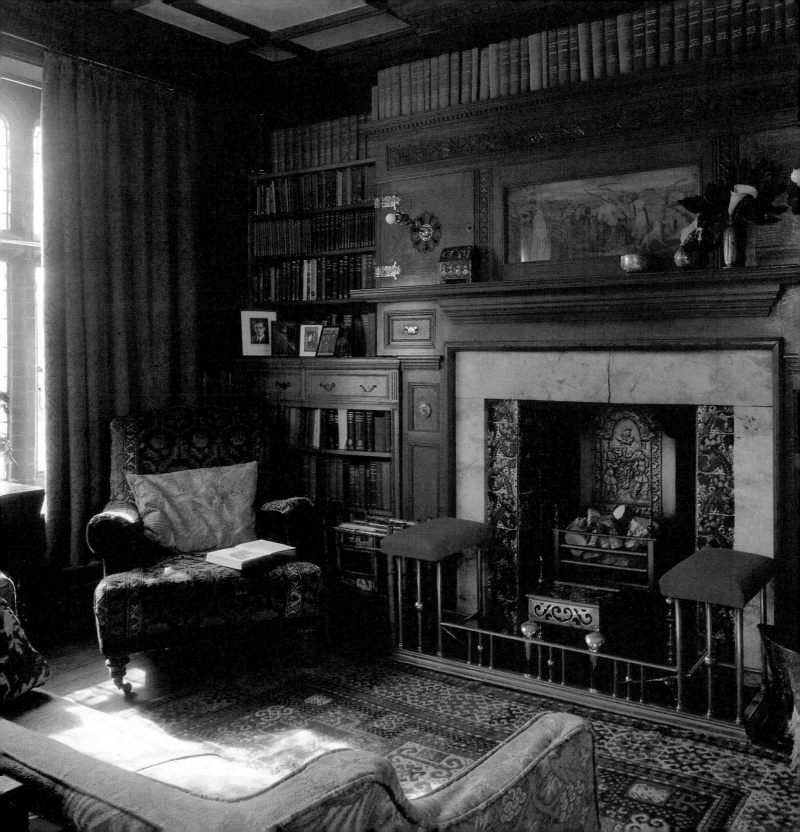

OPPOSITE The Billiard Room, Wightwick. The great floor to ceiling curtains that frame the Gothic windows are in *Bird*, the woven wool double cloth Morris designed for his own drawing room at Kelmscott House. The wallpaper is *Pimpernel*, and the carpet is the *Lily* pattern Kidderminster, 1877.

For curtains with modern headings or those intended for contemporary rooms, or for period treatments where a pelmet will eventually cover the curtain heading, a track is the best option. Sold in plastic or aluminium, track is unobtrusive and can be shaped easily to fit most windows and alcoves. The metal variety is recommended for heavier, lined curtains. For cased headings options include thin metal rods or brass bars. Alternatively, you can use expanding wire supported by hooks and screweyes, or sprung poles which fit inside the window reveal.

LINING

The practice of lining curtains has many advantages to recommend it. A lined curtain wears better, blocks light out more effectively, deadens sound and prevents heat loss, acting both as a draught excluder and insulator. Lining protects fabric from excessive exposure to sunlight and gives a curtain a professional finish, making it hang better. Some heading styles, particularly the more formal varieties, only look effective if the fabric is lined. Blackout lining can be added if light must be excluded totally, in a bedroom, for example. Interlining with soft wadded material ('bump') gives curtains a plump, padded appearance and adds to heat and sound insulation.

Nowadays we tend to think of lining only in these practical, rather mundane terms, but to previous generations, lining fabric was as much part of the final decorative effect as the main facing fabric. Lining, far from being restricted to the dull off-whites, creams and buff sateen fabrics so common today, was available in colours and cheerful prints which accented and complemented the principal curtain design. What our predecessors appreciated was the fact that windows are viewed from *two* sides – from the outside as much as from the interior – and instead of presenting the bland blank look of pale dull linings turned out to face the world, their windows had a much more interesting and lively aspect.

William Morris designed four prints specifically for use as lining fabrics. These were *Wreathnet* (1882), a dense design of wreathed leaves, *Borage* (1883), a crisper, more upright pattern, *Eyebright* (1883), a small floral repeat, and *Flowerpot* (1883), a rather stylized small repeat of flowers in a pot. These were produced in 27-inch widths, in order that two widths could be fitted across a standard 54-inch width of wool. Of these four prints, only *Borage* is still in regular production but there are similar designs available from other sources which could be used as substitutes if this particular effect is desired, as well as plain cotton in solid colours.

Different effects can be achieved by trying out various combinations of lining and main fabric. In some ways, the idea is not dissimilar to the contrasts that can be created in tailoring with, for example, a printed lining showing inside a jacket or a flamboyant back to a waistcoat. In the case of curtains, the lining fabric is often of a simpler design than the facing fabric and generally of less sumptuous material, so that if the main fabric is wool or linen union, the lining is usually a thinner, lighter cotton. But it can also be striking to combine a heavy, self-patterned facing fabric, such as a figured damask or woven wool, with a more obvious print. Earlier in the nineteenth century, sprigged

ABOVE *Borage*, a lining fabric designed for curtains, 1883.

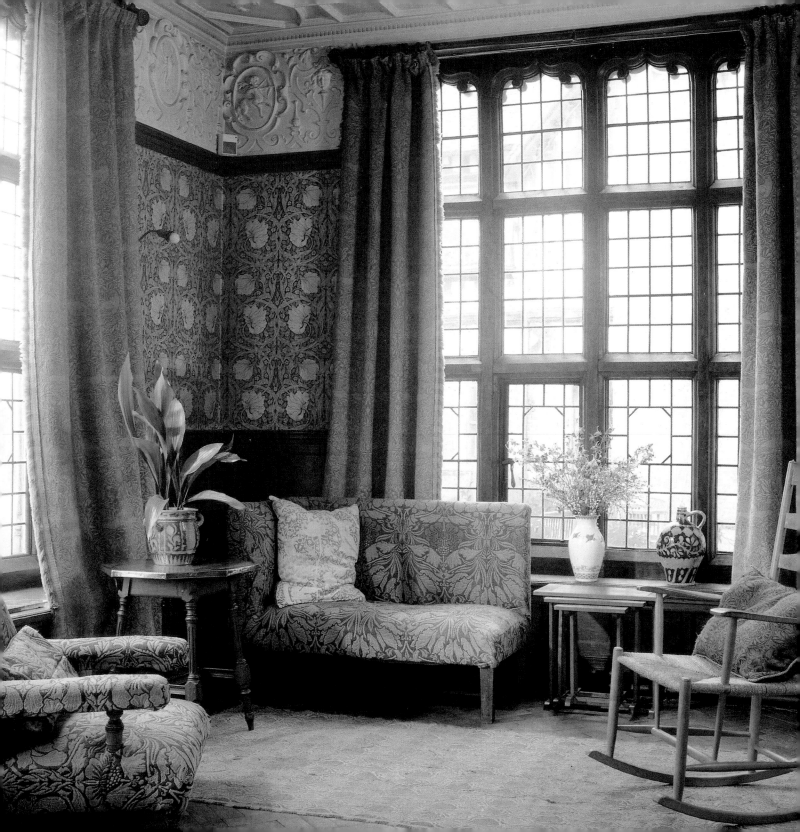

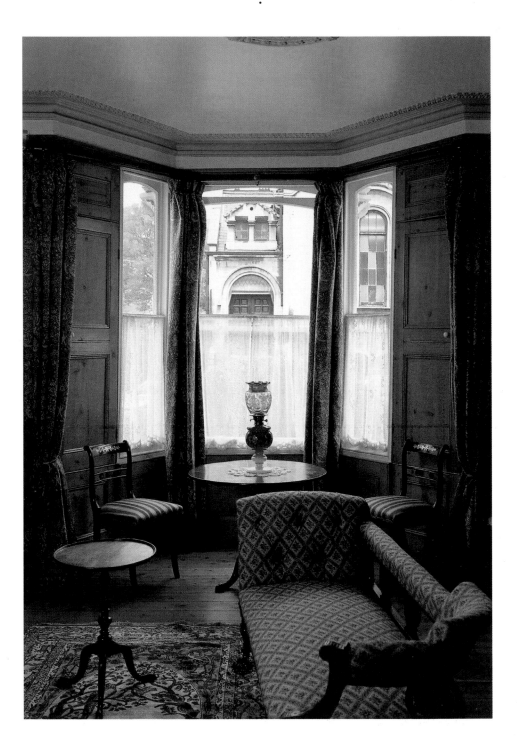

RIGHT Unusual window shapes and styles pose their own curtaining problems. One solution for curtaining a bay window is to frame the central window panel, as here, and hang curtains outside the recess to frame the entire bay. Half panels of lace provide privacy during the day.

cottons were often used as lining material and patterns resembling these can be found today in many stores.

As well as cheering up the view from the outside of the house, when the curtains are caught back by tiebacks lining can be turned over to display a contrasting edge or band. You can also make up curtains so that lining material extends around to the front. If no interlining is used, a plain coloured lining under a light printed fabric will suffuse the material with a tint when the sunlight shines through. Rose-coloured lining under a pattern with a mainly white background can have a really warming effect on the light on a dull day.

Simplicity and lack of pretension are the hallmarks of Morris interiors. Grandiose effects with drapery, intricate trimmings and any of the fussier furnishing styles are at odds with the basic character of the designs. But there are a number of finishing touches which complement rather than detract from the patterns, some of which were supplied originally by Morris and Co. as part of their curtain-making business.

Although the majority of Morris curtains were simply hung from rings with the heading on display, they could easily have been combined with a plain pelmet or valance. Pelmets are of especial use in rooms with high ceilings, to help adjust the proportions of tall windows and give curtains a professional, finished appearance. Box pelmets, where fabric covers a pelmet board, provide the opportunity to display the same fabric flat as that which is gathered and draped in the curtains. Alternatively, a toning plain shade could be used, perhaps coordinated with fabric tiebacks. These tailored pelmets have a formal look, unlike gathered pelmets which are softer and less structured in appearance. Gathered pelmets are shallow lengths of fabric pleated and hung in the same way as curtains. Both gathered and flat pelmets can be shaped, to follow a curve, for example, or they can be combined with a solid pelmet made of a narrow margin of wooden cornicing or moulding.

Morris and Co. supplied matching tiebacks and tassels for their curtains, as well as braid and fringed trimming for their woven fabrics. Tiebacks determine how much light is admitted to the interior, drawing curtains back from the glass, holding them in position and helping them to retain their shape. Depending on their position, tiebacks can alter the basic silhouette of the curtains, from low-waisted to high-waisted, although they are generally set about two-thirds of the way down or at sill height.

Tiebacks can be made in a wide range of materials and styles. Thick tasselled cords were popular in the nineteenth century and are still sold today. Shaped fabric tiebacks (stiffened with buckram) in the same material as the curtains or in a toning plain shade are soft yet tailored-looking. Solid hold-backs – curved brackets and bosses behind which curtains can be draped – are another option.

The Victorians enjoyed lavish trimmings on all their furnishings – fringes, tassels, braid, frills and flounces. Morris and Co. did trim their curtains but with a commendable restraint compared to the prevailing fashion, using simple braid and shallow fringing. At

PELMETS, TIEBACKS AND TRIMMING

its best, trimming gives fabric furnishings a certain crispness and clarity of line, adding detail, textural interest and a sense of movement. At its worst, too much trimming can look fussy and overdone.

Morris fabrics do not require a great deal of further embellishment but can be effectively highlighted with some kind of edging. Braid, gimp, ribbon and bias binding can all be used to outline the edges of a curtain. Colours can be selected either to blend in with one of the principal shades in the pattern or to make a sharp accent to it. Fringing, around the base of the curtain and at the leading edges, is another sympathetic type of trimming. Avoid deep showy gold fringes and choose soft cotton or wool fringes in complementary shades.

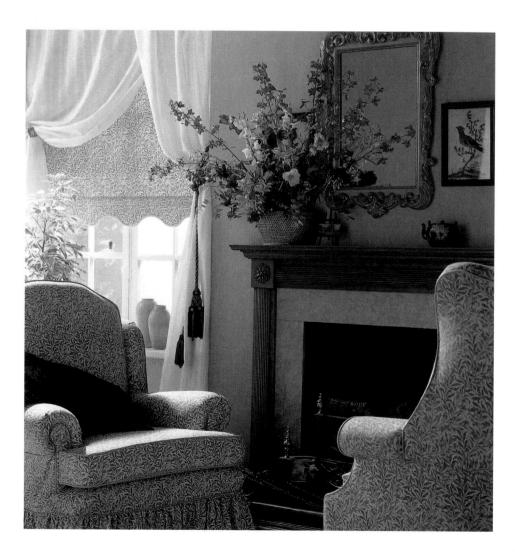

RIGHT Any pattern which works well as either a fabric or a wallpaper is often a good choice for a roller blind, where it will be displayed flat. *Willow Bough* is a case in point, here combined with outer drapery of white self-striped fabric and trimmed with a scalloped edge.

BLINDS

Blinds have a number of advantages which have made them an increasingly popular choice. They require less fabric and are hence both cheaper and easier to make than curtains. They work very well in small rooms and on small windows, where a greater amount of draped material would be overpowering and they represent a good solution for many awkward or inaccessible windows – such as those which slope, those that are positioned high up or are deeply recessed.

Although blinds have acquired a modern image, they are by no means a new decorating phenomenon. The forerunner of today's fabric blinds was the 'sash', a sunshade made of fabric stretched over a frame which first appeared in the seventeenth century. Roller blinds were invented in the mid-eighteenth century and by Victorian times had become quite elaborate, with painted designs and all the usual trimming. And, although festoon or Austrian blinds reached a height of popularity at the end of the nineteenth century, they date back much further, to swagged Georgian drapery.

William Morris fabric works very well made up as blinds, particularly in the elegant restrained style of Roman blinds. If you choose the right pattern you can also make successful roller blinds. Again, there is also nothing to prevent you from using Morris fabric to make festoons if you wish, but it must be said that this style is very far removed from the way the fabric was originally intended to be used.

Roller blinds can be made from any firm closely woven cloth, such as cotton. Special stiffener can be applied to the fabric if you need extra strength – it is important that the fabric should not stretch or sag. Small repeat designs are often the most effective. Upright patterns are probably better than those with a strong diagonal stress, which are not as effective used flat.

Roman blinds are less severe-looking than roller blinds but just as practical. The blind is attached to a wooden batten which screws to the window frame. Cords run vertically through rings at the back of the blind to pull it up in soft horizontal folds. Laths may be slotted in at intervals down the blind to give crispness to the folds. You have to exercise a degree of care when choosing fabric for Roman blinds. Any pattern with large circular motifs generally looks slightly odd when pleated up horizontally. Most Morris fabrics, with their basic 'net' or 'branching' designs, work perfectly well. Roman blinds, like curtains, are better lined. The lining can be turned over the edge of the blind to make a contrasting border. Bias binding in a matching or accenting shade could also be used.

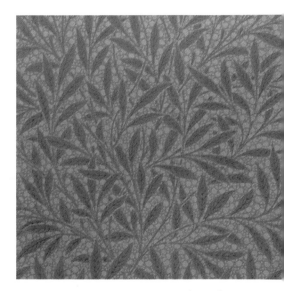

ABOVE *Willow* one of the most popular and enduring of all Morris's patterns, designed in 1874.

CHAPTER FIVE

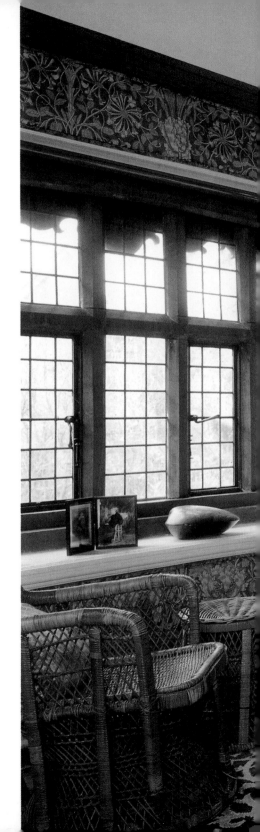

The wind's on the wold
And the night is a-cold,
And Thames runs chill
Twixt mead and hill,
But kind and dear
Is the old house here,
And my heart is warm
Midst winter's harm.

For the Bed at Kelmscott

OPPOSITE The Honeysuckle Bedroom,
Wightwick, named after the wall hangings
of *Honeysuckle* printed linen.

142

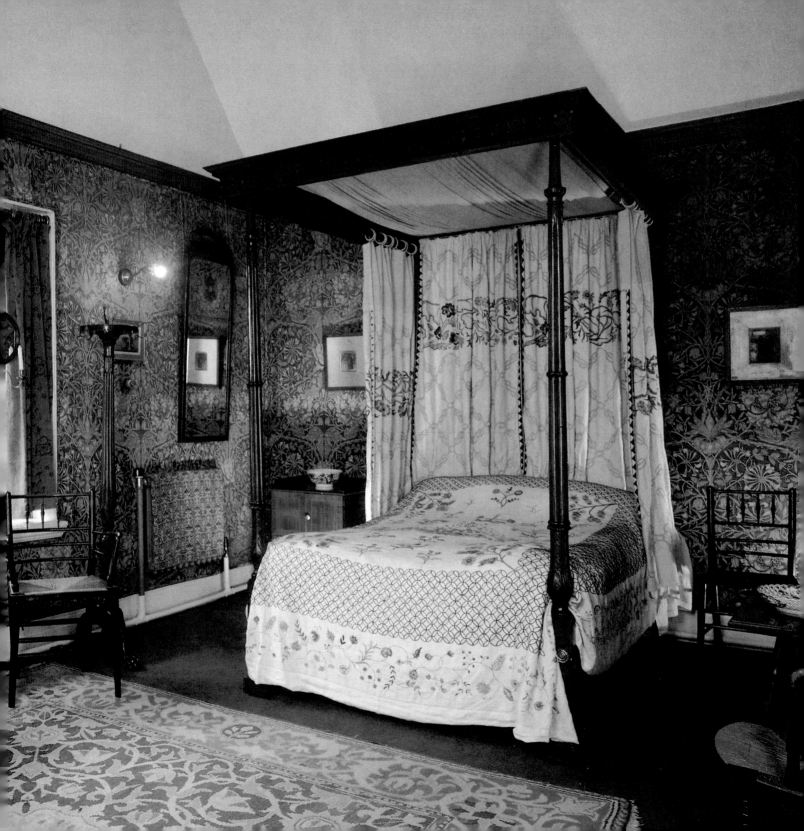

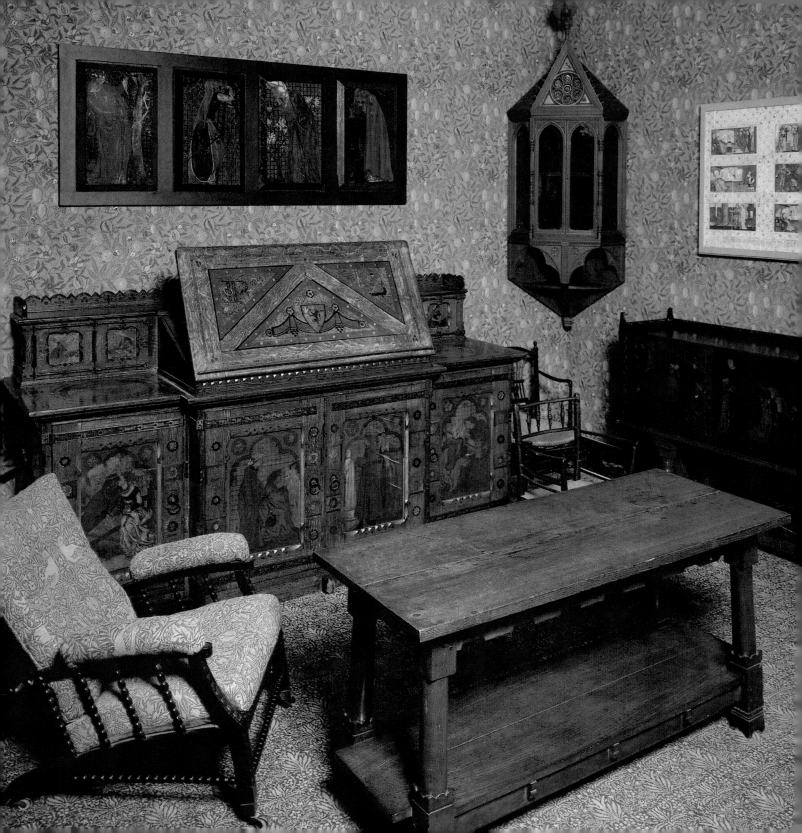

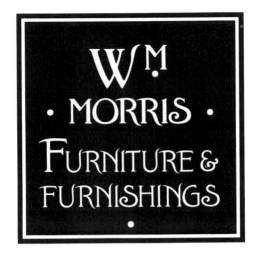

W^M · MORRIS · FURNITURE & FURNISHINGS

ILLIAM MORRIS INSPIRED A MOVEMENT IN DESIGN WHICH HAD AN IMMENSE impact on the way houses looked. As the artist Walter Crane wrote: 'Plain white or green paint for interior woodwork drove graining and marbling to the public-house; blue and white Nankin, Delft, or Grès de Flandres routed Dresden and Sèvres from the cabinet; plain oaken boards and trestles were preferred before the heavy mahogany telescopic dining table. . . .' By the end of Morris's life at the end of the century, the Victorian interior with all its gloom and clutter was giving way to lighter, emptier rooms.

Furniture was changing, too. Morris declared that 'if our houses, our clothes, our household furniture and utensils are not works of art, they are either wretched makeshifts, or, what is worse, degrading shams of better things.' This notion that the everyday was worthy of an artist's or designer's attention had two effects. One was to elevate the status of ordinary objects, a development that would eventually be taken further by the designers of the Modern Movement. The second effect was to stimulate what became known as 'art produce' or what we would call today 'designer furniture'.

William Morris's designs – for wallpaper, fabric, carpets, furniture and other elements of interior furnishing – arose from a consistent philosophy. Morris had a vision of how houses could look and believed in the importance of the decorative arts in bringing beauty into the lives of ordinary people. As the years went by, rather than being tempered by time, his ideas became progressively more radical, until he appeared to advocate bare walls and minimal furnishing – an odd, contrary stance for the founder of a leading decorating firm.

Along with the Morris patterns and furnishings went a style of dress. Intellectual young women could be identified by their plain medieval-style robes, often in sage green, embroidered very simply with floral designs and with a row of decorative buttons down

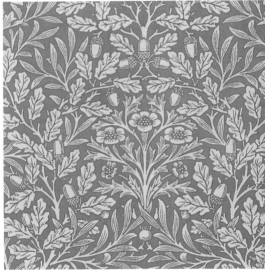

ABOVE *Acorn*, a design for wallpaper from 1880.

OPPOSITE A collection of early furniture and furnishings by the Firm in the Victoria and Albert Museum including Sussex chairs and the *George and Dragon* cabinet, designed by Webb and painted by Morris 1861.

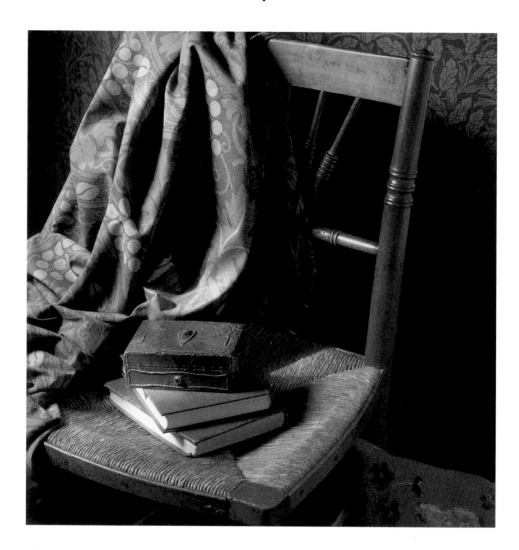

RIGHT A length of *Kelmscott Vine* is draped over the chair; in the background *Acorn* fabric is used to cover a screen. Simple farmhouse furniture from the turn of the century goes well with Morris patterns and makes an acceptable substitute for genuine antiques.

the back. 'Those were the days of green serge gowns and Morris papers,' commented Elizabeth Wordsworth, the first principal of Lady Margaret Hall, Oxford. A string of beads, often amber, completed the look. Ten years earlier, in 1869, Henry James, while dazzled by Jane Morris's beauty, was taken aback by her style of dress, remarking on her 'long dress of some dead purple stuff, guiltless of hoops' and her 'dozen strings of outlandish beads' in lieu of a collar. In dress, as in decoration, Morris and his circle were ahead of their time.

In the late 1870s Morris saw some of his original design ideas adopted and fashionably adopted by a small informed section of the public. The 'aesthetic movement' took Morris's ideal of art for everyone and transformed it into a mystic appreciation of

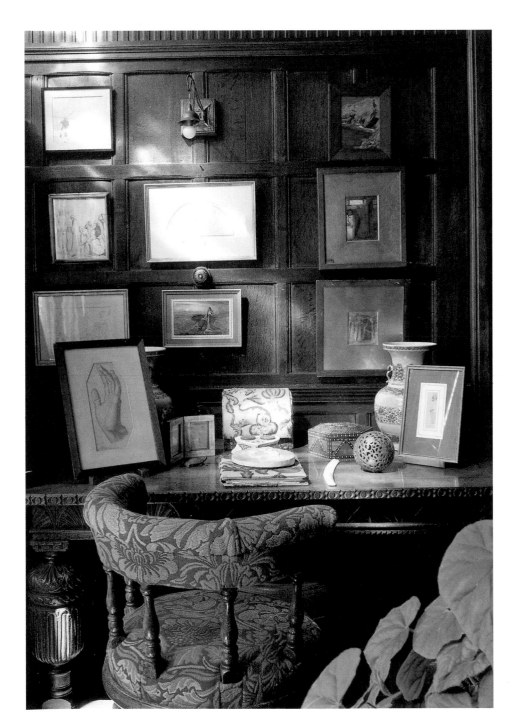

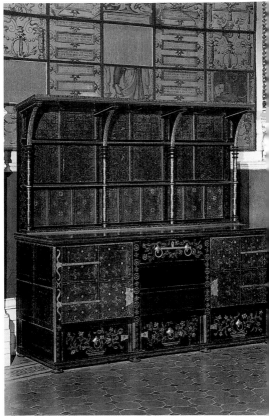

ABOVE A sideboard with embossed leather decoration designed by Webb. This design sold well.

LEFT Wightwick Manor. The chair is upholstered in *Tulip and Rose* (1876), a pattern used for carpet and different fabrics. Large scale prints often work particularly well as upholstery.

beauty. The elevated sensibilities of the Aesthetes, satirized in Gilbert and Sullivan's *Patience*, were at odds with Morris's robust, down-to-earth approach. Nevertheless, the popularity of Morris wallpapers and chintzes among this influential group brought the activities of the Firm to wider public attention.

The Aesthetes' interior style was marked by a preference for 'greenery-yallery' paintwork and Japanese prints. They shopped at Liberty, where their refined tastes could be satisfied by the Oriental artefacts and 'art produce' furniture that Arthur Lasenby Liberty provided. Kensington, where many would-be aesthetes lived, was known as Passionate Brompton and its inhabitants, the Passionate Bromptons or 'PBs', were as instantly identifiable as any Yuppie or Sloane Ranger.

Much more serious and longer-lasting in its effect on design than the style of the Aesthetes was the Arts and Crafts movement, which was directly inspired by Morris and the Firm. It is difficult to categorize this broad international movement since it encompassed a whole range of approaches to design and resulted in very different-looking exteriors, as well as interiors. But the main Arts and Crafts figures were architects who, like Webb at Red House, concerned themselves with design of every detail from door catches to furniture. The concept of the home as a unified design marks the beginning of the trend against Victorian collecting and eclecticism.

FURNITURE FROM THE FIRM

The only furniture Morris designed himself were the pieces he and Burne-Jones had made for their rooms at Red Lion Square. The measurements Morris gave to the cabinet-maker were wrong and the settle turned out to be even more massive than its designer had intended. Like much of the furniture for Red House, these pieces were painted with scenes from mythology.

Morris categorized furniture as being of two types. The first type included 'chairs, dining and working tables, and the like, the necessary workaday furniture in short, which should, of course, be well made and well proportioned, but simple to the last degree . . .' (*The Lesser Arts of Life*). The second type he termed 'state furniture', in other words 'sideboards, cabinets, and the like, which we have quite as much for beauty's sake as for use'. 'State' furniture should be elegant and elaborate with carving, inlaying or painting: 'these are the blossoms of the art of furniture'. Morris and Co. proved to be influential in both spheres. Their marketing of simple cheap chairs based on country models fostered the fashion for plain vernacular styles, while their more decorated 'state' pieces inspired the work of succeeding designer-craftsmen.

Much of the earlier furniture produced by the Firm consisted of one-off commissions, highly decorated, elaborate and costly. On the commercial side, in 1862 Webb designed a best-selling sideboard of painted and ebonized wood, featuring gilt leather panels. Thirty years later, in marked contrast, he designed a plain white-painted dresser for Standen, equally architectural in conception, but restrained and simple. Webb, of course, had been responsible for most of the furniture for Red House, including a circular table with medieval castellated feet. Other pieces were of the 'state' variety,

OPPOSITE A superb Queen Anne marquetry cabinet in the Drawing Room at Wightwick. The walls are covered in *Dove and Rose* (1879), woven silk and wool double cloth, the detail of the design a perfect complement to the intricate marquetry displayed on the cabinet. The brilliant turquoise of a de Morgan vase sings out against the gentle tones of the fabric hangings.

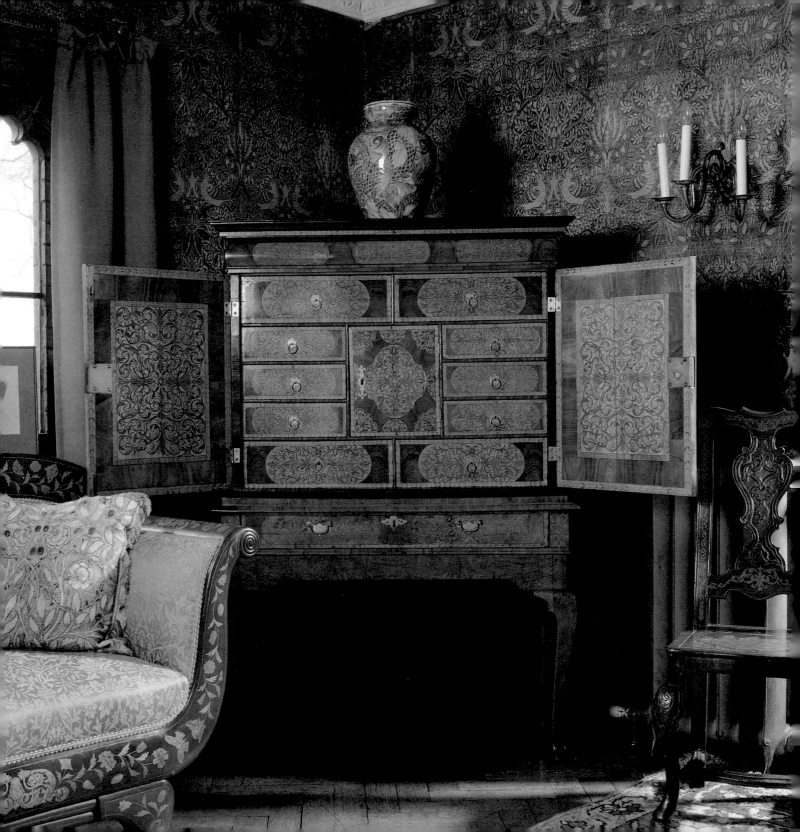

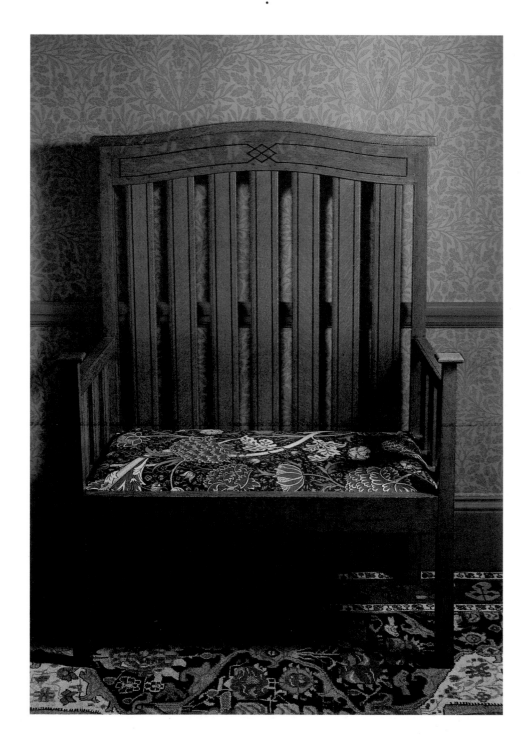

including a hall settle partly decorated by Burne-Jones and Rossetti, and a green-painted dresser for the dining room with pointed arches and trefoil cut-outs. For the Firm, Webb also designed a plainer sideboard and a daybed. Painted furniture, including a blanket chest, was exhibited by the Firm in 1862. To both his contemporaries and the designers who came after him, such as Lethaby and Lutyens, Webb was the embodiment of architectural honesty and attention to detail. As his sketchbooks reveal, Webb was inspired by the shapes and forms found in nature.

Far more strongly associated with the Firm was the range of vernacular chairs, known as the 'Sussex' chairs, which first appeared in 1866. The same year also saw the launch of another popular design, the 'Morris' chair with its adjustable back. Surprisingly enough, the impetus behind both of these designs appears to have been the Firm's new business manager, Warington Taylor. In 1865 he wrote to Webb, saying, 'It is hellish wickedness to spend more than 15 shillings on a chair when the poor are starving in the streets.'

It was not the first or last time that the contrast between the Firm's ideals of art for everyone and the reality of its rather expensive produce was pointed out. After the Firm's appearance at the 1862 International Exhibition, *Building News* commented unfavourably, indicating that Morris designs would 'suit a family which might suddenly be awakened after a sleep of four centuries and which was content to pay enormous sums suitably to furnish a barn.' Taylor was clear that what was needed was 'movable furniture . . . something you can pull about with one hand. You can't stand fixtures now that there are no more castles.' Accordingly, he introduced to the Firm rush-seated chairs he had discovered in Sussex. This vernacular design was subsequently produced in plain or ebonized wood in a variety of styles: as a corner chair, armchair, settle, and a chair with a round seat. One version, with a lyre-back, was known as the Rossetti chair. The 'Sussex' chairs, selling for only a few shillings in some cases, were enormously popular and continued to be produced long after Morris's death.

Taylor also discovered the prototype for the 'Morris' chair in a local carpenter's shop in Herstmonceaux, Sussex. Webb refined the design from the sketch which Taylor sent and it was first produced in 1866. Also available in ebonized or plain wood, the easy chair had a simple frame with arm rests, seat and back cushions. The arms extended back, pierced by holes, and a brass rod could be slotted through to enable the chair to be set in a variety of positions from upright to reclining. Popular and widely imitated, it was available upholstered in different Morris fabrics. Both of these basic designs, with their traditional 'folk' antecedents, were early examples of what would be, in Scandinavia particularly, an important new direction in furniture design. As Taylor noted approvingly about the Morris chair: 'It is original, it has its own style: it is in fact Victorian.' It was authentic, a chair of its time.

In a similar vein was the furniture which Ford Madox Brown designed for the Firm. This included eight chairs, four tables, a piano, bookcases and couches, mostly stained green. Morris furnished his own bedroom with Brown's simple designs. In 1887, Brown designed furniture for an ideal working man's cottage, to be exhibited at the Manchester Jubilee exhibition. These pieces, intended to be simple enough to be copied, also inspired commercial imitations.

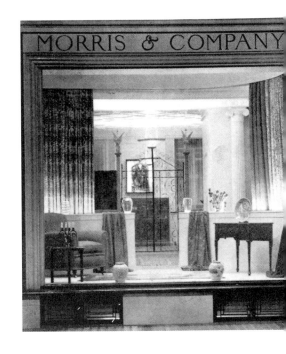

ABOVE The shop front of Morris and Company in the 1920s. The firm moved from the original Oxford Street premises in 1917 to this location in Hanover Square where there was greater display space. Morris designs also sold well in the United States and in Europe. Siegfried Bing, whose shop *Maison de l'Art Nouveau* in Paris was so influential, helped to establish the popularity of Morris fabrics in France, Germany and Scandinavia.

OPPOSITE An Arts and Crafts chair with seat covered in *Cray*. The walls are papered in *Acorn*.

THE INFLUENCE OF MORRIS: ARTS AND CRAFTS FURNITURE

When Morris's health failed in the early 1890, the commercial side of the Firm's furniture production was taken over by George Jack and W. A. S. Benson. By the end of the century, they were producing Georgian revival designs, safely within the bounds of Edwardian taste and supremely unimaginative – designs, it is easy to imagine, which would have been anathema to Morris. Prior to his involvement with Morris and Co., Benson had made his name designing oil lamps and candelabra.

If the spirit of Morris and Co. was not preserved in the Firm's products after Morris's death, it could be found in the work of followers of the Arts and Crafts Movement. W. R. Lethaby, for a time the assistant of Norman Shaw, summed up their beliefs: 'Art is not a special sauce applied to ordinary cooking; it is the cooking itself if it is good.' Together with Ernest Gimson, a protégé of Morris, he founded Kenton and Co. in 1890, which although it lasted a mere two years, was highly influential. Gimson, along with Sidney and Ernest Barnsley, went on to establish a firm in the Cotswolds, founding a tradition of rural craftsmanship which persists to this day. His ladderback chairs and plain tables wedded craftsmanship to rustic simplicity.

The architect C. F. A. Voysey, like Morris, designed everything from furniture to wallpaper, tiles, fabric and carpets. His early designs owe a debt to Pugin, but later work has a purity which to some critics prefigures modernism. Like Webb, Voysey was meticulous in his attention to detail. He believed that 'simplicity in decoration is one of the most essential qualities without which no true richness is possible.' Largely executed in oak, his plain, almost severe furniture has a subtlety which was difficult to copy. Criticized for being 'poor people's furniture for the rich', it was produced in too small a quantity to be cheap enough for the ordinary person.

Much more successful in reaching a broad section of the public was the work of Gustav Stickley. Inspired by classic Shaker designs he had seen on display and influenced by Morris, Lethaby and Voysey, Stickley developed his own 'Mission' style of furniture, sturdy designs in oak which commemorated the pioneer life. His business was established in 1899 near Syracuse, New York and was enormously successful until Stickley was tempted to over-reach himself. Stickley catered for the mass market, recommending his products as 'durable, well proportioned and as soundly put together as the best workmanship, tools and materials make possible'.

Retailers based in Britain included Heal and Sons, established in 1896, and Liberty, which first opened in 1875. Arthur Lasenby Liberty was an energetic, forward-looking shopkeeper who began by selling imported Eastern silks and other wares which attracted the attention of Morris, Rossetti and Burne-Jones. By 1880, Liberty goods were the height of aesthetic fashion. Dhurries from India, metalwork, bamboo furniture and ceramics, as well as fabrics from the Far East, made the store the focus of a design trend. To satisfy growing demand, Liberty began producing their own versions of Oriental-style furniture, as well as copying designs of contemporary furniture-makers. They had particular success marketing a version of the Thebes stool, which was reinterpreted by a number of designers including Ford Madox Brown.

Ambrose Heal began rather later than Liberty, and operated from a different standpoint. A retailer with a good knowledge of design, he was later praised by the architectural historian Nikolaus Pevsner for his 'good progressive furniture', borrowing

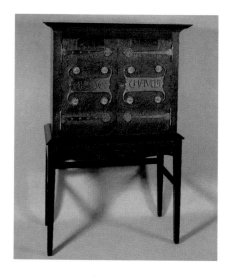

ABOVE Oak cabinet with brass fittings designed by the architect C F A Voysey, 1899. Voysey had a great influence on early twentieth-century furniture design, although his own pieces were usually very expensive and made only in small quantities.

OPPOSITE An oak sideboard from Liberty. Liberty produced a great deal of furniture in the Arts and Crafts idiom. The Mission style chair (right) is by Gustav Stickley.

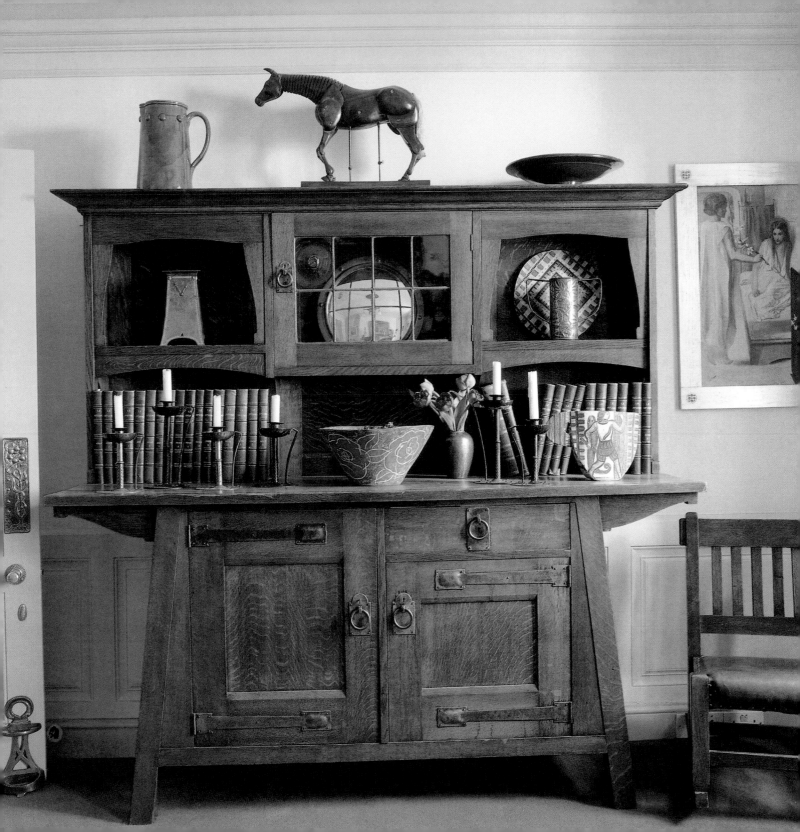

ideas from Pugin, Voysey and Madox Brown, among others. He believed in the ability of the machine, if used properly, to produce work which was both beautiful and useful, forming a link between the ideas of Morris and the commercial world.

WILLIAM MORRIS AND
FURNISHING THE MODERN HOME

Although William Morris might be surprised by the current fascination for reproducing historical interiors down to the last detail, he would probably understand the reasons for it. Morris sought to recreate the richness of medieval decoration in his own work; the designs of the furniture, in particular, show a deliberate attempt to recapture the spirit of medievalism. However, Morris was no slavish copier of past styles and abhorred reproduction of any kind. His work, sometimes denigrated as romantic and regressive, was a criticism of the society in which he lived and a rejection of its values. He might feel some kinship with those who are equally uncomfortable with mass marketed and mass produced goods today.

Morris was the first to make the important connection between beauty and usefulness – the 'form' and 'function' of the modernists; but he also understood the need to preserve continuity by commemorating the past and keeping traditions of craftsmanship alive. Art was not something apart but the 'way in which man expressed joy in his work'.

For those interested in furnishing their house in sympathy with Morris papers and fabrics there are a number of strategies which can be adopted. The first is to acquire original pieces from the period.

Although fine furniture has always been prized, antique collecting really took off at the end of the nineteenth century. The growth of replica or reproduction pieces, supplying the demands of the middle class, fostered a desire among the upper classes to seek out pieces of real, rather than simulated, quality. 'Arts and Crafts' is one of a number of relatively new areas of specialization in the antiques trade today.

Naturally, the one-off commissions which Morris and Co. produced for its wealthy clients, particularly large painted pieces, are extremely rare. Expensive enough at the time, these command astronomical prices when they reach the saleroom, but stop short of the upper limits of the Georgian price bracket. Original stained glass, Webb tables, decorated sideboards and tapestry are available at a price, in an élite market where competition is as likely to come from museums as from private collectors. The particular attraction of the period is that it is recent enough to make possible the identification of different makers, unlike pieces from the eighteenth century and earlier, where provenance is much less certain.

At the other end of the scale are the Sussex chairs, which were produced over a period of eighty years and sold in large numbers. Examples which come to light vary a great deal in terms of condition and this in turn affects price. Those with intact rush seating are more valuable, as are the less usual versions, such as the three-seaters. But this is still not a cheap option. A chair which might have sold for a few shillings in Morris's day may well go for a few hundred pounds now.

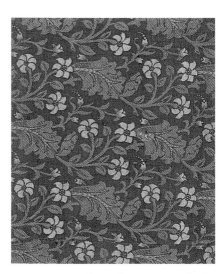

ABOVE *Diagonal Trail*, woven wool, designed by Dearle, 1893.

In a similar spirit to Morris's 'workaday' furniture are examples from Liberty or Heal's from the end of the nineteenth century. Many of these designs represent better value for the collector; they are often good quality, executed in oak, and have lasted well.

The alternative strategy, more practical and less expensive, is to look out for simple, unpretentious styles of furniture, of whatever period, which complement the look. Well-made wooden furniture in country or vernacular styles, not by named designers, can still be found in less exclusive antique shops; there are also contemporary pieces which would do as well. Dressers, chests of drawers, blanket boxes and other forms of free-standing rather than fitted storage can be put with scrubbed oak trestle tables and ladderback chairs for a countrified version of the look. Bentwood furniture – chairs and tables produced by the thousand throughout the nineteenth and early twentieth century to furnish cafés and restaurants – has a certain elegant simplicity that is also compatible, as have Shaker designs. Comfort was not a priority to Morris and his circle; deep-filled cushions and well-stuffed sofas were too reminiscent of the typical Victorian drawing room to find favour, but many illustrations show Morris fabric used to cover chairs and sofas in simple upright shapes. Wooden furniture should be light in tone. Oak is more characteristic than mahogany or the fruitwoods which are so associated with Georgian and Regency styles. Pine can be painted green, stained or decorated; oak lightly oiled.

Another option, but one which inevitably is more expensive, is to patronize the work of young furniture designers, many of whom produce classic contemporary pieces in light-toned woods such as ash and beech. In this area, above all, the tradition of skilled craft work is kept alive.

As far as the actual arrangement of rooms is concerned, Morris's views fit in well with present-day taste. Few people today would actively seek the clutter and density of the High Victorian interior. To Morris, furniture was for use, but that did not mean that it could not be beautiful too. Occasional tables which served no purpose except to hold useless decorative objects, chairs that could not be sat upon, cabinets full of knick knacks that were never used had no place in his interiors.

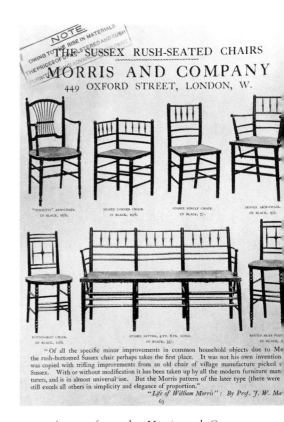

ABOVE A page from the Morris and Co furniture catalogue of about 1910, showing the range of rush-seated Sussex chairs.

SOFT FURNISHINGS

Morris fabric lends itself well to a number of applications, of which window treatment is only one. The Victorian home, as mentioned before, consistently offered plentiful scope for the use of fabric and fabric trimmings, uses which ranged from the practical to the frankly ridiculous. Morris, naturally, had no time for festooned drapery, picture bows and flounced piano legs but even so probably found more ways of using fabric in the interior than some modern homes display today.

The portière or door curtain served an important practical purpose in the Victorian house, excluding draughts and helping to insulate a room against heat loss. In these energy-conscious times, this is a fashion which might well be revived. Portières are particularly useful for curtaining main doorways where these lead directly into a living room with no intervening entrance hall, and for curtaining arched connections between rooms. Any substantial fabric can be used; the Victorians favoured chenille and velvet,

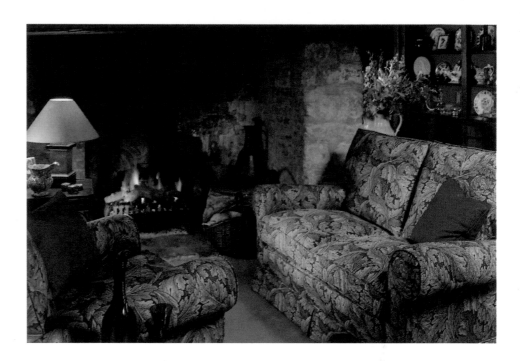

RIGHT The plain lines of a modern sofa and armchair suit a tailored upholstery style. The pattern is *Acanthus*, in linen union.

OPPOSITE Morris's bed at Kelmscott Manor. The bed hangings and valance were worked by Jane and May Morris, together with assistants. The bed curtains, May's design, represent the *Trellis* wallpaper which covered the walls in her nursery. The valance is embroidered with a poem by Morris. Jane worked the cover, which repeats the *Daisy* motif, the first embroidery she and Morris attempted together. The bed hangings were probably made in commemoration of Morris's sixtieth birthday in 1894.

often fringed and tasselled. Morris curtain-weight fabric, lined to provide extra insulation, is ideal. The rod or pole from which the portière is suspended should be taken well above the doorway and extend some distance to either side so that the curtain does not interfere with the operation of the door. The portière often provided the opportunity to display embroidery, and Jane and May Morris worked many such hangings.

Curtained beds are another soft furnishing style which has fallen out of general use with the arrival of central heating. Few Victorian bedrooms had any form of heating beyond a small fireplace, and bed hangings must have been a very welcome means of keeping warm in winter. Morris's four-poster bed at Kelmscott Manor is hung with embroidered bed curtains, topped with a valance and spread with an embroidered cover. The hangings, valance and cover were worked by Jane and May Morris, with assistants, probably to commemorate Morris's sixtieth birthday in 1894. Each bed curtain took three months to complete and was worked to May's design, loosely based on the *Trellis* wallpaper, which was first used in the nursery she shared with her sister. The valance was embroidered with a poem specially written for the bed (and quoted in part at the beginning of this chapter). Jane designed and worked the cover. It featured a flower pattern and is signed 'Si je puis. Jane Morris. Kelmscott', a repetition of the motto 'If I can' which Morris had adopted as his own in the early days at Red House.

Bed hangings are no longer a practical necessity, but can still be a means of displaying fine fabric. The effect need not be overly fussy or even essentially period in mood: Morris fabric lend themselves to tailored styles which are equally at home in

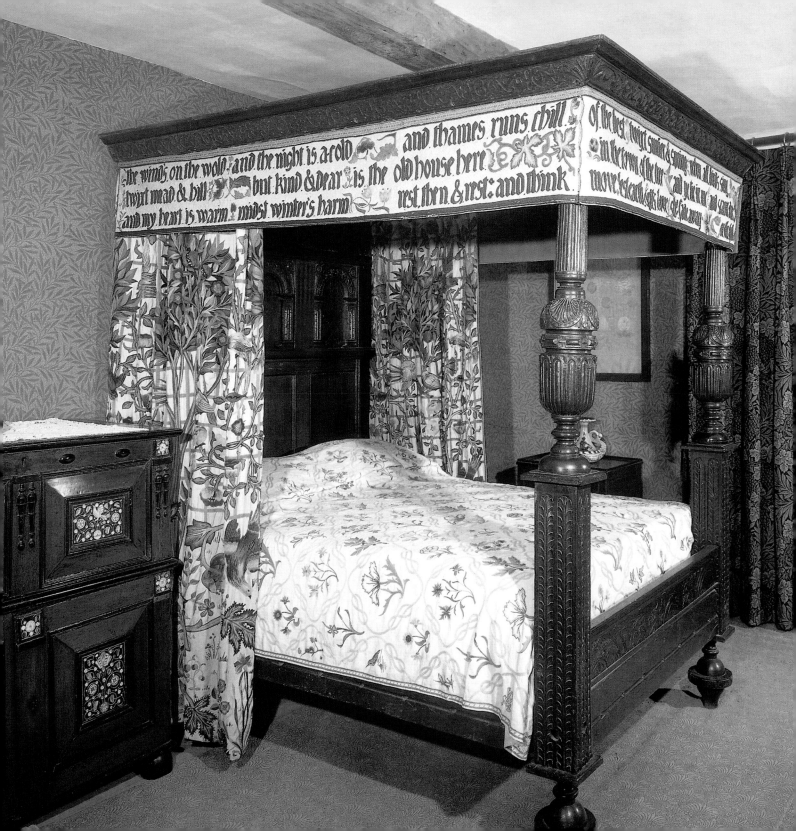

the winds on the wold · and the night is a-cold · and thames runs chill
twixt mead & hill · but kind & dear is the
and my heart is warm · midst winter's harm ·

and thames runs chill
old house here ·
rest then & rest: and think

of the best twixt summer & spring: when all birds sing
in the town of the tree · and ye in me and scarce the
move: lest earth & its love should fade away · and die

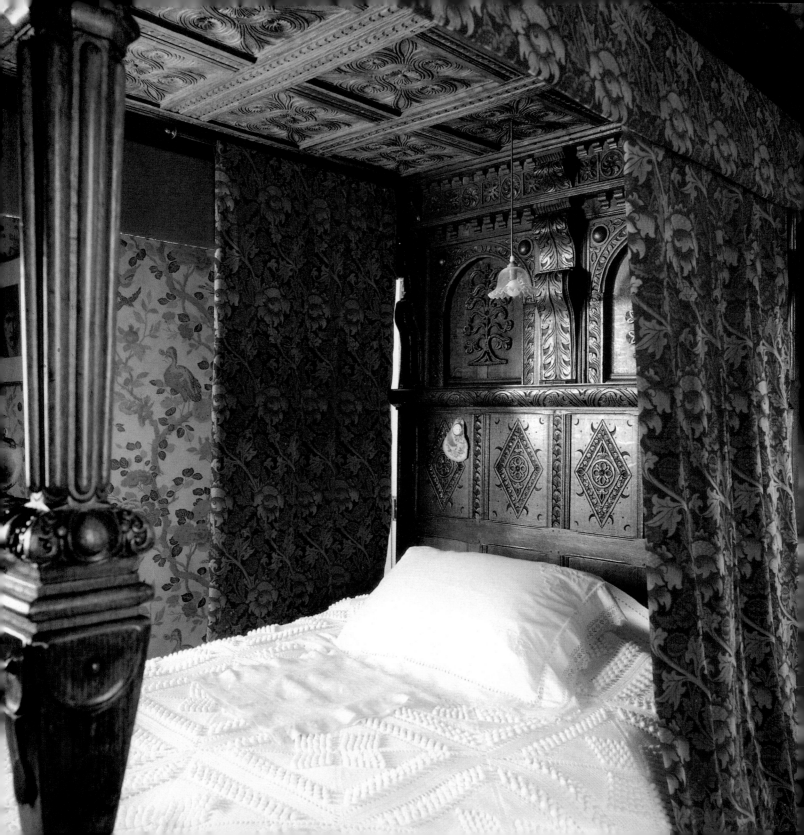

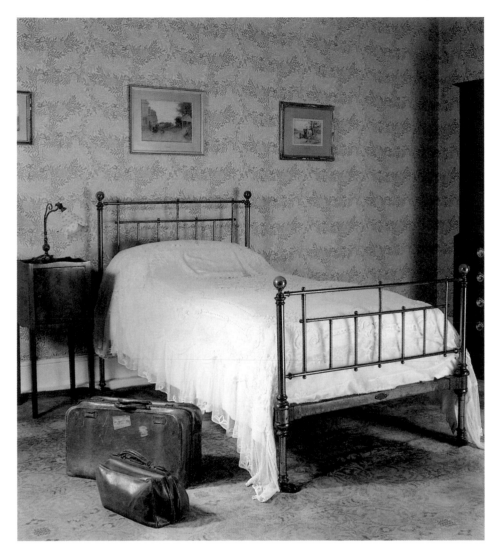

LEFT The Larkspur Bedroom, Standen, with *Larkspur* wallpaper. The brass bed is from Heals, an influential London retailer that was founded about twenty years later than Liberty. Standen was built by Webb in 1882-94, as a weekend home for a solicitor, and was praised at the time for its 'human quality'.

contemporary rooms. Simple fabric hangings convey a sense of warmth and intimacy in a bedroom, and can be suspended from a plain metal frame as well as from the more traditional wooden four-poster. Bed curtains can be simply tied to the top frame or suspended on rings. They should be floor length and will hang better if they are lined. An attractive idea is to choose a contrasting fabric in a smaller scale print for the lining. This particular effect, described in more detail in chapter three, was a common Victorian treatment. A good example are the curtains for the Mackmurdo settle, on display at the William Morris Gallery in Walthamstow, where the main outer curtain fabric is *Tulip* chintz and the lining is *Borage*, a toning print.

OPPOSITE The Indian Bird Bedroom at Wightwick. The bedstead is composed of pieces of Jacobean carving; the velvet hangings are by Morris.

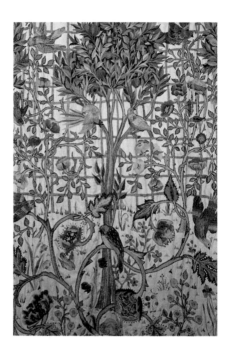

Detail of one of the bed curtains, designed by May Morris for the bed at Kelmscott Manor. Each curtain took three months to complete.

Upholstery is still an important way of displaying fabric. Morris had a considerable impact on the style of upholstery, making it fashionable, for example, to cover furniture year round in cotton rather than merely in the summer months, as had been customary. Many of his chintzes found particular favour as cotton covers for furniture and they are, of course, still suitable for this purpose today. Plain, tailored, rather than flounced, styles of covering should be adopted. Morris fabric was also used for 'close' covering, where the chair or sofa is tightly covered displaying the lines of the piece. Many of the larger patterns look particularly effective used in this way, the bold motifs adding interest to plain firm shapes. Simpler designs should be used if the pattern will be broken up, by buttoning, for example.

Morris understood the importance of upholstery in providing variety and points of interest in a decorative scheme. Over-coordination, where chair matches sofa matches curtains, can have a deadening effect. Instead, Morris advised mixing patterns and colours to give a sense of definition. Since a chair seat is such a relatively small area within a room, it can be in a bright colour or vivid contrasting pattern, serving as an accent which throws the rest of the interior into relief. From the Boston Foreign Fair brochure:

Chairs and sofas give great opportunities for introducing points of bright contrasting colour, and for those high lights and darkest shades which are essential to a complete scheme. Covers need not be uniform. They may be of two or three kinds, according to the size of the room and the number of pieces.

If upholstery can give a decorative scheme a sense of variety, this is equally true of fabric accessories, notably cushion covers. Morris and Co. supplied many designs for embroidered cushion covers, often sold in kit form to be worked at home. The cushion covers, which could also be adapted as firescreens, were very popular with Victorian gentlewomen who spent much leisure time sewing for themselves and their homes. The small scale of these covers means that such work is still a practical possibility today. Individually embroidered or decorated covers give a certain look of richness to a room, as well as contributing different textures, colours and patterns.

Cushion covers also offer the chance to experiment with different fabric effects and combinations. A cover provides a way of introducing a bright contrasting colour to add a vital accent to a room. A sofa, for example, with six cushions, might have two matching the sofa upholstery, one in a sharp accent colour, two in a small-scale print and one in a toning shade. Trimmings should not be lavish or showy. A narrow border of soft wool fringe is very effective with Morris fabric. You can also vary the cushion shape from large square cushions for sofas and armchairs to tubular bolsters for daybeds.

In the Victorian house, most tables were covered in fabric, some in several layers. Morris did a great deal to reverse this trend, leaving plain wooden tabletops on view in a manner that seemed slightly shocking at the time: lack of disguise was an important part of Morris's approach to interior decoration. At the same time, a table top was often a good place to display a particularly fine piece of fabric, a length of embroidery or a beautiful piece of weaving, and there is no reason why the same approach should not be continued today, especially if the table is not in constant use.

The floor occupies a large part of the surface area of a room and its colour, texture or pattern will accordingly have a substantial effect on the atmosphere of the room as a whole. Morris did not neglect this aspect of decoration and, from the mid-1870s onwards, turned his attention to the design of carpets, both machine-made and hand-knotted.

Morris was a lifelong admirer and collector of fine historical carpets from the East. Much of his collection hung on the walls of his houses, as he believed that to use a fine carpet 'as a floor-cloth degrades it especially in northern and western countries where people come out of the muddy street into rooms without taking off their shoes'. Later in life, Morris advised the South Kensington Museum (Victoria and Albert) on the building up of their own collection and even provided financial assistance for this purpose.

His deep appreciation and extensive knowledge of Persian, Turkish and Chinese methods of carpet-making led him to experiment with hand-knotting in an attempt to revive the art in Britain. In 1879 Morris set up looms in the coach house at Kelmscott House; larger looms were established in 1881 at Merton Abbey and the work transferred there. Hand-knotted Morris carpets, however, continued to be known as 'Hammersmith' carpets and carried an identifying mark which consisted of the letter M, with a hammer and waves symbolizing the Thames.

Morris's designs for hand-made carpets were not copies of Eastern examples but intended to capture the same spirit and meaning. He summarized the design of Persian carpets in characteristically evocative terms:

> *In their own way they meant to tell us how the flowers grew in the gardens of Damascus or how the tulips shone among the grass in the mid-Persian valley, and how their eyes delighted in it all and what joy they had in life.*

Carpet-making was labour-intensive and expensive. Most of Morris's larger hand-knotted carpets were special commissions for his aristocratic clients. One of the most famous of the large carpets was the *Bullerswood*, designed for the Sanderson family in 1889. This features bird motifs and was probably a collaboration with Dearle.

The carpet-making shed at Merton Abbey made a picturesque scene. Young women and girls were employed to do the knotting, since their fingers were more nimble. A visitor to the factory in 1883 described it:

> *The strong, level afternoon light shines round the figures of the young girls seated in rows on low benches along the frames, and brightens to gold some of the fair heads. Above and behind them rows of bobbins of many-coloured worsteds, stuck on pegs, shower down threads of beautiful colours, which are caught by the deft fingers, passed through strong threads (fixed uprightly in frames, to serve as a foundation), tied in a knot, slipped down in their place, snipped even with the rest of the carpet, all in a second of time.*

Machine-made carpets designed by Morris were made by other firms. Morris began designing for machine processes in the late 1870s, with the intention of improving on the standard heavily-shaded Victorian design. His stated aim was for 'pure and shapely forms

FLOORING

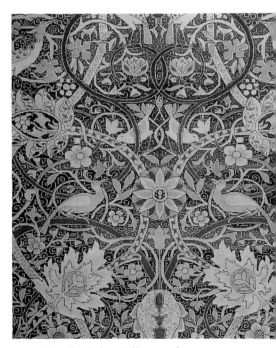

ABOVE Detail of the *Bullerswood* carpet, woven in 1889 for the Sanderson family.

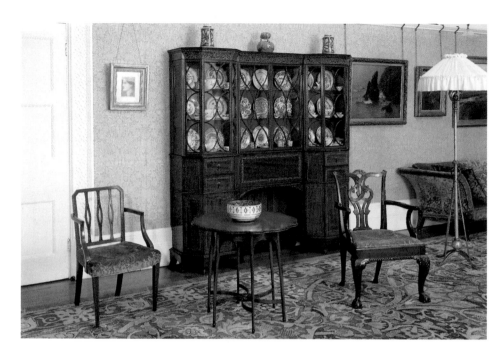

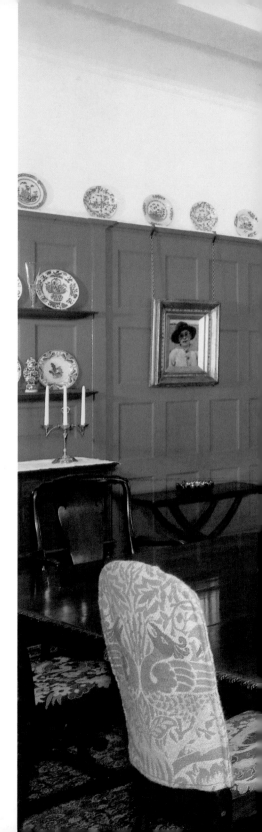

ABOVE AND RIGHT The Drawing and Dining
Rooms at Standen, with Chippendale chairs
and Arts and Crafts furnishings.

with simple colouring'. Designs were produced for five different types of machine carpet and in this area, as in all others, Morris was acutely aware of differences in technique and what impact these would have on pattern or design.

Machine-made Morris carpets found a wide popularity, put to everyday use in wealthy houses, displayed in middle-class drawing rooms and even adopted by the Orient Line in the 1880s for cabin flooring. Particularly popular in the United States were the Kidderminster carpets, also known as Scotch or inlaid. These were hardwearing and dirt-resistant and often used for areas of heavy wear such as hallways, stairs and landings. Of a better quality were the Wilton and Brussels varieties produced in the traditional carpet factory at Wilton, first established in 1701. Brussels carpet, similar to today's cord carpeting, had a surface pattern and was very durable. Wilton was silkier, as the loops were cut to form a dense pile. Wilton was the most popular of all Morris machine-made carpets although it was more expensive and twenty-four designs were produced, including *Lily, Rose, Wreath* and *Bellflowers*, where distinctive flower forms are often set off against a dark indigo ground. Morris also produced designs for different types of Axminster.

The border was an important element in the carpet design. Morris favoured borders where several different pattern elements were combined. Borders were available in

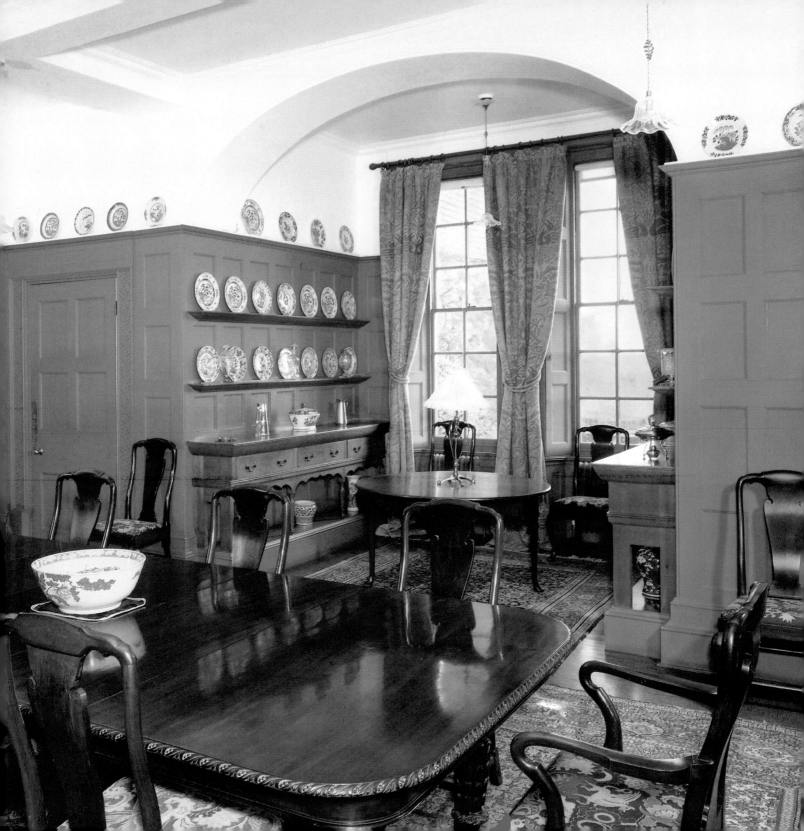

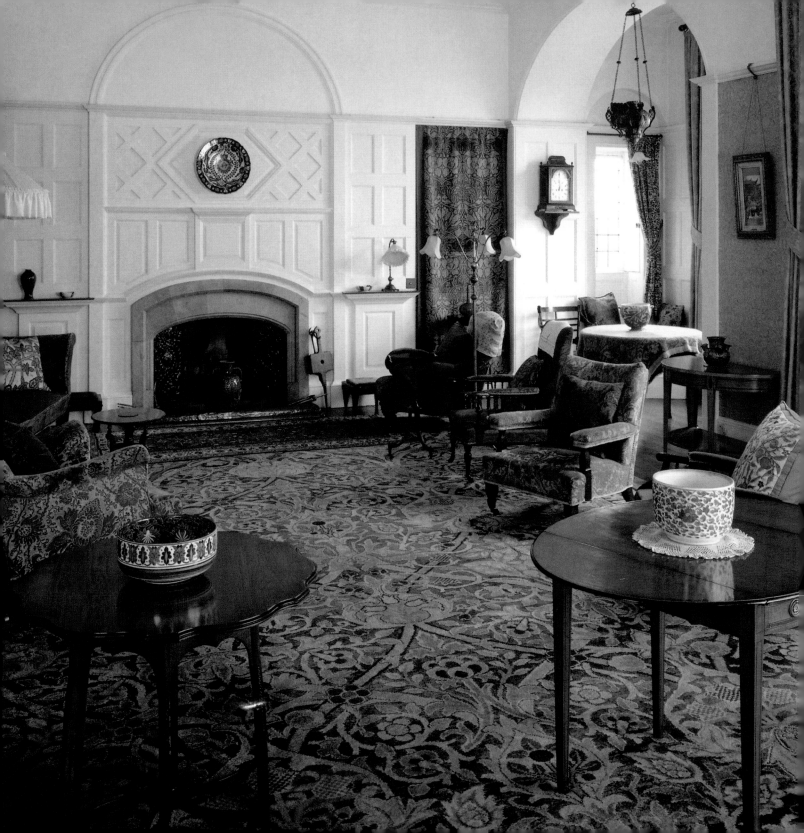

different widths and different designs, including geometric stripes and chevrons. At this time, carpets were not laid wall to wall but were generally bordered squares or rectangles.

Carpet was an important part of this pattern mixture. Today one can choose between modern, sympathetic machine-made carpet designs, many of which are still available with a integral border, or hand-made ethnic rugs of various kinds. There is a huge range of rugs available at a reasonable price, many from India and the Middle East, and these can provide the subtley of tone and compatibility of pattern required. The cheaper types of hand-made rug are the flat weaves, which include kelims and dhurries. Kelims are produced in Turkey and Afghanistan. Vegetable dyes produce rich warm colours which mellow with age; patterns are largely geometric. Dhurries are often made of cotton, and come in a huge range of colours and patterns. Pile rugs, which include Persian and Turkish carpets, vary in quality but tend to occupy the upper end of the price range; some, of course, are collectors' items.

Aside from carpeting and rugs, other types of flooring sympathetic to a Morris interior include plain polished wooden boards, country-style quarry tiles, and various types of coir or natural fibre matting. Woven seagrass, sisal and coir matting is now available in a variety of colours and subtle patterns and can be laid in the same fashion as a carpet to form a natural background for rugs or a hard-wearing alternative to carpet. Victorian encaustic tiles, particularly if laid in an entrance way, would also strike the right note.

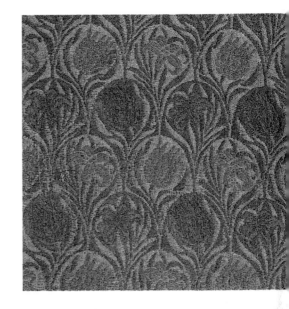

ABOVE Kidderminster carpet in *Lily* pattern, from the Billiard Room, Wightwick.

'Don't think too much of style,' Morris urged an audience in a lecture on art in 1881. The basic honesty of his approach has given his work a spirit of versatility which has led to its long and popular life.

Morris had little use for artifice or simulation and campaigned hard to make the experience of everyday living more beautiful and more efficient, directing people to look carefully at the objects they used and at their surroundings in order to discard the ugly and the useless. His effect on Victorian design and decoration was a kind of visual editing, weeding out the clutter and substituting beauty for pretension and showiness. And although Morris's interests included the literary and the political, he never thought that how we decorate our houses was unimportant, seeing beautiful surroundings – at home and at work – as vital for creativity and happiness.

This attitude of selection and appreciation is more important in creating a 'Morris' interior than tracking down historically accurate door furniture. A positive enjoyment of both simplicity – plain surfaces, natural textures, simple forms – and richness – dense patterns, decorative artefacts, pure colours – are the real components of the Morris interior.

IN KEEPING

OPPOSITE The Drawing Room, Standen. Morris believed that the patterns that one chose to live with should have certain qualities, above all 'something that reminds us of life beyond itself, and which has the impress of human imagination strong on it.'

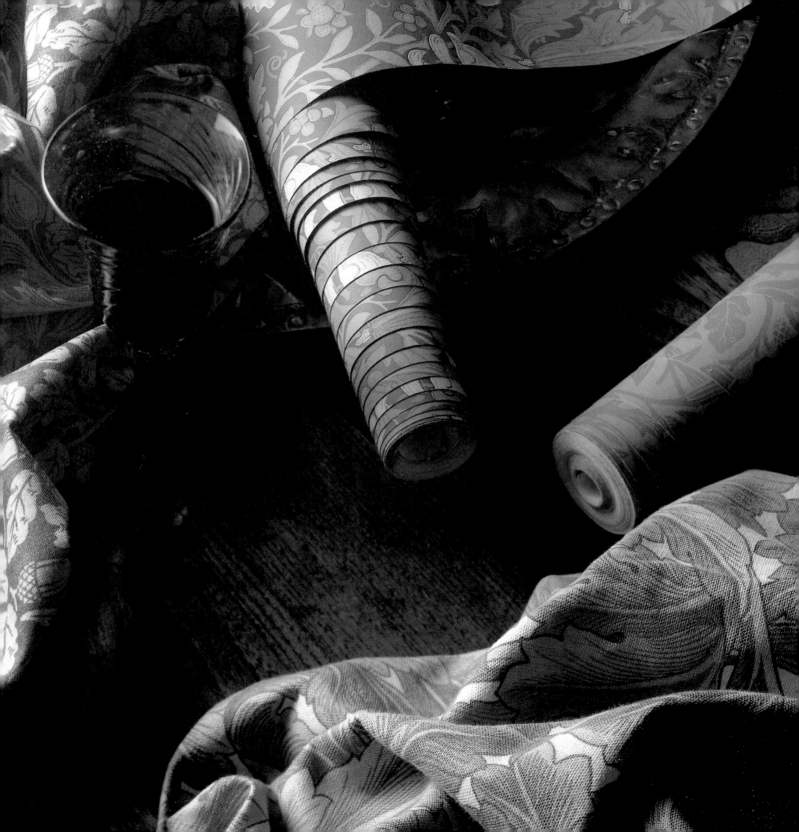

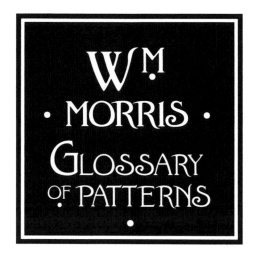

The following section is a glossary of the most common patterns by William Morris and others working with him. The patterns, chiefly for wallpapers and printed textiles, are arranged alphabetically for easy reference. Designs are by Morris, unless otherwise stated. Many of these patterns are still in production today. The dates given refer to the year of registration, as opposed to design, although in many cases they are the same year.

OPPOSITE Complementary colourways in blues and earth tones: *Acorn* and *Acanthus* fabric with *Compton* and *Acorn* wallpaper.

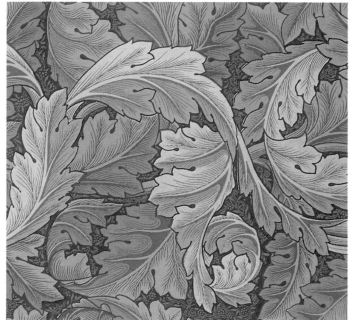

ACANTHUS WALLPAPER (1875)

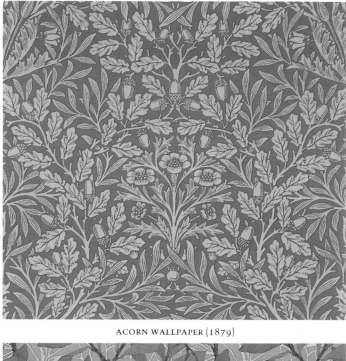

ACORN WALLPAPER (1879)

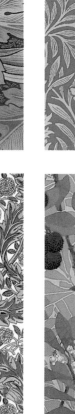

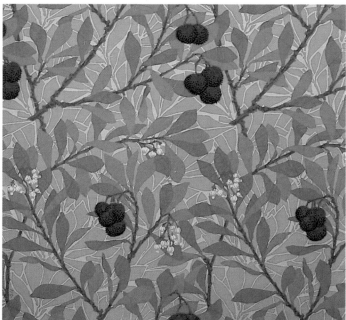

AFRICAN MARIGOLD PRINTED COTTON (1876)

ARBUTUS WALLPAPER (KERSEY, 1913)

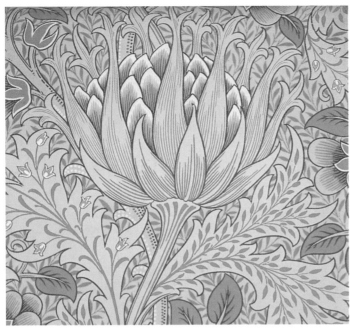

ARTICHOKE WALLPAPER (DEARLE, 1899)

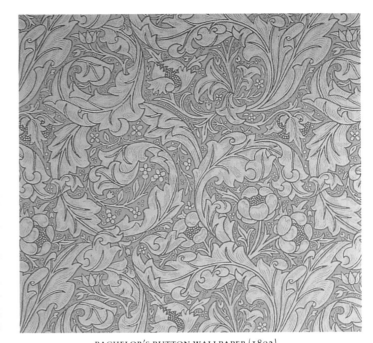

BACHELOR'S BUTTON WALLPAPER (1892)

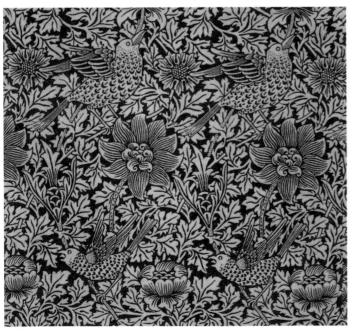

BIRD AND ANEMONE PRINTED COTTON (1881)

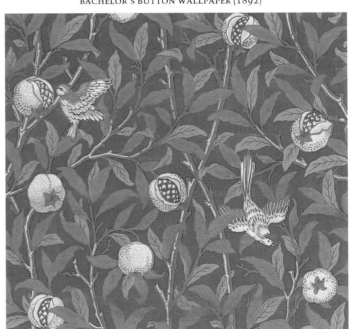

BIRD AND POMEGRANATE WALLPAPER (DEARLE, 1926)

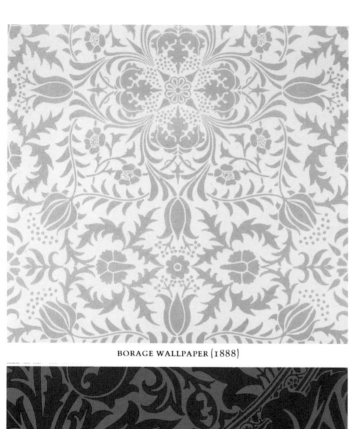

BORAGE WALLPAPER (1888)

BROTHER RABBIT (1882)

BRUGES (1888)

CELANDINE WALLPAPER (DEARLE, 1896)

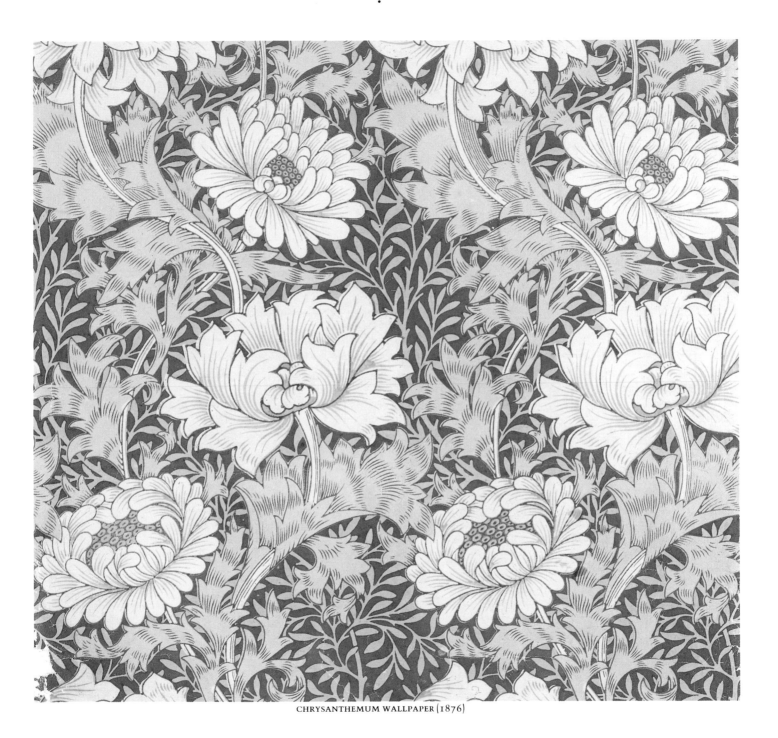

CHRYSANTHEMUM WALLPAPER (1876)

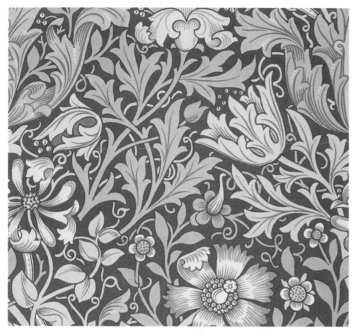

COMPTON WALLPAPER (DEARLE 1896)

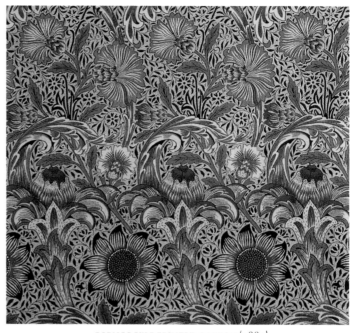

CORNCOCKLE PRINTED COTTON (1883)

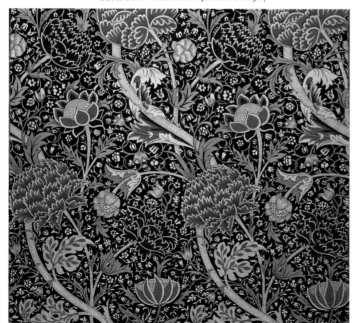

CRAY PRINTED COTTON (1884)

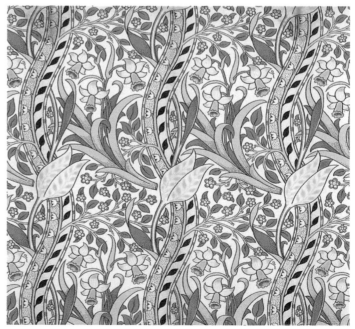

DAFFODIL PRINTED COTTON (DEARLE, C. 1891)

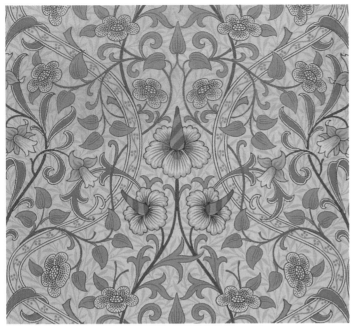

DAFFODIL WALLPAPER (DEARLE, 1903)

DAISY WALLPAPER (1864)

EVENLODE PRINTED COTTON (1883)

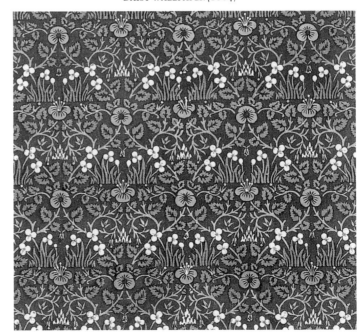

EYEBRIGHT PRINTED COTTON (1883)

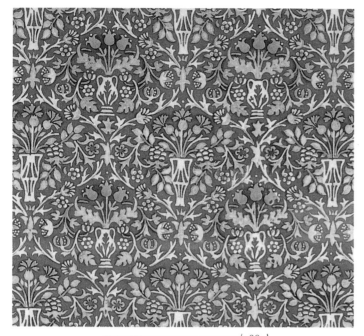

FLOWERPOT PRINTED COTTON (1883)

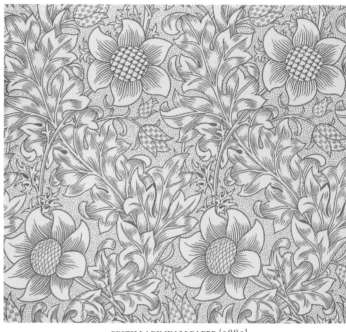

FRITILLARY WALLPAPER (1885)

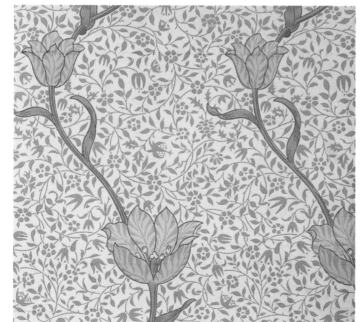

GARDEN TULIP WALLPAPER (1885)

GOLDEN LILY WALLPAPER (DEARLE, 1897)

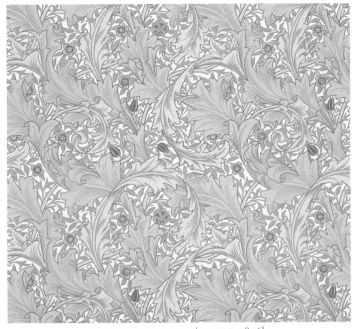

GRANVILLE WALLPAPER (DEARLE, 1896)

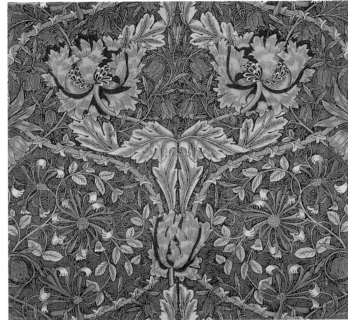

HONEYSUCKLE PRINTED COTTON (1876)

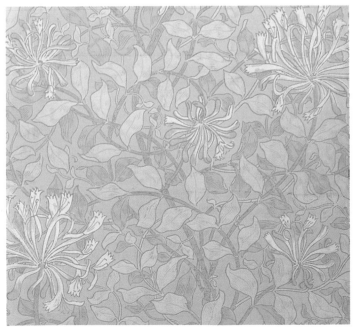

HONEYSUCKLE WALLPAPER (1883)

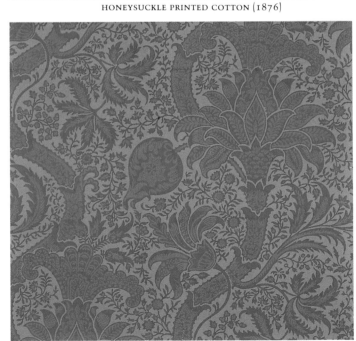

INDIAN WALLPAPER (C. 1871)

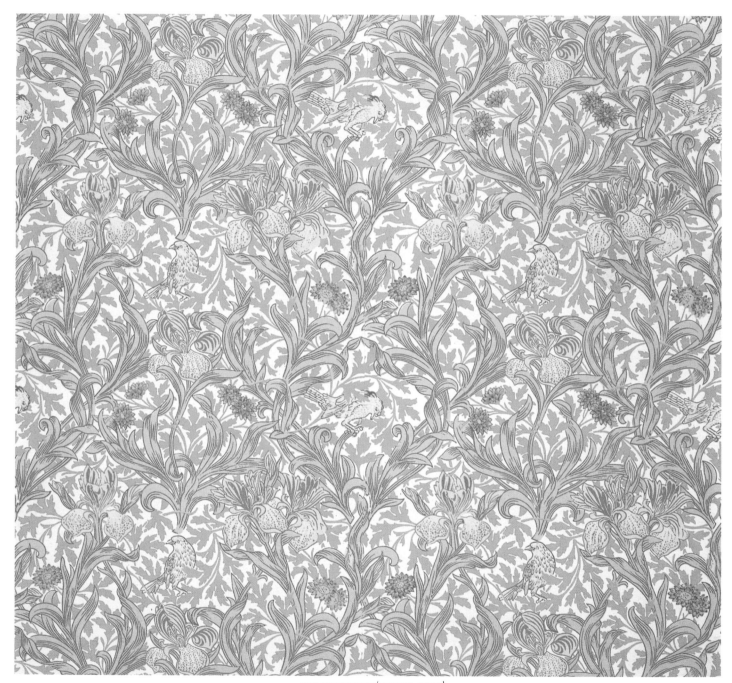

IRIS WALLPAPER (DEARLE, 1992)

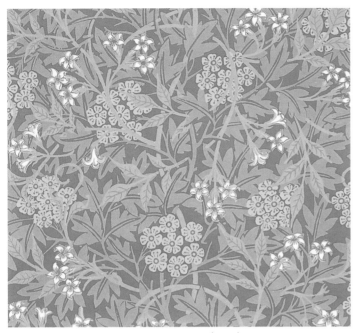

JASMINE WALLPAPER (1872)

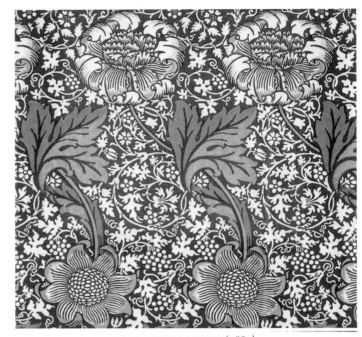

KENNET PRINTED COTTON (1883)

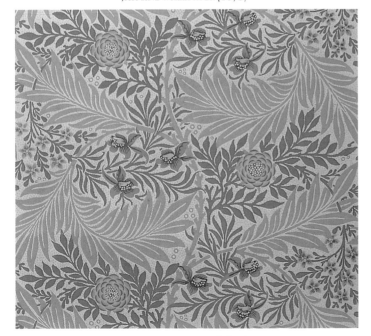

LARKSPUR WALLPAPER (1872)

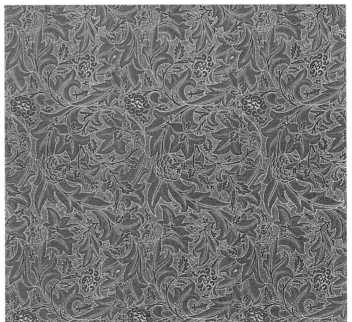

LEA PRINTED COTTON (1885)

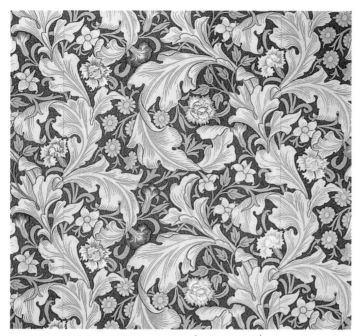

LEICESTER WALLPAPER (DEARLE, 1911)

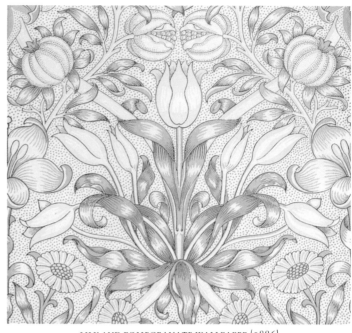

LILY AND POMEGRANATE WALLPAPER (1886)

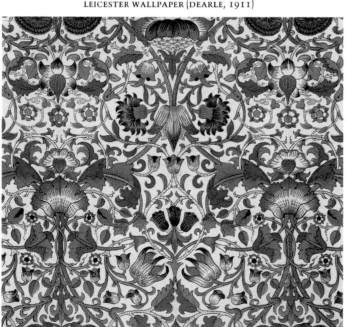

LODDEN PRINTED COTTON (1884)

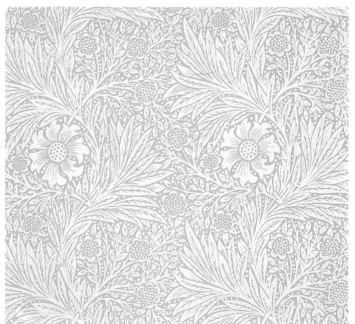

MARIGOLD WALLPAPER (1875)

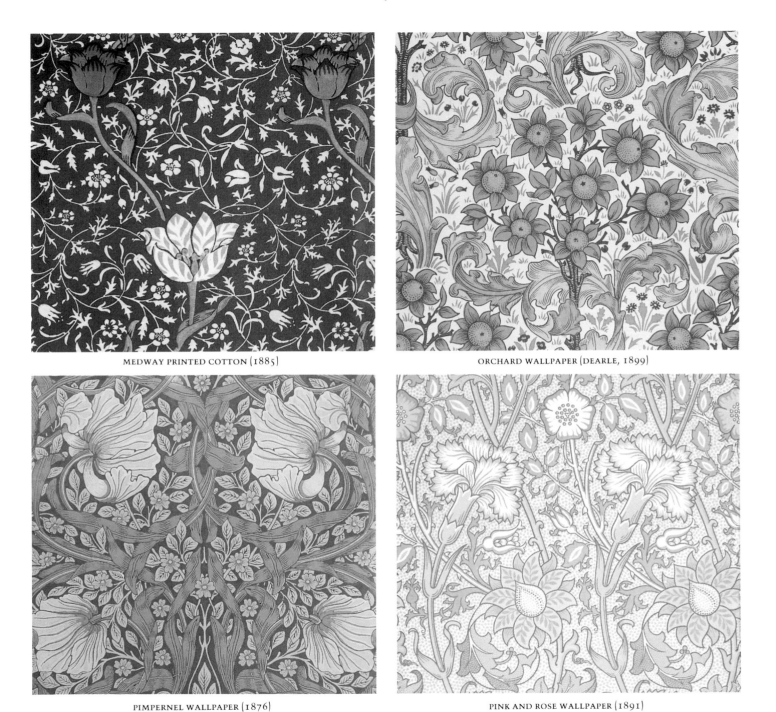

MEDWAY PRINTED COTTON (1885)

ORCHARD WALLPAPER (DEARLE, 1899)

PIMPERNEL WALLPAPER (1876)

PINK AND ROSE WALLPAPER (1891)

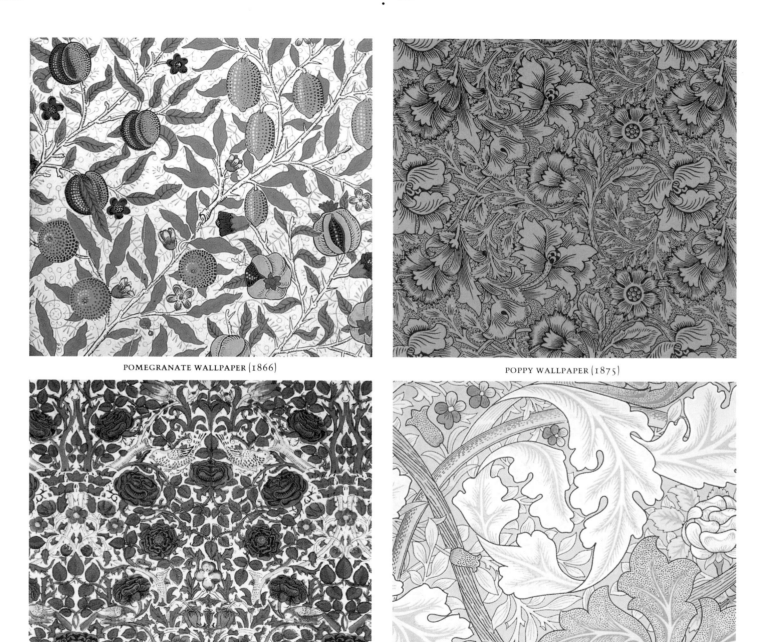

POMEGRANATE WALLPAPER (1866)

POPPY WALLPAPER (1875)

ROSE PRINTED COTTON (1883)

ST JAMES WALLPAPER (1881)

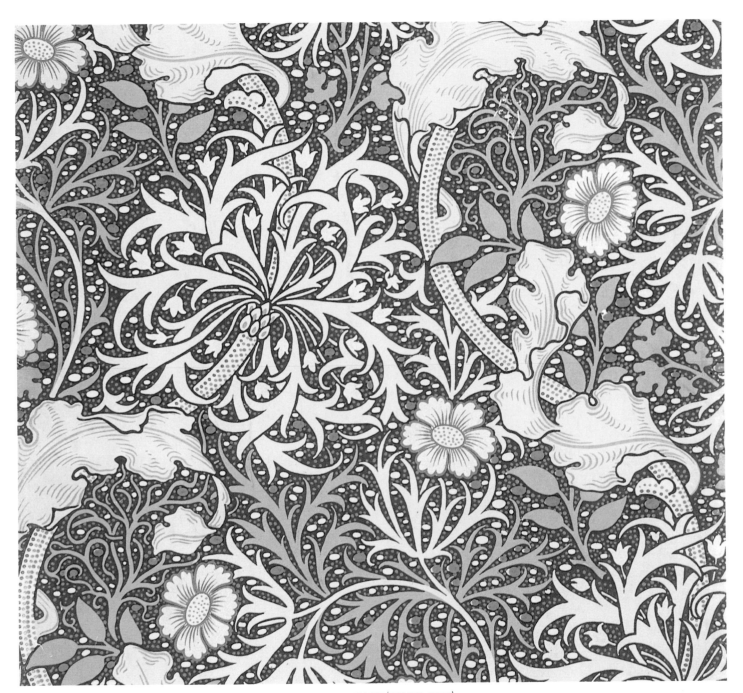

SEAWEED WALLPAPER (DEARLE, 1901)

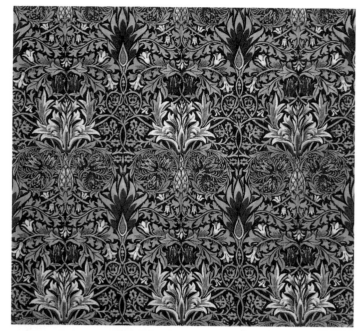

SNAKESHEAD PRINTED COTTON (1877)

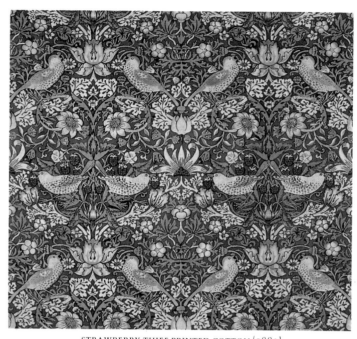

STRAWBERRY THIEF PRINTED COTTON (1883)

SUNFLOWER WALLPAPER (1879)

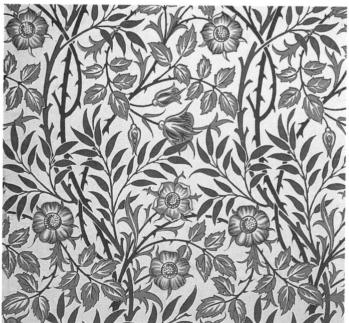

SWEET BRIAR WALLPAPER (DEARLE, 1912)

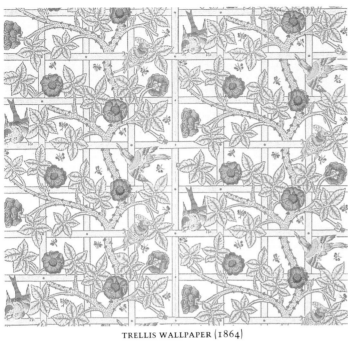

TRELLIS WALLPAPER (1864)

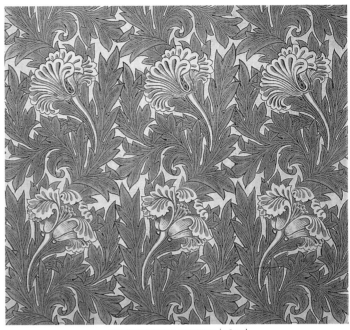

TULIP PRINTED COTTON (1875)

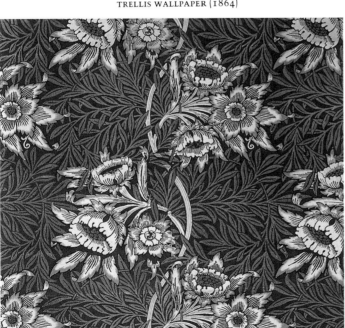

TULIP AND WILLOW PRINTED COTTON (1884)

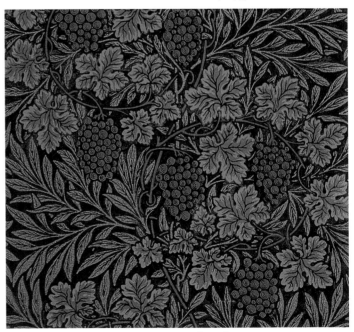

VINE WALLPAPER (1873)

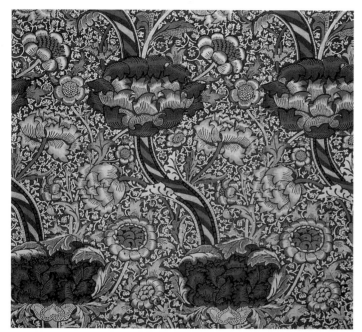

WANDLE PRINTED COTTON (1884)

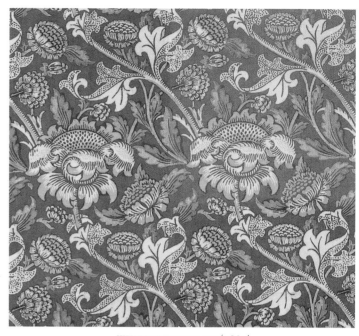

WEY PRINTED COTTON (1883)

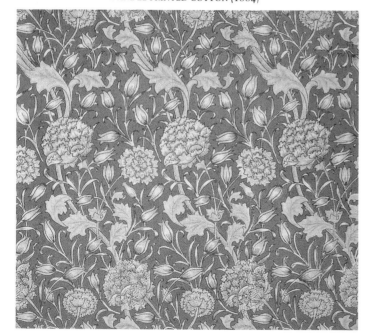

WILD TULIP WALLPAPER (1884)

WILLOW WALLPAPER (1874)

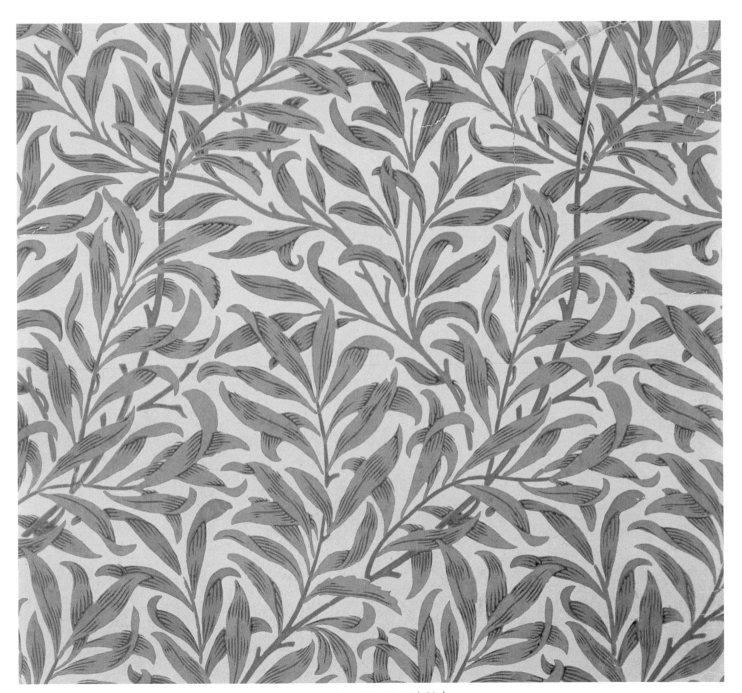

WILLOW BOUGH WALLPAPER (1887)

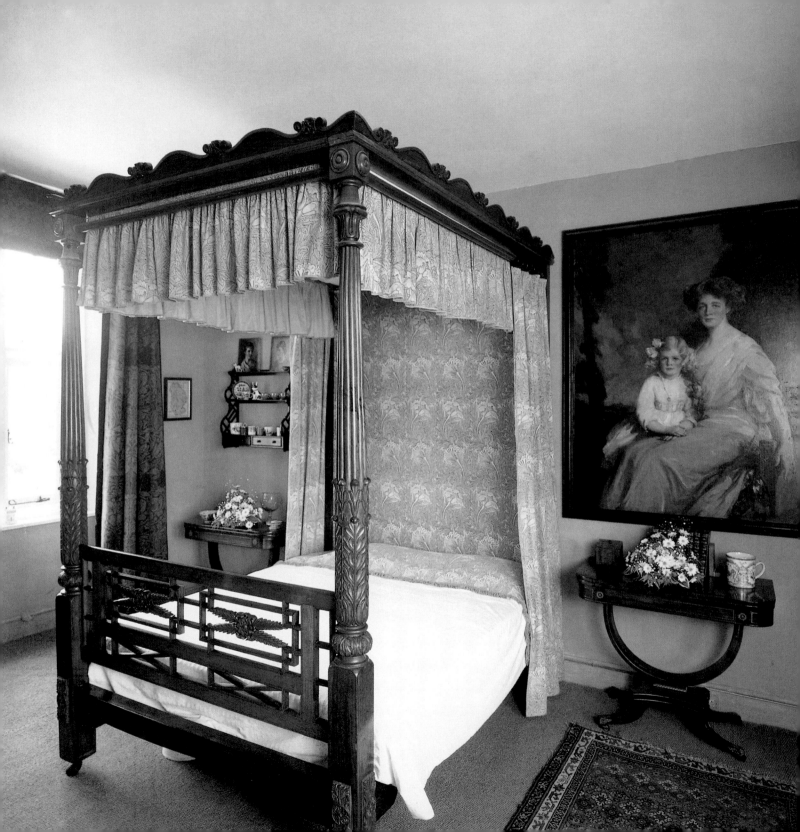

STOCKISTS AND SUPPLIERS

Wallpaper and fabric

Morris & Co.
http://www.william-morris.co.uk
has links to all UK, European and US
outlets stocking Morris wallpaper and
fabric designs.

Arts and Crafts furniture

Paul Reeves
www.paulreeves.london.com
The world's leading dealer in the Arts
and Crafts Movement.
www.artfurniture.co.uk
Arts and Crafts furniture and furnishings

www.millineryworks.co.uk
Arts and Crafts furniture and metalwork

Haslam and Whiteway
http://www.haslamandwhiteway.com
Specialist dealer in 19th century furniture

Tony Geering
http://www.puritanvalues.co.uk
Arts and Crafts specialist dealer

Circa 1910 Antiques
http://www.circa1910antiques.com

COLLECTIONS

United Kingdom

William Morris Gallery
Lloyd Park
Forest Road, London E17 4PP
(Former home of the Morris family 1846-
56. Now houses an extensive collection.)
www.wmgallery.org.uk

Victoria and Albert Museum
London SW7 2RL
(Textiles, tapestries, furniture and embroidery, as well as the Morris Room, formerly
the Green Dining Room.)
www.vam.ac.uk

Kelmscott House
26 Upper Mall
London W6 9TA
(Headquarters of William Morris Society,
which organizes exhibitions and lectures
and publishes a newsletter. Open to public.)
www.williammorrissociety.org/house.shtml

Red House
Red House Lane
Bexleyheath, Kent
www.kelmscottmanor.org.uk/home

Kelmscott Manor
Lechlade, Gloucestershire
www.kelmscottmanor.org.uk/home

Wightwick Manor
near Wolverhampton
West Midlands WV6 8EE
(National Trust property, open to public.)
www.nationaltrust.org.uk/wightwick-manor/

Standen
East Grinstead
West Sussex RH19 4NE
(National Trust property, open to public.)
www.nationaltrust.org.uk/standen/

Craigside House and Country Park
Craster
Alnwick
Northumberland
(National Trust property, open to public.

Lord Armstrong's house containing
several bedrooms decorated with
Morris wallpaper.)
www.nationaltrust.org.uk/cragside/

United States

Cooper-Hewitt Museum
The Smithsonian Institution's National
Museum of Design
2 E 91st Street
New York, NY 10028
www.cooperhewitt.org

The Metropolitan Museum of Art
Fifth Avenue at 82nd Street
New York, NY 10028
www.metmuseum.org/en

Delaware Art Museum
2301 Kentmere Parkway
Wilmington, DE 19806
(Pre-Raphaelite and decorative objects)
www.delart.org

SELECT BIBLIOGRAPHY

William Morris was a prolific writer; since his death, many books have been written about all aspects of his life. The 'Official' biography, begun immediately after his death, was written by John Mackail, the classics scholar who married Burne-Jones's daughter Margaret. In due course, Georgiana Burne-Jones also published her reminiscences, *Memorials of Edward Burne-Jones* (London, 1904), which necessarily contained many references to Morris. A good deal of what Morris had to say about his own life can be found in a long autobiographical letter written in September 1883 to Andreas Sheu, a comrade in the socialist movement.

In the years after Morris's death, his daughter May edited his collected works and published her own reminiscences.

Isabelle Anscombe and Charlotte Gere, *Arts and Crafts in Britain and America.* Academy Editions, 1978

Georgiana Burne-Jones, *Memorials of Edward Burne-Jones*, 2 vols. London, 1904

Jeremy Cooper, *Victorian and Edwardian Furniture and Interiors.* Thames and Hudson, 1987

Helen Dore, *William Morris.* Pyramid Books, 1990

The Encyclopedia of Arts and Crafts. Quarto Publishing, 1989

Penelope Fitzgerald, *Edward Burne-Jones, A Biography.* Michael Joseph, 1975

Mary Gilliatt, *Period Decorating.* Conran Octopus, 1990

Geoffrey Grigson, *A Choice of William Morris's Verse.* Faber and Faber, 1969

W. R. Lethaby, *Philip Webb and His Work.* Oxford University Press, 1935

J. W. Mackail, *The Life of William Morris*, 2 vols. London, 1899

Jan Marsh, *Jane and May Morris, A Biographical Story.* Pandora, 1986

Roderick Marshall, *William Morris and His Earthly Paradises.* Compton Press, 1979

May Morris, *William Morris: Artist, Writer, and Socialist.* Blackwell, 1936

William Morris, *News from Nowhere.* London, 1890

Gillian Naylor, Ed., *William Morris by Himself.* Macdonald Orbis, 1988

Linda Parry, *Textiles of the Arts and Crafts Movement.* Thames and Hudson, 1988

Linda Parry, *William Morris Textiles.* Weidenfeld and Nicolson, 1983

E. P. Thompson, *William Morris: Romantic to Revolutionary.* London, 1955

Aymer Vallance, *The Life and Work of William Morris.* 1897; republished Studio Editions, 1986

Ray Watkinson, *William Morris as Designer.* 1966

William Morris Today, Exhibition Catalogue. ICA, 1984

ACKNOWLEDGEMENTS

AUTHOR'S ACKNOWLEDGEMENTS

I would like to thank Colin Webb, Helen Sudell and especially Louise Simpson, for her generous help and enthusiasm.

PUBLISHER'S ACKNOWLEDGEMENTS

The publishers would like to thank the following for all their help: Bill Batten [photography], Sally and Howard Manton, Heather Dunlop and Lesley Hoskins of Sanderson, Claire Lloyd [art direction], Clare Archer and Lindy Trost [soft furnishings], Wilf and Mark [set decoration], Lynda Marshall [picture research].

PICTURE CREDITS

Illustrations are reproduced by kind permission of:

Arcaid: (photographs Richard Bryant) 2, 59, 116, 147; (photographs Nial Clutton) 90, 138.
Cyril Band (courtesy of the Oxford Union, Oxford): 14.
Bill Batten: 66, 67, 69, 73, 75, 82, 92, 100, 103, 104, 108, 112, 120, 123, 127, 128, 131, 146, 150, 166.
Birmingham Museum and Art Gallery: 28, 173 *Eyebright*, 174 *Flowerpot*, 177 *Kennet*, 179 *Medway*, 182 *Snakeshead and Strawberry Thief*, 183 *Tulip and Tulip and Willow*, 184 *Wey*.
The Bridgeman Art Library: 39, 42 (right), 42 (The Christopher Wood Gallery), 46, 61 (The Victorian Society), 76 (The William Morris Gallery, Walthamstow), 97, 98 (The Victoria and Albert Museum, London), 106 (The William Morris Gallery, Walthamstow) 115, 124 (The Metropolitan Museum of Art, New York), 152 (Cheltenham Art Gallery and Museums).
Sonia Halliday and Laura Lushington: 18, 19.
Kelmscott Manor (The Society of Antiquaries of London): 25.
A. F. Kersting (courtesy of The Society of Antiquaries of London): 34, 49, 157, 160.

The Landmark Trust: (photograph James Morris) 109.
The Macdonald Group: (photographs Trevor Richards) 43, 47, 95, 122; (courtesy of the Society of Antiquaries of London, photographs Trevor Richards) 22, 96, 99; (courtesy of the Sandford Berger Collection, Camel, California, photographs Patrick Treganza) 74 and 76; (photograph Reeve Photography) 114.
National Monuments Record: 53, 58, 89, 91.
National Portrait Gallery: 9, 15, 16.
The National Trust Photographic Library: 36; (photographs Andreas Von Einsiedel): 7, 8, 36, 44, 62, 63, 70, 72, 77, 85, 86, 87, 119, 132, 135, 137, 143, 149, 154, 158, 165, 178, 184 *Wild Tulip*; (photographs Mike Caldwell): 164, 159; (photograph Jonathan Gibson) 162, 163.
St Brides Photographic Library: 17, 33.
The Sanderson Design Archive: 37, 68 (top), 87, 168 *Acanthus and Arbutus*, 169 *Artichoke*, 173 *Daisy*, 175 *Honeysuckle wallpaper*, 177 *Jasmine*, 179 *Pimpernel*, 180 *Pomegranate*, 181 *Seaweed*, 182 *Sweetbriar*, 183 *Vine*, 184 *Willow*, 185 *Willow Bough*.
Sanderson Press Office: 83, 93, 115, 121, 130, 140, 156, 169 *Bachelor's Button*, 170 *Celandine*, 174 *Golden Lily*, 175 *Granville*, 176 *Iris*, 179 *Marigold*, 183 *Trellis*.
Diana Tonks (photograph Stewart Downie): 186.
Victoria and Albert Museum (by courtesy of the Board of Trustees): 20, 21, 23, 30, 52, 79, 88, 109 (bottom), 136, 144, 145, 147, 161, 168 *Acorn and African Marigold*, 169 *Bird and Pomegranate*, 170 *Borage and Bruges*, 171 *Chrysanthemum*, 172 *Compton and Daffodil*, 173 *Daffodil*, 174 *Fritillary and Garden Tulip*, 175 *Honeysuckle printed cotton and Indian*, 177 *Lea*, 178 *Lily and Pomegranate and Lodden*, 179 *Orchard and Pink and Rose*, 180 *Poppy and St James*, 182 *Sunflower*.
Fritz von der Schulenburg: 78, 117, 134, 153 (courtesy of Andrew Wadsworth); 80.
Weidenfeld and Nicolson Archive: 56, 57, 64 (The Society of Antiquaries of London), 65 and 101, 107 (private collection), 110, 151.
Elizabeth Whiting (photograph Peter Aprahamian): 55.
The William Morris Gallery, Walthamstow, London: 11 (left and above), 24, 26 (right and left), 29, 32 (left and above), 49, 50, 68 (bottom), 111, 154 (top), 169 *Bird and Anemone*, 170 *Brother Rabbit*, 172 *Cray and Corncockle*, 173 *Evenlode*, 177 *Larkspur*, 180 *Rose*, 184 *Wandle*.
Cover © Andreas von Einsiedel/Corbis

INDEX

Numbers in italics refer to illustration captions

Acanthus design, 68, 101, *154*, *167*, *168*, 187
Acanthus and Vine tapestry panel, 109
Acanthus Damask fabric design, *130*
Acorn design, 68, 74, 105, *145*, *146*, *151*, *162*, *167*, *168*, 187
African Marigold chintz design 67, 168
Anaglypta, 40
Arbutus wallpaper design, *168*, 187
Art Nouveau, 101, 109
Artichoke wallpaper design, *169*
Arts and Crafts Movement, 38, 121, 123, 124, 125, *126*, 148, *162*, 188
Avon chintz design, 76

Bachelor's Button design, *169*, 187
The Beauty of Life (Morris), 42, 84
bed hangings, *154*, 156, 159, *159*, *160*
La Belle Iseult (painting by Morris), 16
Benson, W. A. S., 84, 152
Bird design, 48, 52, *52*, 64, 83, 106, *136*
Bird and Anemone design, 68, *68*, *169*, 187
Bird and Pomegranate design, *169*
Bird and Vine design, 87
Blackberry design, *130*, 187
blinds, 141; festoon or Austrian, 141; roller, 40, 129, *140*, 141; Roman, 126, 141; tailored fabric, 125
Borage design, 136, *136*, 159, *170*
Borage Ceiling design, 187
Brer Rabbit design, 64, 68, *170*
Brown, Ford Madox, 13, 18, *134*, *145*, 151, 152, 154
Bruges design, *170*, 187
Bullerswood, Kent, 57
Bullerswood carpet, 57, *161*
Burne-Jones, Sir Edward, *11*, 12, 13, 15, 18, *19*, 20, *20*, 21, 29, 31, 32, 33, 38, 54, 64, 148, 152
Burne-Jones, Georgiana, *11*, 16, 21, 29, 33

café curtains (half-curtains), 130
carpets, 9, 28, 29, 31, 40, 52, 53, 54, 57, 63, 66, 88, 161-5; Axminster, *162*; borders, 162, 165; Brussels, 162; *Bullerswood*, 57, 161, *161*; Hammersmith, 54, 57; hand-knotted, 161; *Holland Park*, 91; Kidderminster, *136*, 162, *164*; *Lily*, *136*, *145*, 162, *164*; machine-made, 161-2; Persian, 48, 106, 161; *Swan House*, 91; *Tulip and Lily*, 52; *Tulip and Rose*, *147*; Wilton, 162
Castle Howard, York, 54
Celandine design, *170*, 187
Chaucer, Geoffrey, 12, 15, 24, 33, 52

Christchurch design, *92*, 187
Chrysanthemum design, 69, 101, *171*, 187
Clouds, Wiltshire, 57, 79, 93-4
Cole, Henry, *20*
colour-fastness, 123
colour schemes for walls, 92-8
Compton design, *57*, 67, 69, *69*, *102*, 105, *130*, *167*, *172*, 187
coordinated patterns, 66, 79, 81, *102*, 126, *130*, 160
Corncockle design, *172*
cotton, 123, 126, 129, 136, 139; printed, 28, 30, *32*, 41, 53, 68, 72-7, 123, 129, 148, 160
cotton sateen, 126, 129
'country cottage' style, 57
Cragside, Northumberland, *37*
Crane, Walter, 145
crapaud easy chair, 41
Cray 'river' chintz design, 68, *70*, *72*, *74*, *111*, *151*, *172*, 187
Cullinan, Ted, 64, 68
curtains, 40, 59, 60, *70*, 123, 124, 125, 129-36, *136*, *138*, 161; bed, *154*, 156, 159, *159*, *160*; café (half-curtains), *130*; 'glass', 40, 124; headings, 129-30, *136*, 139; interlining, 136, 139; length, 133; linings, 129, 136, *136*, 139; pelmets, tiebacks and trimmings, 139-40; pleated, 130; portières (door curtains), 40-1, 155-6; tracks, poles, rods, hooks and rings, 133, 136, 139, 156; under-, 124, *124*, 129
cushion covers, 160

Daffodil design, *53*, 67, *172*, *173*
Daisy design, *20*, 21, 24, 66, 101, 105, 106, *154*, *173*, 187
damask, 40, 105, 106, *136*; St James, *106*, 123
Dante Alighieri, Beatrice, 15, *46*
D'Arcy, William Knox, 91
Dearle, J. H., 31, 54, *91*, *107*, 161; designs by, 65, 68-9, *70*, 78, 83, *91*, *101*, *104*, 109, *109*, *113*, 123, *130*, *154*, *169-82 passim*, 187
designer furniture, 145, 148
dhurries, 152, 165
Diagonal Trail design, 84, *154*
Diapers wallpaper design, 101
Dove and Silk fabric design, *148*
dressers, 52, 148, 151
dyeing, dyes, chemical or aniline, 28, 40, 74, 123; indigo, 28, 29, 74, 76; natural or vegetable, 28, 29, 30, 64, 74-6, 123, 165

The Earthly Paradise (Morris), 6, 24, 26, 32, 33, 35, 111
Elm House, Walthamstow, 10
embroidery, 16, *20*, 21, 31-2, 54, 59, 66, 98, *154*, 156, 160, *160*
Evenlode design, 68, *74*, *173*
Eyebright design, 136

fabrics, 28, 29-31, 54, 57, 63, 64, 68, 71, 122-4, 155; accessories, 160; bed curtains, *154*, 156, 159, *159*, *160*; colour-fastness, 123, curtains, 129-36; hand-printed, 72, 76-7, 126; hanging, 105-11; lining, 136, 139; machine-printed, 76, 77, 126; portières, 40-1, 155-6; production of printed cottons, 72-7; range of materials, 123, texture and tactility, 79, 122-3; turn-over structure, 68; window treatments, 124-9; *see also* carpets; curtains; dyeing; printed cottons; tapestries; wallhangings
Fairfax-Murray, Charles, *20*
Faulkner, Charles, 12, 21, 113
Faulkner, Kate, *20*, 187
fireplaces, 39, 45, 59, 87, 90, 121, 124; tiles, 6, 46, 111, 113, *115*; Wightwick Manor inglenook, *133*
firescreens, 160
floor coverings, 40, 161-5
Flower, Wickham, 54, *57*
Flower Garden design, 54, *57*
The Flowerpot (embroidered panel), *20*
Flowerpot design, 136, *174*
Foliage design, 69, *108*, 187
The Forest tapestry, *57*, 88, 109
frieze papers, 111
friezes, 54, 88, 90, 111, 113
Fritillary wallpaper design, *174*
Fruit or *Pomegranate* design, 24, *25*, *37*, 54, 66, *102*, *145*, *180*, 187
furniture, 9, 15, 16, 19, 21, 57, 145, *146-8*, 148-55, *154*; Arts and Crafts, *37*, 59, 72, 78, 148, *151-2*, 152-4; bentwood, 155; covers, 160; designer (art produce), 145, 148; from the Firm, 148-51; furnishing the modern home, 154-5; Japanese 'art', 41; Kelmscott House, 48, 52; Liberty's and Heal's, 148, 152, 154, 155; Morris & Co. catalogue, *154*; 'Morris' chairs, 24, 48, 151; painted, 15, 45, 46, 52, 151, 154; Red House, 16, 45, 46, 52, 148, 151; Red Lion Square, 15, 148; replica or reproduction, 41, *154*; state, 148, 151; Sussex chairs, 24, *74*, *105*, *145*, 151, 154; V&A, *145*; Victorian, 41; Voysey's, 152, *152*; 'workaday', 148, 151, 155

Garden Tulip design, *174*, 187
George & Dragon cabinet, *145*
'glass curtains', net or muslin, 40, 124
Golden Lily design, 60, *78*, 123, *174*, 187
Golden Stem design, *70*
Gothic Revival, 13, 42
Granville design, *92*, *123*, *175*, 187
Great Tangley Manor, Surrey, 54, 57, *57*

headings, curtain, 129-30
Heal & Sons (Ambrose Heal), 152, 154, 155, *159*
Holland Park (Ionides's home), 54, 109
Holland Park carpet, *91*
Holy Grail tapestries, *91*, 109
Honeysuckle designs, 28, 68, 101, *115*, 126, *142*, *175*, 187
Howard family, 31, 54, 111
Howard, George, ninth Earl of Carlisle, 54, 123
Hunt, William Holman, 13

Indian design, *72*, *83*, *101*, 102, *175*, 187
indigo-discharge printing, 76
indigo dyeing, 28, 29, 74, 76
interlining, curtain, 136, 139
International Exhibition (1862), *17*, 19, 20, 151
Ionides, Alexander, 54, *57*, 88, 109
Iris design, 126, *176*, 187

Jack, George, 84, 152
James, Henry, 15, 146
Japanese decorative arts, 41; prints, 41, 148; spindle 'art' furniture, 41
Jeffrey & Co., printers, 63-4, 66, 71, 126, 187
Jasmine design, 28, 68, *68*, 101, *177*

kelims, 126, 165
Kelmscott House, Hammersmith, 29, *29*, 31, 32, 33, 43, 83, 109, 188; Dining Room, *Pimpernel* paper and Persian carpet, *48*, 52, 106; Drawing Room, *Bird* hangings, *48*, *52*, 106, *136*; interior decoration and furnishing, 48, 50-2
Kelmscott Manor, Gloucestershire, 26, 28, 33, 67, 68, 81, 83, 87, 188; Attic Room, *97*; Drawing Room, *48*, *48*, 123; Gere's drawing of east front, *26*; Green Room fireplace tile border, *113*; interior decoration and furnishing, 46-50; Morris's four-poster bed, *154*, 156, *160*; Tapestry Room, *35*, 50, 106; white panelled walls, *48*, 93; white wool curtains in drawing room, *48*, 123; *Willow* bedroom, 81, 98, woodcut of, *9*

Kelmscott Press, *11*, 33, 68
Kelmscott Vine design, 83, *146*, 187
Kempe, C., *133*
Kennet 'river' chintz design, 68, *177*
Kenton & Co., 152

lambrequin (pelmet), 40, *124*
Larkspur design, 28, 68, 101, 102, 126, *159*, *177*, 187
Larsson, Carl, 97
Lea fabric design, *177*
Leicester wallpaper design, *178*
The Lesser Arts of Life (Morris), 87, 125, 148
Lethaby, W. R., 123, 162
Liberty's (Arthur Lasenby Liberty), *128*, 148, 152, 152, 155, 187
Lily design, 101, *136*, *145*, *164*
Lily and Pomegranate design, *178*
Lily Border design, 187
Lincrusta, 40
lining, curtain, 129, 136, *136*, 139
linoleum, 40
Little Scroll design, 98
Lodden design, 66, *178*, 187
Loop Trail design, 187

Mackail, John, 16, 29-30
Mackintosh, Charles Rennie, 109
Mackmurdo settle, *159*
Mallow wallpaper, 101, 187
Malory, Thomas, 12; *Morte d'Arthur*, 15
Manchester Jubilee exhibition (1887), 151
Mander, Sir Geoffrey, 57, 87
Marigold design, *113*, *121*, *178*, 187
Marx, Eleanor, 32
matting, coir or natural fibre, 165
Medway design, 179
Merton Abbey workshops (Surrey), 29-31, 76, *115*; carpet-making, 161; dye book recipes, *74*; hand block-printing of chintzes, *32*; Pocock's painting *The Pond at Merton Abbey*, *30*
Michaelmas Daisy design, *104*, 187
Millais, Sir John Everett, *The Return of the Dove to the Ark*, 13
Millefleurs woven wool design, 87
Minstrel Figure tapestry, *107*
Modern Movement, 9, 145
Morgan, William de, 6, 20, 67, 113; earthenware tiles, *115*; vases, *83*, 148
Morris, Jane (*née* Burden), *11*, 20, *26*, 33, 46, 52, 146;

death of William, 33; embroidery work, 20, 21, 45, 105, *154*, 156; marriage to William (1859), 15-16
Morris, Jenny, *11*, *26*, 28, 33
Morris, May, *11*, 20, *26*, 31-2, 33, 52, 68, 81, 98, 106, *106*, *154*, 156, 160, 187
Morris & Company, 28, 33, 93, 94, 111, 113, 126, 139, 148, 156; curtain-making service, 129; embroidery kit, 20, 160; furniture, 148, 151, 152, 154, *154*; Hanover Square shop front, *151*; interior design and decoration commissions, 53-7, *57*-8, 70, 88; Merton Abbey workshops, 29-32, 76; stained glass, *17*, *19*; 'Morris' chairs (designed by Webb), *24*, *48*, 151
Morris family, photograph of, *11*
Morris, Marshall, Faulkner & Company, 18-21, *24*, *145*
mural painting, *11*, 15, 16, 19, 111, 113

Naworth Castle, 31, 54
News from Nowhere (Morris), 9, *9*, 26, *26*, 33, 48

Oak silk damask design, 106
Orange Border design, 187
The Orchard tapestry, 109
Orchard wallpaper design, *109*, 179
Oxford, 12-13, 53
Oxford Union murals and decorated ceiling, *11*, 15

Palace Green (No. 1: Howard home), 54, 111, 123
Passionate Bromptons (PBs), 148
pattern/pattern-making, 63-83; combining or mixing, 81, 83; coordinated schemes, 66, 79, 81, 126; as decorative strategy, 79, 81; in the interior, 79-83; Morris's views on, 69, 71, 101-2, 124, 125; wallpaper production, 71-2; *see also* fabric designs; wallpaper designs
Peacock and Dragon design, 48, *48*, 83, 106
pelmets, 40, 41, 124, 125, 129, 130, 136, 139
Persian Brocatel design, *91*
Pevsner, Sir Nikolaus, 45, 152
Pimpernel design, *48*, 52, 87, 102, *136*, 179
Pink and Rose design, *76*, 179
Planet design, 187
pleated curtains, 130; box, 130; pencil, 130; triple and pinch, 130
Pomegranate see *Fruit* or *Pomegranate*
Poppy design, 101, *180*, 187
portières (door curtains), 40-1, 155-6
Powdered design, 98

Queen Square, *17*, 21, *24*, 29

Queens' College, Cambridge, fireplace tile panel, 113, *115*

Red House, Bexleyheath, 9, 15, 16, *24*, 43, 46, 52, 59, 67, 93, 97, 148, 188; *Daisy* bedroom hanging, 16, 18, 45-6; decoration and furnishing, 16, 18, 45-6, *46*; designed by Webb, 9, 15, 16, 46, 67, 148; frescoes in drawing room, 111; furniture, 45, 46, 52, 148, 151; Morris and Jane move to, 16, 46; Morris moves to Queen Square from, *17*, 21, 24; settle, 16, 46; stained glass window, *122*; Upper Landing, *43*, 94
Red Lion Square, the Firm's premises at, 18; Morris's studio/rooms, 15, 148; settle, 16
reproduction or replica furniture, 41, 154
restoration, Morris's views on, 9, 32, 46, 48, 97
Rose design, 101, *180*, 187
Rossetti, Dante Gabriel, 13, 15, 16, *17*, 18, *19*, 21, 26, 50, 52, *72*, 87, *115*, 152; *Blue Silk Dress (Mrs William Morris in a Blue Silk Dress)*, 24; *Day Dream*, 20
Rossetti, Elizabeth/Lizzie (née Siddal), 15, 16, 26
Rossetti chair, 151
Rounton Grange, 54; Drawing Room, *57*
rugs, ethnic, 52, 79, 83, 126, 165
Ruskin, John, 12, 13, 38, 42; *The Stones of Venice*, 13, 33

St James design, 88, *106*, 123, *180*
St James's Palace, Armoury and Tapestry Room, 24, 106
St Mark's Venice, 32, 48
Sambourne, Linley, 53-4, *54*, 60
Sanderson, Arthur & Sons, 63-4, 66, 102, 126, 187
Sanderson family, 161, *161*
Scroll design, 68, 101, 102
Seaweed design, 65, *101*, *181*
Seddon, J. P., *145*
Shaw, George Bernard, 43, 52
Shaw, Richard Norman, 53, 105, 152
Sickert, Helena, 52
sideboards, Arts and Crafts, *72*, *152*; designed by Webb, *147*, 148, 151
silk, *57*, 88, *91*, 122-3, 148
Snakeshead design, 28, 68, *182*
Socialist League, *29*, 32, 33
Society for the Protection of Ancient Buildings (SPAB), 9, 32
South Kensington Museum (now V&A), 63, 68, 161, 188; early furniture by the Firm, *145*; International Exhibition (1862), *17*, 19, *20*, 151; William Morris Room, *20*, 24

Spray wallpaper design, 102
stained glass, 9, 18, 19-20, 24, 31, 46, *54*, 130, 154; All Saints, Selsley, *17*; Red House, *122*; St Peter and St Paul, Cattistock, *19*; Wightwick Manor Library, *134*
Standen, Sussex, 15, 57, 67, 83, 148, 188; Dining Room, *162*; Drawing Room, *162*, *164*; *Larkspur* bedroom, *159*; *Willow* bedroom, *118*
Stanmore Hall, Drawing Room, *91*; *Holy Grail* tapestries, Dining Room, *91*, 109; Small Drawing Room, 88
stencilling, 88, *94*, 113
Stickley, Gustav, 152, *152*
Strawberry Thief fabric design, 30, 64, 66, 68, *182*
Street, G. E., 13, 15
Sunflower design, 68, *78*, *182*, 187
'Sussex' chairs, 24, *74*, 105, *145*, 151, 154, *154*
Swan House carpet, *91*
Sweet Briar design, *90*, *113*, *182*, 187
Swivel fabric design, 83

tapestries, 9, 28, 31, *35*, 50, 57, 66, 98, 106, 109, 111, 154; *Acanthus and Vine*, 109; collaborative, 109; *The Forest*, *57*, 88, 109; *Holy Grail*, 109; *Minstrel Figure*, *107*; *The Orchard*, 109; *The Woodpecker*, *106*
Taylor, Warington, 21, 24, 151
Tennyson, Alfred Lord, 9, 12
Textiles (Morris article), 64, 122
tiebacks, tassels and trimmings, 139-40, 155, 160
tiles, tiled panels, 9, 20, 24, 40, 46, 111, 113, 117, *117*; earthenware (De Morgan), *115*; fireplace, *6*, 46, 111, 113, *115*; quarry, 165; Victorian encaustic, 165
Titanic suite, 110
Trellis design, 24, *24*, 66, 67, 83, 101, 126, *154*, 156, 183, 187
Tulip design, 28, *28*, 83, *118*, 159, *183*, 187
Tulip and Lily carpet, 52
Tulip and Rose design, *147*
Tulip and Willow design, *183*
'turnover' or mirror repeat, 68

undercurtains, *124*, *124*, 129
Utrecht Velvet fabric design, 110

velvet, 41, *63*, 68, *110*, 155, *159*
Venetians wallpaper, 101
Victorian interior, *39*, 41, *41*, 42, 45, *78*, *101*, 121, *124*, 145, 155, 156
Victorian Society, *54*, 54
Vine design, 68, 101, 102, *183*, 187

Voysey, C. F. A., 152, *152*, 154

wallhangings, 16, 18, 24, 31, 45, 50, 57, 81, 98, 105-11; *see also* fabric designs; fabrics; tapestries
wallpaintings, 15, 19, 111, 113
wallpapers, 24, 28, 39-40, 53, 63-8, 98-105, 122, 148; frieze papers, 111; hand-printed, 71-2, 104, 187; machine-printed, 104, 105, 187; Morris's views on, 69, 71, 101-2; production, 71-2; turnover or 'mirror' repeat, 68
walls and finishes, 87-117; colour schemes, 92-8; fabric hangings, 105-11, 113; frescoes, *54*, 88, 90, 111, 113; proportion and detailing, 89-92; stencilling, 88, *94*, 113; tiles, 111, 113, 117; wallpainting, 15, 19, 111; *see also* tapestries; wallpapers
Wandle 'river' chintz design, 68, *184*
Wardle, George, 28, 30
Wardle, Thomas, dyeworks of, 28, *74*, 76
weaving, 28, 29, 31, 64, 68, 123
Webb, Philip, 15, 18, 20, 33, 46, 52, 59, 93-4, 151; animal drawings, *19*, 20, 24, 64, 67, 88; furniture designed by, 16, 21, 24, *145*, *147*, 148, 151, 154; houses designed by, 24, 54, 57, 123, *159*; Morris's collaboration with, 24, 31, 45, 54, 52; Red House designed by, 9, 15, 16, 46, 67, 148; tiles, fireplace, 113, *115*
Wey fabric design, *184*
Wightwick Manor, 57, 188; Billiard Room, *87*, *136*, *164*; Dining Room, *63*; Drawing Room, *6*, 148; Great Parlour, 9, *84*; Hall alcove, *133*; Honeysuckle bedroom, *142*; *Honeysuckle* wall covering, *115*; Indian Bird Bedroom, *159*; Library, *134*; Oak Room, *70*, *72*; staircase, *44*; *Tulip and Rose* chair, *147*
Wild Tulip wallpaper, *63*, 68, *184*
William Morris Gallery, Walthamstow, 159, 188
Willow design, 28, 48, 66, 68, 81, 98, 105, *118*, 126, *141*, *184*, 187
Willow Bough design, *44*, 81, 83, 90, 93, 98, *98*, 105, *107*, *118*, 140, *185*, 187
Willow Bough Minor design, *121*, 187
windows/window treatment, 59, 121-41; blinds, 40, 125, 126, 129, *140*, 141; glass curtains, 40, 124; lining, 129, 136-9; painted glass (Kempe), *133*; pelmets, tiebacks and trimmings, 124, 139-40; proportion, 129; undercurtains, *124*, *124*, 129; using William Morris fabrics, 124-9
The Woodpecker tapestry, *106*
woodwork, 40, 53, 59, 94, *113*, 145
Wreathnet lining fabric design, 136